CRYING AND BABIES

CRYING AND BABIES
HELPING FAMILIES COPE

JOHN KIRKLAND

CROOM HELM
London • Sydney • Dover, New Hampshire

Croom Helm Ltd, Provident House, Burrell Row,
Beckenham, Kent BR3 1AT
Croom Helm Australia Pty Ltd, First Floor,
139 King Street, Sydney, NSW 2001, Australia

British Library Cataloguing in Publication Data

Kirkland, John
Crying and babies: helping families cope.
1. Stress (Psychology) 2. Mother and child
I. Title
155.9'0880431 BF575.S75

ISBN 0-7099-1564-0

Croom Helm, 51 Washington Street, Dover,
New Hampshire 03820, USA

Library of Congress Cataloging in Publication Data

Kirkland, John, 1945-
Crying and Babies.

Includes index.
1. Crying. 2. Infants (Newborn)–Care and Hygiene.
3. Infants–Care and Hygiene. 4. Parent and Child.
I. Title.
RJ253.K57 1985 649'.122 85-4139
ISBN 0-7099-1564-0
ISBN 0-7099-1565-9 (pbk.)

Phototypesetting by Bryce Francis Ltd, Wellington, NZ
Printed and bound in Great Britain
by Billing & Sons Limited, Worcester.

CONTENTS

COPYRIGHT

My thanks are due to the following publishers and authors for their generous permission to include their materials in this book. The copyright holders must be consulted prior to any further use.

Alma Publications (Box 7.1) and Maureen Minchin, *Food for Thought.*
American Psychiatric Association (Box 7.4)
Department of Health, New Zealand (Box 7.3)
Janet Hambly (Intervention 10.7)
Margaret McCall (Intervention 9.4)
Chris Meddick (Intervention 9.5)
New Zealand Federation for Deaf Children Inc. (Box 7.2)
New Zealand Federation of Parents Centre (Box 8.3) and Parent Centres Bulletin.
AH and AW Reed Ltd (Box 1.1) and Jenny Phillips *Mothers Matter Too.*
Wiliams and Wilkins (Box 3.1) and R.S. Asnes and R.L. Mones.
VORT Corporation. (Boxes 9.1 through 9.9 are Copyright © 1979 by University of Hawaii at Manoa reprinted from *HELP Activity Guide* by Dr. J. Kirkland by permission of VORT Corporation, P.O. Box 60132, Palo Alto, California 94306, U.S.A.)

ACKNOWLEDGEMENTS

The word-processing skills of Julie Vickers and Glennis Fairley converted my untidy handwriting into readable typescript. They managed numerous drafts cheerfully.

As Dean and H.O.D., Raymond S. Adams allowed and encouraged me to continue working with crying babies within an academic community.

I am grateful to colleagues and friends at the University of Guelph (particularly Margaret McKim and Griffith Morgan) and Richard Barham who arranged for an envigorating year spent in Canada.

Cry study students in England, New Zealand and Canada are acknowledged as a source of inspiration.

Siobhan Norrish and staff at the Family Unit provided many crying babies, sound advice and a place for me to work; all are appreciated.

Elaine Hefford and Raewyn Morris kindly took time to read drafts and help clear up ambiguities and tidy my style.

I am very grateful to Jillian Cleghorn who did both the art work and the pasteup. Peter Herbert and Robert Roberts assisted by giving time to answer my constant questioning about printing; as did Walt Abell and Ted Drawneek with computing.

Both Tim Hardwick, editor at Croom Helm, and Frances Kelly, my London agent, made this book into a reality.

Finally to those many parents of crying babies who so generously gave me both time and opportunities to study their little ones I express sincere gratitude.

To our teachers;
crying babies.

PART I

INTRODUCTION

1 THE NEED FOR BOOKS OF THIS SORT

Crises in development

Captain Mark Phillips was quoted in a magazine article as saying that "The skill of being able to ride is being able to adapt yourself to ride from one horse to another. Eventually you learn which buttons to press. But if you jump onto another horse it's a different ball game — but the principle's still the same. You've got an accelerator, a brake and a steering wheel. They'll just be in different places" (1).*

Something very similar applies to babies. Although they are all quite alike in some respects they each have distinctive personalities as well. Those who deal with babies can recognise which buttons make them go fast, slow and change direction. It takes time to pick up these skills. While this sort of thing can be recognised in those who appear to have a certain touch, it is important that parents and others who handle the day to day business of living with babies be encouraged to enjoy the benefits of mutual understanding which can occur during development.

Unfortunately it is often the case that authors of books aimed at parents with young children make the assumption that all one needs to do is present the evidence and things will take care of themselves. Often this is not the case. Besides having the "facts" people frequently require gentle guidance as to a safe course to follow. Simply put, people do not live by facts alone. They need a certain spirit of understanding and shared compassion.

There are excellent preparation for parenthood classes available in some localities. Yet, even given the most up-to-date information in an educationally relevant manner adjusted to the psychological needs of those attending, there are events following birth for which no amount of teaching can adequately prepare a new parent. These are the crises in development; sudden, shocking and scaring. In the early weeks the crisis may well be continued infant crying. Later it might be night waking. Then

* References are listed for each chapter at the end of the book.

later still there are the so called temper tantrums. These may be followed by bed-wetting. And so they go on, crisis after crisis.

For some families these crises are more devastating than for others. We do not yet know enough about events which trigger crises that punctuate the flow of development. And since we do not know enough there are literally dozens of suggestions arising from different theories proffered by well-meaning people whose task it is to help relieve the suffering which seems to be brought on by crises of this type.

There are at least two quite different sorts of approaches which ought to be considered when offering guidance. One deals with the mechanical aspects of the developing organism. Consider the straight forward observation that all humans are basically bags of chemicals. The largest bag which encloses the others is our skin, a surface to prevent drying out in the sun and dissolving in the rain. Within this bag are many other bags, like bones which give support enabling other bags (muscles) to act in a co-ordinated manner providing movement and locomotion. And so on. The main point of this illustration is to stress the importance of realising the body is a machine. As the body grows in shape and size different parts of the machine become tuned for particular performances. At around five months a baby will begin to roll over for instance. Many of these developments are set by internal time clocks which are genetically programmed. As will be discussed below, the "medical" approach to people is mostly by way of a machine which is malfunctioning. The second approach can be summed up in a brief comment "Humans are bags of chemicals, with will". There is a sense of purpose which may be realised, sets of plans which can be designed or decisions which can be made. So beyond those bags of chemicals is a spirit of being. People think, can think about thinking and may even write this down for others to think about too. They can join in with one another; link their ideas, share their feelings and tell others about their fortunes and misfortunes.

A crisis in development occurs when tension reaches such a level that any increase in stress will either threaten or bring about a disruption in the ongoing system. Some crises can be quite beneficial. For example if the ongoing system is not working to the benefit of those involved an opportune intervention will be a crisis in development since it is aimed at breaking a disruptive cycle. All interventions are aimed at particular crises and may themselves become a crisis for those who are willing to use them. The main difference is that the interventions are designed to have predictable consequences. They are intended to make events more manageable and can clear channels of communication between the consultant and parent as well as between parent and baby.

NOTE: Throughout this book the term "consultant" is used to describe those helping others cope with crying babies in families. This broad term is intended to be neutral, and may be personalised by many different people drawn from a range of contributing professional and volunteer groups.

Three to thirty weeks

The eight month zone between three and thirty weeks is one which is covered by many baby and child care books. Attention is typically directed toward outlining those things which can be done to baby. While it is recognised by these authors that babies exist in family settings, there has, until recently, been an almost exclusive focus on the mechanics of parent-infant relationships. Emphasis is typically placed on the baby; how to prepare this and that, what to expect as baby's skills advance during development, patterns of interaction which may be observed as baby grows older and so forth. These are important topics.

Parents are people too. They have needs and wishes and desires which are very much a part of their own existence. These cannot be hung up on a peg in a cupboard and the door closed until the childrearing years are over. When there is a developmental crisis like continued baby crying for which there seems to be no relief these personal feelings are even more forceful. There are now at least two crises, the infant's and the parents'. The skill of any consultant lies in being able to select from a repertoire of interventions the ones which do justice to the situation. These need to meet the crisis of contributing members, enabling each to adjust and proceed with the business of growing together and forming healthly attachments.

This book is aimed at consultants working with both parents and babies who are trying to make it through this indeterminate zone, a minefield which stretches from the end of the post-birth honeymoon (around three weeks) until the beginnings of speech and independent moving about (around eight months).

The general assessment scheme will be applicable to those who deal with other developmental crises at different ages. Perhaps some of the interventions will be useful for other settings as well. Even so, this book is aimed primarily as helping those who are involved with assisting parents cope with their crying babies through the weeks when this crisis is particularly bothersome. The effects of some babies' crying will be felt much sooner than three weeks and for others it could go on for almost two years. This may mean being involved for earlier and/or longer than the time period mentioned here. A consultant needs to assess each situation and select interventions from what is available even if it means extending the age range downward or upward for the materials offered in this book. The main thing is that the interventions are here and organised for practical use.

Involvement with action plans

Many professionals are apt to encourage their patients or clients to become dependent upon them. When this happens decisions cannot be made without an additional consultancy. It is an easy trap to fall into. Without thinking about the effects of an intervention a consultant can easily create a situation which fosters dependency.

The aim of the interventions designed for this book is toward encouraging independence. Whilst there may be a brief period during which a parent relies heavily upon the advice offered by a consultant, this is a transitory phase. There are some parents, it should be recognised, for whom the visiting consultant may be the only adult person who is willing to offer a chance to talk at a reasonable level of intelligence. Although this may appear to be a dependency relationship it is nothing short of having company and an opportunity to talk things over.

A dependent relationship between adults can easily become unhealthy. An alternative concept is "interdependency". Here each person needs the other but at the same time can carry on independently. This is one way of thinking about consultant-parent relationships. There is a mutual understanding and co-operation as the task at hand is dealt with. Each person brings their capabilities and together a course of action is mapped out. If this is done within a reasonably open framework then neither party needs to feel guilty if things do not turn out as anticipated. Having the freedom to make decisions, the information available to help work these out, and the confidence to put them into action promotes a sense of well-being and confidence.

Some, however, may liken a consultant to an agent in a chemical reaction which simply activates at a faster rate a process which is going at a slower pace. This is known as a catalyst. Throughout, however, the catalyst is not itself affected by the reactions which seem to go on all around it. When consultants do allow themselves to be drawn into a reaction they are no longer catalysts but active ingredients. It's all very well considering the idea of a catalyst in a cold laboratory-like mechanical fashion. In the dynamic world of people what helps to bring about change is itself changed. If it is not, then the person is redundant and a workbook or recipe would have been just as useful.

Perhaps the critical issue here is not about "dependency" at all. It is one of involvement. For instance how do you maintain your own interest in a new case when the case itself looks like an old and rather familiar problem which you have seen many times previously, maybe even on the same day? There is a subtle distinction between fostering a relationship which is totally dependent on your presence and direction and one which has as its goal the mutual development of participants. To an observer there may be little difference between these two modes at the onset. But as the process continues it will become apparent that the former is not going anywhere at all as it is stale and closed. For the other there is a sense of purpose, of rhythm and movement since here the interventions are implemented to encourage activity, openness and discovery as the developmental processes are realised.

One of the essential characteristics of the second approach is that consultants are aware of what they are intending to do. They have a set of plans from which a selection may be made. If a consultant knows what is planned there is no need to be flustered and it is possible to apply that essential human virtue, compassion. Taking an interest in a case involves two complementary aspects. First, a knowledge of what is possible, based on a sound plan of likely outcomes from assessment. And second, a desire to promote a sense of worth for those who are at their wits' end. This book addresses itself to the former, trusting that consultants will adopt a humane attitude which will engender a spirit of co-operation through mutual respect.

Families affected

Practically all families with a baby are involved in coping with crying at some time or another. Many manage to handle the crying satisfactorily or at least without detriment to the health of those living with the baby. There are others for whom this particular crisis is devastating. It erodes into all of the corners of existence, eating out and weakening the bonds which were quite adequate previously for meeting family needs.

Typically the crying is coupled with other disruptive behaviours like excessive activity, negative moods, poor feeding and irregular sleeping. From numerous researchers (2,3,4) working in different countries it would seem that around 10% of babies are affected in this manner. It is useful to remember that these babies have a clean bill of health. That is to say there is nothing wrong with them from a medical point of view. Since there is no common organic disorder which can be diagnosed nor a prescription drug provided to alleviate infant distress then it is commonly assumed by many doctors that there is nothing "wrong" with baby and it is the mother who is to blame. Although this view is still commonly held it is gratifying to know that the research evidence against it is slowly trickling through.

Another reason for the sheer lack of effort directed toward this family health topic is the political powerlessness of mothers with young babies. It is enough that these parents are struggling to stay afloat in the house setting by meeting daily demands without trying to raise community consciousness on this matter. Fortunately many mothers are able to voice their disapproval and be heard. They are assertive enough to indicate that urgent assistance is needed. One grass-roots group in England named itself as Cry-SIS and the members have not forgotten the horror of trying to manage with their crying babies.

When babies do grow older and the first crisis is passed safely the difficult times and trying hours with a screaming infant can be put aside. It is rare for these to be forgotten. With any group of grandmothers there are two questions which guarantee discussion. First, "Tell me, if you will, about your birthing experiences?". And, second, "What was it like trying to cope with a crying baby?". There is now a great deal which can be told to them of developments which have occurred in the past decade with regard to issues surrounding birth. In that domain women have not continued to suffer in silence, erroneously believing that their personal experiences during delivery were unique and not to be talked about. The veil of awe, mystique and reverence has been replaced by a keen desire to know who is doing what and why. Expectant parents can now actively participate in birth as most of their mothers could not.

A similar unveiling has not yet occurred with regard to coming to grips with infancy. Here, as it used to be for birth, parents are having to go it alone. So long as infant mortality rates are not jeopardising national health statistics it would appear there is no need to provide services for parents who are supposed to be able to manage because it is something for which they are innately equipped. Just as the positive results of active birth involvement are clear to any who wish to look, so too it is to be expected that support for infant-trapped parents will make important differences to family well being.

What is available

"Crying" or its synonyms are not indexed in many medical paediatric text books and when they are the reference is typically to "crying cat syndrome". From these sources one could conclude that baby crying is not a phenomenon doctors are trained to deal with. Many popular books aimed at parents do contain a section on crying. Much of this is biased because the authors are often passing on their own pet beliefs. Perhaps one of the better treatments is offered by Penelope Leach (5).

To find out what had been written for parents on this topic a group of students in one of my cry classes drew upon information from over 70 published sources. After an initial survey six main headings were decided upon. These were; causes in infants, remedies for infants, causes in mothers, remedies for mothers, types of cry and finally, effects of crying.

In order to summarise the main points made by these authors seven separate sections were designed within each of the six headings listed above. Each of the examples provided below is drawn from the "causes in infants" heading.

1. Medical. Dealt with topics with which a medically qualified person may become involved and treat. Tend to be "internal and pathological" in nature, e.g. anal fissure, constipation, ear ache.

2. Maturational. Captured those items for which the most suitable "remedy" was the passing of time, waiting for some changes to occur as participants developed, e.g. colic, growth spurt, teething.

3. Physiological. This overlaps with the medical section and contained matters which were "internal but normal", e.g. hunger, thirst.

4. Temperamental. Geared toward the "personality" of participants, typically internal and stable over time, e.g. delicate emotions, temper.
5. Learned. Included those items which are primarily socially determined and "acquired", e.g. habit, "testing" cry.
6. Inflicted. Listed those things which are fairly reactive and direct, e.g. frequent small feeds, too hot, wet/dirty.
7. Emotional. These involved feeling e.g. pain, anger, boredom, disappointment, fear.

Both the six headings and seven sections are provided here so others can use them to categorise advice which is found in other sources. From this survey of the available literature it would seem that after carrying out the usual routines of cuddling, feeding, burping and changing there is little practical advice available for either those who are guiding parents or for parents themselves about how to sustain healthy involvement with distressed babies.

Consequences of neglecting this topic

Since there is little systematically organised material available to guide those who are dealing with crying babies many consultants get by on bluff and waffle. Common explanations include those indicated in the previous section. There are two outcomes which consultants dealing with parents of crying babies seek to alleviate and/or prevent. Both can lead to death. One is depression, the other is baby bashing.

Depression The following extracts are from an excellent and highly readable book entitled *Special Report on Depression Research* (6). On pages 3–6 the following paragraphs are quoted from the section headed with the question "What is Depression?"

> Feeling sad, blue, down and dejected is a normal part of the spectrum of human emotions. We are familiar with such feelings in ourselves, and in those we know well. Transient unhappiness follows many of life's disappointments, losses and letdowns. Missing out on a new job opportunity, breaking up with a lover, moving to a new city, all can initiate a brief period of pain and sorrow. But most normal people bounce back from these experiences with renewed enthusiasm and gusto once the initial sense of loss wears off. Even those who experience profound grief at the loss of a loved one do not stay in a perpetual state of mourning. They do show many signs of clinical depression temporarily — crying, withdrawal, apathy, sleeplessness, loss of appetite and weight — but usually within a reasonable amount of time they resume their normal life pattern.
>
> What distinguishes normal depressed feelings from the disorders known as depression is the persistence and severity of change in usual

function. Instead of being transitory, the symptoms of depression last inordinately, for months, perhaps years without treatment. The symptoms are of several types: mood disturbances (such as enduring feelings of sadness, hopelessness), disturbances of biological functioning (sleeplessness, loss of appetite, loss of sexual drive, apathy, tiredness), and disturbances of thought (morbid preoccupations, delusions, hallucinations). Although depressive disorders, like normal depressed feelings, may be precipitated by losses, stresses, and unpleasant experiences, they may also occur in the absence of any single event, or in response to events that are objectively minor.

The psychological themes underlying these disorders may include sadness, helplessness, hopelessness, loss of self-esteem, loss of initiative and creativity, guilt feelings, self-punishment, social withdrawal, and preoccupation with suicide. In some cases, anxiety, hostility, over-indulgence, transient paranoia or other delusions, and various psychosomatic complaints may be present. Sleep disturbances, early morning awakening, lowered sexual drive, poor appetite and weight loss, complete inability to experience pleasure (anhedonia), or a general slowing of thoughts, speech, and movement may also occur in depressive disorders.

The symptoms of depression vary with personality and are also clearly a function of culture, since all behaviours, including depressive behaviours, are expressed in the context of a set of rules governing what is normal for the group. It is perhaps not so obvious that the expression of depression and mania may vary even within subcultures in the United States, in different areas of the country, in diverse socioeconomic or religious groups, or in the several minority groups.

In the same Special Report the following paragraph is cited from the section entitled "Causes of Depression".

Depression is currently viewed as having multiple causes which may be different for various groups of individuals, and in the end, different for each individual because of his or her idiosyncratic genetic makeup and life history. According to the vulnerability concept, individuals are born with low or high biological susceptibility to numerous disorders (e.g. different thresholds for the development of disorder). Whether illness develops, and when, depends on how the entire body adapts to internal and external stresses. Some of the bodily effects of diet, physical illness, exercise, learning, and stress are permanent and irreversable, especially in early life.

The ideas from different theories about depression have been summarised as a diagram which first appeared in a book aptly entitled *Mothers Matter Too* (7).

Box 1.1

Some theories on the cause of depression in women at home

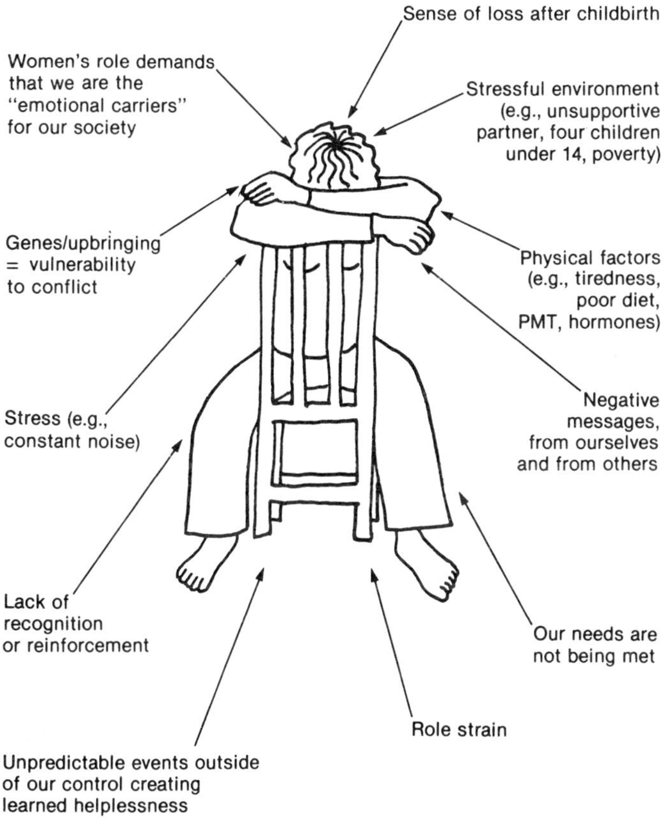

Source: Phillips (7)

Although there are many classifications for depression Katharina Dalton (8) distinguishes between several types which tend to occur in the first year following birth. First there is the *maternity blues*, a short-lived mild form of depression which lasts for about a week and is all over two weeks after birth. Next is *postnatal exhaustion* which comes on slowly, commencing either immediately following birth or emerging over the next few weeks, and has gone by about the time of baby's first birthday. *Postnatal depression* may begin immediately after birth or be a continuation of maternity blues, presenting itself with typical symptoms of depression. It may commence with ceasing breast-feeding, though for others will end with stopping breast-feeding, or may start with recommencing with the oral contraceptive or coincide with the days prior to the first menstrual period. Finally Dr. Dalton introduces *puerperal psychosis* which are severe cases where mothers are hospitalised often within a day or two of its emergence, and for whom in a majority of cases an illness punctuated the first two weeks after birth.

Whilst there is little doubt that many mothers experience depression in some form or another in the 3–30 week zone following delivery this is only gradually becoming recognised by health care agencies. What is done about this is another matter. While many procedures have been documented for other groups, mothers have typically been ignored, although there are exceptions.

A complex set of interactions occur between the various bodily changes associated with depression. Treatment tends to mirror the emphasis which a particular theory places, whether it be for changes in neurotransmitters, neurohormones, emotions/cognitions or behaviours/actions. Given that one set of changes influences another, then provided we are aware of these reciprocal effects the most satisfactory course of action lies in doing what one can within the constraints of skill, urgency and observable outcomes. In the present book emphasis is directed to the latter pair, emotions/cognitions and behaviours/actions.

Baby bashing

For decades developmental research and theory concerned itself mostly with these effects arising from differences in adults and/or situations of growing children. From the early 1970's a trend began which altered this view. Now it is generally accepted in the academic literature that the young are likely to influence those who look after them (9). In other words, as parents involve themselves with babies, then at the same time and in their own ways babies change how they are handled. For those who have been working closely with babies this "discovery" is hardly surprising. A quiet, easy going baby makes quite different demands from a noisy, irritable one. One consequence of this sort of thinking about the influences infants have on their parents is a reconsideration of the notion of baby bashing. Inconsolable crying is possibly one of the main triggers for acts of violence, a point which has been made elsewhere (10).

It takes less than a second to bash a baby. The rapid change from gently fondling an infant to feeling like hurting it is a horror known to many parents. People who have never been near to the edge of abuse may find this notion difficult to grasp. But there are those who have trodden the narrow way and only just restrained themselves from injuring their helpless young. Some parents are haunted for years by the ghosts of what could easily have been a family tragedy.

To be trapped at home with a young and difficult baby places an adult under a strain which is seldom recognised as intense by those who have never been in a similar situation. The line between feeling sudden intense hatred toward and actually striking an unmanageable baby can be so fine as to be almost transparent. There are occasions when the chief villain is the situation.

Although it is likely that most parents do not show physical aggression toward their infants during bouts of passionate anger, it is not known to what extent infants are at risk from these parents. Further, we are only beginning to find out about the sorts of things which parents coping with babies feel are important. The idea that motherhood is somehow "natural" is a difficult one to displace. How many damaged infants do we need to count before listening to the plight of parents? Some bruises take years to heal.

Unfortunately many of the schemes which have been designed to provide indications about which infants might be at risk from physical abuse by their parents are not particularly useful. Professionals can create careers for themselves by specialising in "abuse" (11). Yet, in spite of all the support and studies mounted so far, only a few provide promising leads.

Before it was well known that we were involved with baby crying and its effects at Massey University, Anthony Hill and I designed a questionnaire on baby bashing. After trying out earlier versions of the questionnaire on different groups of parents so as to tidy it up, a final version was carried by a national women's weekly magazine. The following paragraphs outlines results we obtained from that survey.

One reason for designing the questionnaire was to find out from mothers the sorts of things which led them to feel like smashing up their babies. It is known from the abuse literature that some adults' personalities can be biased toward unleashing acts of aggression. But little is known about mothers who are otherwise quite "normal", but occasionally feel like striking out.

In the questionnaire "bashing" was defined as "extreme physical abuse and violence toward babies". When we sent an earlier version of the questionnaire to professionals so as to obtain some critical comments many suggested we drop this extreme definition. We didn't. Mainly because the mothers who had helped in the survey design told us that was exactly how they felt at times. We defined a "baby" as an infant up until its first "birthday".

We formed two main groups of mothers on the basis of their replies. One was made up of those people who both felt like and said they did abuse their babies. A second group consisted of mothers who felt like being violent but did not abuse their infants. Many of these mothers would have been looking back, so it must be kept in mind they were remembering their pasts.

For purposes of reporting, the questions and answers are grouped into three main clusters. In the first one general background information was obtained. On the basis of these replies it would appear that many parents believe others feel like smashing up their babies; that the high risk times are in the afternoon-to-evening period; the early months are the roughest; and that there is a two-thirds bias towards both males and to first born, whether male or female.

The second cluster looked into the different ways that mothers tried to cope. Our results are quite clear: inexperienced and tired mothers try to manage mostly by leaving and/or ignoring their restless, crying babies. Typically the comforts used by both groups included cuddling, feeding, talking/singing, rocking, walking and toys, in that order. With our interest in baby crying the answer to the question "What did the baby do to make you feel like this?" was crucial. For over half of the answers from both groups the reply was simply "crying". This is not at all surprising for parents, yet strangely many of the contemporary "risk" models designed to predict abuse omit this more than obvious cause. One possible reason for this omission may be that even if crying was acknowledged little can be done about it anyway. This book is intended to change this situation and provide a source of things which can be done.

In the final cluster we found out about other people who may have been called upon to help out. The answers here paint a grey picture. Most had no other adult (except, perhaps for a partner about whom we did not enquire) who helped out during their bleak times. Perhaps "help" was not requested of others who may have been available. Then, going on, most mothers didn't leave their babies with anybody else, yet suggested a break from baby could be beneficial. And, clearly, there are no services about which mothers agree could be helpful. Mind, they may not have tried these; we did not ask them. Although doctors, nurses and paramedicals are top of each group's listing they do not achieve a majority vote. Perhaps they had been tried and found wanting.

There are dozens of "reasons" which could be offered for the lack of clear differences between the two groups of those who did abuse and those who felt like being violent. Perhaps the wrong sort of questions were posed. Or, mothers may not have answered honestly, since it was their reporting which we relied upon. Maybe they had forgotten. Possibly mothers did not classify themselves correctly. How about these being non-representative samples, or even faulty coding on our part? And so it could go on and on. It is not too difficult to put aside that which is disagreeable, to dismiss it as inconsequential.

However, it is my belief that thousands of women would agree with these results. Simply put, it is that there are no clear distinctions between those who feel like smashing up a baby and those who go ahead and do so. Coldly, the point is that on the basis of our questionnaire replies, there are no readily apparent differences between a group of mothers who did bash their babies and a group who felt like doing so.

We need to know more about the fine line which divides mothers' (and fathers' as well as other providers') feelings of violence from the actual event. How can we hold the hand which may rock the baby too hard; or restrain the fist which flies out; or slacken the grip which shakes a baby's shoulders too vigorously ......? These, and others, are the questions which press tightly. We need answers. In the meantime we have to do the best we can with the facilities available.

What mothers have written

The following extracts from letters show how mothers view their crying babies. Some of these letters came as a result of the "baby bashing" and "colic" surveys, others from general correspondence. They each point to the sheer enormity of the problem and of the urgency of some solution or resolution. These letters are included because I believe these views are important. Indeed, I would welcome additional mail on this topic. Dip into the letters, but be warned, they could be too "heavy" to tackle in a single sitting.

1. Baby cried especially at night normally around dinner time. He seemed colicky. Inspite of medicines he seemed to get worse. Sometimes I used to be quite rough in putting the medicine into his mouth. I started feeling more and more detatched from him. Since my husband was a man that couldn't cope with a child crying, I had to shut myself in a room with baby and pace the floor with him, for hours. I believe baby could feel lack of love from me. He became so much worse that I spent most of the day and night walking the floor with him. At times I only had one hours sleep, and during these times I wanted to throw the baby against a wall. These feelings were so strong and real, that I found it a little hard to distinguish which thought was most real.

2. Please note that at the time this happened my baby was about six months old and although it was him crying constantly that made me so tired it was the elder boy — then two and a half years — that I hit, till I

was afraid to go near him in case I lashed out. The bruises and gashes he received from my actions, I told my husband were collected in falling down the steps.

3. Once, maybe twice, maybe three times I just handed the child to my husband and walked out — always night time — walked the streets for hours and hours — would come home, amazed I could face it all like a new woman.

4. When my baby cried and I didn't know what to do the resentment built up towards the child. I also felt I couldn't discuss this (way I felt) with my husband as he was such a calm passive person and could tolerate so much more than I, and this built the resentment up more. I can't describe what held me back, perhaps it's guilt. I don't know but in the end I realised I had to talk to someone and I was lucky I had a very understanding G.P.

I talk a lot to other girls who have these same feelings and I must say that it's talking about and knowing that someone else has these feelings that helps one get over it.

5. I feel that in the early months after my baby's birth I could have become one of the 'baby-bashers'. I was fortunate enough to have the care of an excellent psychiatrist and a very thoughtful husband and thankfully such a thing never happened. Prior to my having a baby I was very anti-baby-bashers, but now having been through a possible situation myself I can understand the emotional side and be a little more tolerant.

6. If only there was somewhere locally one could take the children even for an hour or two sometimes, at a reasonable charge rate even, it would be a godsend for desperate mothers, and no doubt save a lot of child bashing.

7. After having two very normal little baby girls, I gave birth to another daughter nearly 19 years ago. The birth was easy but from the first day our baby cried nearly all the time. Her head would be bathed in perspiration whenever she was brought along at feed times. I tried to breast feed but found that with the worry of the baby, the other two to care for as well as the farm cooking etc, to cope with, that the baby had to be weaned. The crying continued night and day and the doctor told me to feed the baby every time she cried! I think I probably made the condition worse by doing this but at least she was quiet while the teat was in her mouth. With my husband's help I managed to get over those first three months but I did break out in a horrible nervous rash that was so itchy I scratched myself raw. The doctor prescribed tranquillisers for me at that stage. Our daughter progressed slowly — was slow to smile, crawl, walk and talk and always found school work difficult. She often had prolonged bouts of vomiting and stomach pains but even after a day or two in hospital they found nothing. She still gets odd bouts of stomach pains but has a job in an office and seems to be coping reasonably well.

8. I remember listening with horror to a minister preaching a sermon on the trials of family life many years ago. He had a baby son with a similar trouble as ours and he freely admitted that he felt like holding him by his ankles and crashing his head against the door. I felt revulsion for the minister then, but I understand his feelings now, and I appreciated the memory of his sermon when I was sorely tired by being helpless in the face of our child's constant screaming.

9. The teething period with both children was hard. The frustration of not knowing how to comfort them also because they seemed to cry more at night, lack of sleep made me irritable. With my second child my husband and I took turns in getting up and 'walking the floor' which helped tremendously.

My neighbour had a child a few years older than mine and we talked the situation over. I discovered my doubts and fears were quite normal.

10. I feel I could write a book on the subject! My grandmother keeps saying to me, when I complain of something, "its a long row to hoe", or "we all go through it". That makes me mad because you don't know how many others have suffered, you want constructive help right then and there, not to be told that in 15 years time you will be able to lie in bed and have breakfast in peace for the first time!! You can't even visualise that far ahead. I live day by day and don't make plans too far ahead.

11. I feel that a lot of my problems were caused at the Maternity Hospital where we very rarely saw our babies, no cuddles after feeding, not allowed in the nursery between feeds, no teaching of how to hold or bathe baby, in fact it was hell. When I got home she just cried all the time and as I was breast feeding the strain stopped milk flowing. When I asked for help I got criticism and felt guilty as it seemed to be all my fault and so I so started to take it out on baby. God knows I tried so hard but I feel the original bond was broken through lack of contact after birth.

12. I spent most of my days crying in the bedroom and refused to leave the house. I avoided contact with the child as much as possible, I recognised what was happening and told my doctor quite frankly what was going on. He gave me tranquillisers which didn't help at all.

13. My sleep was in short spells during nights. I would frequently return to bed in tears of exhaustion and frustration. It was during this time I desperately felt the answer would be to grasp girl twin by her ankles and bash her against a wall. Am thankful now and was then, immediately I got a hold on my feelings, that I did not allow my desperation to take charge. However, I can readily understand and feel sympathy for so called baby bashers.

14. Have thought about this a lot during the past year as before this, my first baby, I had despised baby bashing and bashers and now feel I can quite understand it.

I think perhaps motherhood in particular and perhaps parenthood generally is over glamourised. Everyone clucks away about a new baby and often offers no practical help. I know, without my mother's help in the first two weeks I would have gone crazy. I never had the rests suggested during the day, nor could I manage normal household necessities, let alone extras (visitors, baking etc). All this boiled down to lack of knowledge and experience. Before the baby comes one is lulled into thinking they eat and sleep, as nowadays in smaller families most mothers-to-be have had little experience of new-born babies around them all day and night. Also I think there is pressure to perform — be a model mother, housekeeper, wife, etc. When the emphasis should be on peace and happiness — it matters not that the house is messy and meals are late or thrown together if everyone's happy surely. And if visitors come to criticise they aren't worth knowing. However, we mothers break ourselves to conform and either suffer ourselves or take it out on children. Pride too I think stops people reaching out for help to 'pregnancy help' or neighbourhood coffee groups and Leagues — just a break and "tea and sympathy". We also carry on this keeping up appearances to friends, neighbours, parents especially in-laws and the pressure from this and sometimes over-expectant husbands is too much.

A lot of husbands too are raised by apparently super-capable mums who expect their daughters-in-law to cope entirely alone — never heard of fathers changing nappies, put other or this child to bed, bathing them etc. So husband sits down in front of TV and frowns at or yells to wife about noise, lack of quality of dinner etc. and never raises a finger except to complain.

Mine fortunately was not like this, though a reluctant or disgusted look from him was enough to push me over the edge on a bad day. But no thanks to his mother who is men-on-the-pedestal type person.

However, I have seen women worn to a frazzel managing alone because of that kind of husband and then left alone when everything has wound down because hubby's gone to the pub or footy meetings etc. So to top it all off she has no adult stimulation to equalise everything again.

Rather than people offering suggestions like 'time you weaned him' (when you are both quite happy with the status quo), 'time you used a potty', 'shouldn't he be walking/talking' why not say 'I'll mind him for an hour or so while you, shop, read, sleep, see a movie, visit a friend etc'. Amazing how different you feel towards junior (and he you) after a short separation. I'm lucky for that.

15. Tonight I have been sitting back watching our son, who is 14 months old happily playing with his Dad. He gives us so much pleasure now but the first eight months were nothing but unreasonable torture for us, his parents.

I remember hearing some months ago about the study you are doing on 'crying'. I hope that it is not to late to contribute.

At this stage I won't analyse anything, although on looking back I do have a few thoughts on why we might have had a crying baby. I'll just write about it as it happened.

We had been married four years; I was eager to start our family. My husband agreed but did not have the same enthusiasm. As my pregnancy progressed he became more interested and excited. I read books on childbirth, breast feeding and attended excercise and parent classes. I was lucky enough to have a natural labour and delivery (without drugs). Our son was born a very healthy 7lb6oz. We were thrilled. I felt marvellous and prepared to look after my baby 24 hours a day. The hospital thought otherwise and insisted on taking him to the nursery for part of the day and at night. I pressed my point to the staff which was that I felt I would like to learn how to care for him with them as a back-up if needed. Eventually I was allowed 24 hour rooming in but it was an unpleasant experience as I was alienated by the staff. Still, we coped.

It wasn't until he was about two and a half weeks old that it all started. It was an ordinary sort of start to the day. Then before lunch the crying began. He wouldn't stop and nothing would pacify him, not feeding, rocking, cuddling or leaving alone. It was not a quiet cry either it was a full throated scream that seemed to come from his whole body. He finally settled about 10pm. We were rather tense by that time but thought he would probably be back to his usual self by the next day (just as well we didn't know what was ahead). The next day was the same and the next and the next. There were screams upon screams. He hardly slept during the day and woke every two hours at night. Feeding at night was the quickest and easiest way to get him back to sleep.

After three days I took him to the doctor. He could find nothing wrong but prescribed a syrup. This was given 15 mins before a feed. It helped although I was reluctant to rely on it.

The weeks went by and the tension in our household grew as the screams echoed through the house. He would sleep for 30 minutes then wake suddenly just bellowing. If he was left, he would be brilliant red and soaked with perspiration. He never seemed to be out of my arms. I was feeling exhausted but wouldn't leave him with neighbours or friends as at that time I couldn't bear the thought of inflicting them with this red faced yelling monster.

My husband was good and helped in the house but he hated the crying and would get very angry and uptight. When the baby wasn't crying we would talk and wonder why??? We knew that parenthood was not all roses but this!!! We were hardly living.

Occasionally my husband would babysit while I went for groceries. But even that was no break because I would rush into the shop and grab things off the shelves as quickly as possible always dreading what would be going on at home. I wasn't afraid that he would physically hurt the child but I always expected a repeat of the very first night that I left him to go next door. I had been there for about one and a half hours when the phone rang and my husband said to come home. When I opened the door a bundle of noise was dumped into my arms and my husband said "I can't stand this" and walked out (only for 30 minutes). We talked about it later and kept reassuring each other that things would get better. Six weeks was often a turning point (so they said). Six weeks came and went!!!

I felt like a miserable failure of a parent. I sought advice from everyone. What was I doing wrong? He was so healthy putting on loads of weight and very alert. Why did he wake every two hours during the night? I'd try forcing him to go longer between feeds in the day (4 hours) but that only produced more crying in him and anxiety in me. One day I got angry! I lay him on the floor hoping he would enjoy a kick. He kicked all right and yelled. I was sitting on the couch looking down and saying "please, please shut up you're nothing but a mouth" and at that moment I was really close to hurting him. All I could see was this great cavern of a mouth and the noise pounded into my head. There was nothing remotely human about it. I put my foot under it and flipped it onto its stomach. "Perhaps you'll like it better that way" I said "Oh dear, you don't". I'll just grind my foot into you and stub you out then. I didn't! but I hated the baby and I hated myself for being so useless as a mother.

When he was three months we shifted from the town where he was born. I thought that soon he might get better because three months was another turning point. Nothing changed. We weren't a family, we were three unhappy people who existed. The tension was incredible when he was awake and we would just flop when he was asleep. My husband would walk down the drive home after work, full of apprehension as to what he'd meet. More often than not it would be a harassed wife on the verge of tears with half the tea cooked or none at all.

I found that going out of the house every day helped. Our son always seemed to enjoy the stimulation of different people and different places and was often quite amicable until we were home. Soon I got harder and if I was trying to cook dinner I would dress him in winter woollies and put him in his bouncinette outside on the doorstep. I'm sure the neighbours enjoyed their evening serenade and I felt so much better with the door between me and the noise.

At about four months we tried him on solids to see if that would help. He enjoyed the food but it made no difference to the amount of crying. He became chronically constipated though. He would not have a bowel motion unless he was given an enema or suppository. These were prescribed by a doctor and I gave him one every three days to retrain the bowel. After a few weeks of this, pureed prunes for breakfast were enough to keep things moving. We went to a paediatrician who said there was nothing physically wrong but thought he might have a lazy bowel. He did not think that this would be the cause of his crying.

Time went by and our boy was growing and learning. He enjoyed playing with toys but only if someone was there interacting with him. Never would he play by himself. At six months he could pull himself along the floor on his stomach. A lifesaver was a bouncer that is hung in a doorway. Harnessed into this he would jump vigorously often smiling. Nights were a little easier, we were usually up two or three times. It was no use shutting the doors and letting him scream himself to sleep. He was a very strong little boy who could rage on for an hour, no trouble. We would be wrapping our pillows round our ears and tossing and turning until we'd end up yelling at each other. Finally one of us would get him. My husband, who is usually an easy going man, would storm into the bedroom and vent his anger by hitting the bedding on the cot and at times would slap the baby on the legs. Before the baby arrived I would have said that it would be me that would lash out rather than him. But I couldn't be bothered hitting, it would use up to much energy and I felt too drained for that. It was easier at night to be unemotional and do what had to be done then sleep. I felt the opposite during the day. I was always rushing to get things done. In the afternoons I would jump into the car and away. As I drove I would be rushing, foot always hard down on the accelerator and my heart was always beating fast.

By age seven months the bouts of crying were not so frequent. He still woke at least twice a night. I went to the doctor for tranquillisers because I felt that the night waking was habitual and I hoped this would break the pattern. He had a prescribed drug every night for two weeks. We slept. It was beautiful, our first night of uninterrupted sleep in eight months. When we discontinued the tranquilliser, he still slept the whole night. I weaned him from the breast. Ever since then he's never looked back. We're really proud of our boy. He's still very active. When he walked at ten months people said "now the trouble starts, he'll be into everything". I'm always hauling him out of some mischief but that doesn't worry me in the slightest because he's happy. "Crying" is a thing of the past.

Gosh! I have gone on, Haven't I. Once I started it all just poured out. Hope its all of some help. I think it is essential to realise the implications of the crying baby especially in families with other stresses. An unhappy marriage or financial worries would be more than enough to tip the balance and result in battered or abandoned babies or suicidal mothers.

2 INTENTIONS AND LIMITATIONS OF THIS BOOK

Tool kits and themes

The people who are usually called in to attend maintenance problems around the home are trained to recognise difficulties and may even fix these on the spot. To do so they need vehicles equipped with enough tools to tackle common jobs. An electrician for instance has usually both a vehicle with basic facilities and a kit with screwdrivers and the like, carried about on person to save needless trips back and forth to the van or truck. The equipment can be used to test, repair, replace and service most domestic electrical installations. If the job is too complicated either specialist help may be sought or the unit taken to a workshop.

Something similar goes on when dealing with babies in crisis. Like an electrician a consultant is trained to make decisions based on an examination of the presenting symptoms. At times specific tools will be needed in order to probe into what is going on. Tools can be designed both for specific and general tasks. Extending the above illustration, interventions may be likened to an electrician's screwdriver which can only be used on a few head slots, or a multi-meter which with a flick of a knob can be used to test a wide range of circuits for different effects.

Having a set of tools is only part of the equipment. Although the different interventions can be seen by others, in the same way as an electrician's equipment may be seen, it is how these are used which makes sense in the long run. One has to go beyond the tools and see how these can be employed to the best effect by putting a plan into action.

A plan is like a musical theme: it offers a set of working instructions for which there is general pattern. Once a personal theme is grasped then variations may be created upon it. Although there are likely to be a wide range of tunes which can be realised from a single theme (some of which may even appear to be contradictory) there is, nonetheless, an underlying unification which gives a purpose to the interventions selected. This book provides themes which consultants may use as a basis for creating interventions which maximise strengths and interests.

Assumptions and bias

All people have assumptions and biasses about the way the world is constructed. While this book is not designed to alter your beliefs and values, it is appropriate that you be aware of some of mine. Even though you may be able to identify these by a careful reading of the text to make this task easier I'll note a few down. The main reason for this statement is to help make sense of the book; as a student said to me once, "Once I could see where you were coming from it all fitted into place".

Briefly, I believe that people are active, can have plans, think about these plans, tell others about them and think about alternatives. People can anticipate events and these will influence what they do in the present. People can have different views of the same thing and can talk about these differences. Feelings are just as important as thoughts but have a language system which we are just beginning to find out about, mainly because we have attempted to use the languages of reason and logic for phenomena which are both unreasonable and illogical. I have an optimistic view of humans and believe that we can achieve a good deal more than we often settle for.

Metaphors

When writing about how pre-school children acquire the capability to read, Sylvia Ashton-Warner (1) characterised her discovery of a child's key vocabularly with epigramatic statements such as "a word walks hand in hand with its image". The images which adults use in their personal communication stem from metaphors. If you tune your ear to these then keys which open a communication channel will be provided. According to one dictionary (2) a metaphor is "the application of a word or phrase to something that it does not apply to literally, in order to indicate a comparison with the literal usage ...". In his typically poetical style Lewis Thomas captures this point nicely by noting "we have language and can build metaphors as skillfully and precisely as ribosomes make protein" (3, p.14).

There are two main metaphors which commonly deal with human development. It is helpful to know about these since their orientations are poles apart and their implications far reaching. If you apply the wrong metaphor in a situation, one that does not match a parent's position, then your time is wasted. One skill a consultant acquires is to tease out which metaphors apply and then select interventions to fit. This way activities will make sense to participants.

Of course you will run into difficulties if you do not have the flexibility to switch from one metaphor to the other in order to suit particular cases. Providing background training in metaphor identification is beyond the scope of the present book. In Box 2.1 are listed the characteristics of the two dominant metaphors, the machine and the plant. You can inspect these features and perhaps spot your own preferences.

Box 2.1

Summary of differences between two human development metaphors

	Metaphor	
	Machine	*Living Organism*
1. causes of action	external	internal
2. behaviour change	quantitative	qualitative
3. the whole	sum of parts	greater than sum of parts
4. measurement	interval	ordinal
5. design	cause and effect	part of evolving whole
6. activity	pushed	spontaneous

It is not hard to see how these metaphors are expressed by different professionals. For instance the mechanical one is endorsed by those who represent classical medicine and behaviourism. Consequently there is little doubt it makes sense to those who share this metaphor but is quite disastrous for those who do not.

To go beyond this dual-metaphor dilemma is to create another, one which can accommodate each of them. This is important since there are times when one rather than the other metaphor is relevant. A lot of time has been wasted by protagonists arguing over which of these metaphors has the greater merits in understanding human development.

As one attempt to go beyond this opposing pair, Margaret McKim and I decided to apply a different metaphor to babies in their families. We took our cue from a comment by Ernest Bruckler who said "More than the land, the sea is a metaphor for everything". The imagery which does justice to both of the other metaphors (machine and plant) is suggested by water, moving sea water which can swirl into tidal rock pools of varying depths. Our metaphor is *pooling*. On the surface one can deal with the mechanical aspects of interaction. At the first meeting with a family this is often the most satisfactory place to begin since the parents want something which can be done immediately, right at this moment. Literally, this is testing the water.

Others may want to plunge in, having tried enough options already to know that they are now aiming at getting a better feel for their situations. These people are familar with surface buffeting, have survived and are now aiming at a deeper understanding of the dynamics which are influencing their growth together.

There are more features to the pooling metaphor. For the present however the point is that it provides one way of dealing with the conflict between the mechanical and the organismic. By using the idea of pooling and by modifying it to suit personal needs, the classical two-metaphor developmental paradox can be resolved. Further, an awareness of alternative metaphors will make it easier to deal with cases in which contradictions abound. By deciding which metaphor parents are adopting consultants are provided with a means of selecting interventions which fit individual situations. Often people are not aware of their metaphoric orientation.

Since action plans have as their source one of a few basic metaphors, this means there is more to practical consultancy than simply taking any intervention and applying it without regard for the needs or preferences of those with whom one is working. Knowing a person's perspective means knowing their metaphors. Only then can one get alongside and help to make sense out of surrounding chaos. Through drawing from different perspectives (medical, paramedical, psychological, social work, etc) educational schemes may be designed by professionals to meet in a practical way the needs of those having to cope with crying babies.

Neither a theory nor a research text

This book is not intended to draw together various theoretical positions. All the same it is not possible to avoid an introduction to some ideas which are behind the various interventions. The use of metaphors in the previous section is theoretical in the sense that these are assumed to provide an insight into the relevance of selecting particular strategies. An intervention applied without a broader, theoretical, understanding is like a ship without a rudder. Making the easy distinction between theory and practice is of little use since these are complementary aspects of the same thing.

One further distinction may be of use here. Computers which play chess are excellent at weighing up the probable outcomes from several alternative projected moves quite quickly. These programmes can hold far more information than any person. Yet people can still beat the machines, even when playing chess according to the rules. The machines, it seems, are excellent tacticians. They can size up many situations and move to accord them with maximum gain. People can be either tacticians or strategists. A strategist plots a course of action using additional criteria and goes about playing the game with an underlying theme which forecasts general and overall themes of which the individual moves are part.

In human development, first time parents without experience tend to be like tacticians. From the available information they act often without grasping the significance of underlying movements provided, for example, from biological urges. With experience parents may become strategists. Hence, as the saying goes "the time to begin having a family is when you should stop", the point being that after having raised children parents would go about it quite differently given another chance. There is a trap here. If a parent has had a couple of easy babies and then meets a "difficult" one then many of the previously worked out strategies just will not apply.

By searching through the many theories which have been formulated to account for the development of babies in families, anybody can find support for a particular action. This is not very helpful, darting from one to another in an attempt to justify what is done. For example if a person wishes to find a theory which would warrant leaving a crying baby alone then dial up a behaviourist. At the other extreme if a person wanted to justify always picking up a crying baby then select an attachment theorist.

With experience, and an openness to learn from meetings with mothers and crying babies, consultants will become strategists; able to identify what can be done to fit in with developmental and family themes. Simply being able to cite a particular theoretical position is of little use. All the same it can be helpful to know what others have already written on a subject as their insights can illuminate likely stumbling blocks.

Most of the research which has been published on this topic demands a fairly sophisticated level of statistical comprehension and some of it is badly done anyhow. Both theories and research are important. In our own work these areas make up two legs of a stool. The other leg which is emphasised in this book deals with application. Although not dealing directly with theory and/or research this book would not exist if these aspects were ignored. As some of you make use of the intervention you will begin to make changes and observe the outcomes. In other words, if an enquiry approach is maintained then people can come up with their own views as to why things work (this is a theory of sorts) and of the variations which may be applied in different situations (which is research). It is by searching for explanations and noting how fluctuations can be of service that educational strategies emerge. This book is aimed at setting this into motion.

Ethics

A consultant's sphere of responsibility includes both families with irritable babies as well as professional codes of ethics. In essence, the underlying theme of any code of ethics is respect for both the profession and for the receivers of any services. When designing and applying an intervention a problem often faced by consultants is how to get the most from theoretical and research findings when these are adapted and applied in practical settings with minimal risk.

Consultants, especially those who are volunteers, can be quite lax about attending to professional codes of ethics. Codes are designed to maintain standards within a profession, to provide guidelines for practitioners as well as a means of judging services, and to offer a framework for handling complaints.

Medical and paramedical groups publish ethical codes for their members. So do those who offer other services. For example the following quotation is from the American Psychological Association's *Specialty Guidelines for the Delivery of Services by Clinical Psychologists* and makes it clear what, in part, clinical psychological services are. These are, in part,

> Interventions directed at identifying and correcting the emotional conflicts, personality disturbances, and skills deficits underlying a person's distress and/or dysfunction. Interventions may reflect a variety of theoretical orientations, techniques and modalities . . ." (4).

If a consultant belongs to several professional associations or societies, many codes of ethics are likely to apply. This can be quite confusing, especially if there appear to be minor contradictions. These statements are intended as guidelines; a practitioner still needs to make informed decisions with respect to the law and those attended.

Many ethical safeguards may need to be implemented. In our own work the following two are applied. First, by asking those whom we consult to complete a consent form. This serves as a helpful reminder about the limits of involvement. Since it is easy to slide into assuming an authoritarian position where practically any question at all may be asked, a consent form provides basic rights and helps consultants to "mind their own business".

The consent form which we use is shown in Box 2.2.

Second, this form and each of the interventions are submitted to and cleared by an Ethics committee established within the University. Many institutions now have similar groups which handle topics such as these. One distinct possibly which has to be considered is if something untoward happens. An extreme example would be an infant death which is "blamed" onto consultants by parents who claim to have been following directions.

Other consultants

Crying babies and their families can be subjected to a kaleidoscope of professional services. The range of possibilities becomes clearer when various assessment procedures are followed and contra-indications are

Box 2.2

Consent Form

Involvement with babies

Please read carefully the following:

I understand that any information provided is confidential to professional persons involved, that I am free to refuse to answer any questions which are embarrassing or which may intrude on my privacy, and that I may withdraw my consent and discontinue participation at any time without prejudice.

I also understand that people involved in professional training sometimes have access to the material and that information gained may be used for instructional and research purposes but that the names of participants are not released.

I herewith consent to participate.

______________________________	______________________
Signature of Parent-guardian	relationship to baby
______________________________	______________________
Signature of Researcher-clinician	Date

Name and address (printed)

____

____

____

____

detected. These may extend from marriage counsellors through to neurologists.

Already, as part of a professional group, many consultants will be familiar with both services and agencies available in their local communities. In addition, established protocol will exist for making referrals to other consultants.

For those who are not affiliated to or work from a "known" community group, remember it is very easy to upset others who intimate that the territory has been staked out and that any interference with the established order will not be tolerated. In short, you'll need to establish a reputation by action. Even though many families are affected, in the first instance tackle only enough cases that can be comfortably handled in order to work out your own strategies. The word will soon get around that you are offering assistance to those coping with crying babies. Your actions will speak for themselves.

There are three groups to whom information may need to be supplied. One consists of other members of your profession. To these case reports, observations, ideas, interventions and the like can be presented at society meetings and conferences or published as journal articles, letters, book chapters. This is highly specialised and tends not to make a lot of sense to those outside of the profession. A second group consists of families, those who are direct recipients of the service offered. For this group a different type of documentation is provided. Further details about this are provided below.

An intermediate group, between professional colleagues and families is made up of other professionals, the news media, and so forth. For this group at least two modes of communication are used and ought to be provided for. One is verbal, and can take the form of an interview in a face-to-face setting or by telephone. The second is by way of written enquiries. For this group I have prepared a two-page statement which can be quoted. A simply worded document of this sort is most useful for eliminating possible sources of error. The statement I use is shown in Box 2.3.

Box 2.3

About CrySOS clinics for people with crying babies

CrySOS Questions

If you answer *Yes* to five or more of the following comments a CrySOS clinic may be able to offer practical assistance.

—On most days my baby has bouts of non-soothable crying (mostly around early evening).
—During most nights my baby wakes crying.
—Overall, my baby cries more than an average baby.
—My baby has a "difficult" personality.
—After feeding, changing, and burping, my baby continues to cry after being picked up.
—I have to try and cope with my crying baby alone.
—Baby crying upsets me.

Discovering how to cope with baby crying
is one task in the understanding of parenthood.
But this does not have to be done alone.

Background

The term CrySOS (said as "crisis") was formed by adding to the word "cry" the international distress signal. This captures nicely what we deal with in clinics: parents who are at their wits' end, driven with feelings of desperation by their difficult babies.

Although these "troublesome" infants account for as much as 10% of the baby population it is a common belief nowadays that parents should be able to cope alone. At one time extended family members (such as grandparents), or friends, or neighbours provided mothers with essential social support. Today this is less often the case. Unfortunately many parents have few others to whom they can turn with confidence. Beyond a family doctor people are expected to manage without a whimper.

Many cannot. CrySOS clinics are designed to provide parents with professional support, to help them to "make it" rather than "break it" with their demanding babies. Clinics are designed to apply research findings. Consultants and parents work together with baby in a joint undertaking.

Philosophy and Purposes

The clinics' philosophy is an optimistic one. Simply put, it is that people can make a difference for good in their situations. This tends to happen when threads of meaning are drawn from surrounding family chaos. By joining with parents, consultants are able to deal with each unique situation through helping parents:

- —recognise the disruptions crying babies create;
- —to understand their feelings of helplessness;
- —to appreciate why they feel the way they do;
- —to take part in procedures designed to introduce patterning to their daily activities;
- —to recognise their strengths;
- —to remain healthy.

Above all, clinics are geared toward preventative maintenance enabling parents to survive until the next day, the next week, the next month without damaging themselves or their infants.

Service

CrySOS is an idea rather than a place. So long as the broad clinic philosophy is applied it does not matter where this happens. However, consultants are able to work only in face-to-face settings. Communication by other means, whether telephone or letter is not undertaken.

Intervention

CrySOS clinics deliver self-help educational services. Our intervention procedures have been designed within a broad social-psychological framework. Parents are encouraged to seek "medical" clearance from their Doctors. Whilst some of our procedures have been refined over the years there are others which are still undergoing modification. The clinics apply research findings in a practical manner and may provide us with insights for future studies.

Referrals

Parents, usually mothers, find out about clinics from friends, doctors, or other health and social service professionals. The initial meeting can take upwards of an hour. A second meeting is typically planned to take place in the following week. Families graduate from our programmes when parents are no longer upset by baby.

Since the clinics are designed especially for crying babies, families are referred to other agencies if non-crying issues seem to be disrupting family life.

Further Information

Requests for additional materials may be directed to:

(put your name, agency, address, phone)

No answers

This book is intended as a guide to help people orchestrate themes which can be put into action. Short of killing them there is no single cure for all crying babies. As consultants work through their plans it will be found that some interventions have a much higher success rate than do others. Success can be attributed to many things; parents may have become more capable, an intolerance could have been discovered and appropriate remedial action undertaken, an infection identified and medication prescribed to counter this successfully, and so on. Any strategy needs to have a certain amount of openness built in so that unexpected events can be accommodated and used to advantage.

This book is incomplete. Perhaps it can never be finished. Parents and babies will continue to change at a faster rate and to offer more challenges than may be resolved by theoretically inspired research. What can be achieved is a better set of guidelines.

The cases which are the most difficult to handle are those that seem to "break the rules". Here, in spite of what would be expected, quite the opposite occurs. For instance a parent writes that a night-waking crying baby quite quickly stops this after having been left alone. Initially the parents believed that picking baby up and offering comfort was in baby's best interests. This was routine for an exhausting eight months. Then one night neither parent could rally to the night-cry and did nothing. The crying went on for a time and then stopped, never to happen again at night. Stories like this are uncomfortable. For there are other families where babies were left, quite deliberately, but did not seem to stop their night crying. How then does one make a decision based on a particular family's needs, expectations and capabilities which at the same time fits in with guiding strategies for action available to a consultant? To simply leave all babies, as advocated by some of the more extreme behaviouristically-inclined operators, to cry it out because others have done so without apparent bad effects, is to ignore many characteristics of human nature of which the need for making bonds of attachment is one.

Most people who have lived with or worked among crying babies have their own pet theories about what is going on and should be done. Cases can be quoted for whom the advice applied, apparently with success at every turn. If it was that simple the crying baby crisis would have been resolved long ago. A professional not only makes suggestions but has a broader scheme within which the advice is placed. It can be justified on grounds other than it works, if it is part of a broader plan.

3 TYPICAL "ISSUES"

Spoiling

Questions and comments along the following lines are not unusual. "If I always pick up my crying baby won't she cry more often, just to be cuddled?" "How do I know my baby won't learn bad habits? He may never give me a moment's rest if he's picked up each time he cries." "If my baby is crying at night she stops as soon as I pick her up. But I want her to learn to sleep through." "He now knows that if he cries I'll pick him up. I wish I'd never begun this business. Now I can't leave him at all."

Some babies like lots of cuddles. Others seem to be more "distant" and appear not to enjoy close comforting except during routines like feeding. Overall, babies are designed for being with adults. It has been suggested that humans ought to be born at around 46 weeks' gestation. Yet babies are born when they are, since any increase in size would jeopardise their mothers' health. Of course there are some big babies, but, on the whole infants tend to be of an optimum size. Consider one implication of this idea. If babies are born sooner than they ought to be then they are still attached even though physically separated.

Humans belong to the group of animals which cling, follow closely and protest loudly when left alone. Evidence to support this classification can be obtained from analysis of milks from various species, spacing of feeding, and the capability to regulate temperature. From an evolutionary viewpoint humans do not belong to the drop-and-leave species where the young feed on protein enriched milk taken between long spells, are able to move about soon after birth and may be killed by predators if they are noisy during mother absence. The compensation of reduced birth size, adjusted to fit delivery mechanisms, is evident for human babies in extreme vulnerability during the first few months. They are totally dependent on adults during this time.

It is children who may learn bad habits, so when these have been identified interventions may be tailored to meet the needs of those who show concern. Babies are not children. Babies are unlikely to show evidence of bad habit learning until the latter half of their first year.

There are some general developmental patterns of infant behaviour that are characterised by a sudden onset, continuation over a few weeks, and a final falling away to vanish from sight. As already mentioned, night-waking and stranger anxiety tend to show this trend. So too does infant crying. If these are biologically based crises, complete in themselves, then it may be thought that nothing need be done at all since in their own time they will simply disappear. For a few babies this may be the case. For most though, it is how these crisis displays are managed when in their prime which seems to have consequences for later development. There is an inter-meshing of developmental themes occuring. The upshot of this may not be evident until much later. All the same, parents are the only agents who cause subsequent developmental crises. It may be more appropriate to consider basic themes. Some arise from the biological unfolding of participants and others from their social interactions and expectations.

Most authors agree it is not possible to spoil a young crying baby by picking it up. Infant crying in the early weeks is a biologically-based signal which demands adult attention. It is when the crying does not stop after following the standard repertoire of cuddling, feeding, and changing that aid may be sought.

Claims about spoiling are often an indication of disruption: the adults have "better" things to do with their time than simply messing about with babies. Consultants ought to be familiar with the questions parents may raise about imagined "dangers of spoiling" and be prepared to answer these doubts in ways which meet the uncertainties voiced. A straight forward statement of the "facts" is unlikely to be adequate.

Infantile Colic

There are advertisements from around the turn of the century encouraging people to purchase anti-colic nipples for use when bottle feeding. These advertisements still appear. The better teat has not yet been invented to prevent colic.

For a Crying Baby Questionnaire from which over 450 replies were obtained, colic was defined as "rhythmic attacks of screaming which cannot be explained by any known cause or reason for discomfort". The following comments are based on results obtained from that survey.

Two-thirds of the mothers indicated their colicky baby was first born. There were no male-female differences. Over 80% of the babies had at least one colic attack each day. These attacks had a regular pattern. They occurred mostly after feeding in the late-afternoon to evening period. For over half, these attacks lasted between one and four hours, while for almost a third, daily colic sessions lasted beyond three hours' duration.

Half of the colicky babies commenced their crying before twelve days of age, and three-quarters were well underway before three weeks. Only a quarter had stopped by three months. This result gives rise to some doubt about the common phrase "3-month colic". In fact half the babies continued until four and a half months. Surprisingly, a quarter of the babies were still crying from colic attacks after nine months of age. It seems that one hope of many parents caught with a colicky baby, that it will cease at three months, appears unfounded. This news is not good news. There is a major caution in presenting these results. That is, these trends are based on group-analyses and an individual baby could perform quite differently from what these summary figures show. In other words: hope must be sustained.

If we knew what caused colic in babies we might be able to do something about it. But we don't. In the questionnaire mothers were asked about likely causes. Around a third of them related this to "wind", either as a "build-up", or an "inability to bring it up". About equal numbers (10%) indicated causes in; too much milk too fast, an underdeveloped digestive system, or tension in the home setting. As for possible remedies, it is clear mothers of colicky infants are willing to try many "cures". A quarter "paced the floor". Other commonly listed attempts included; boiled water, back-patting/massaging, carrying, movement, warm hot water bottle or bath, cuddling, and mother excluding certain "windy" foods from her diet (eg. cabbage, peas, dairy products). However the main response was medication (85%). Yet in spite of medication being highly nominated it was not found to be a successful arrestor of colic bouts. When asked what successfully stopped colic, "medication" came third in the priority listing, following "nothing" and "time/natural growth".

To extend answers provided under the "causes and cures" questions, two items tapped other approaches. In one, parents were asked what suggestions could be provided to a mother with a colicky baby. The highest response class was to "find a sympathetic doctor/paediatric nurse" (20%), followed by "medication" and "leave baby with trusted friend" (10% each) and then front/back pack, relaxation, patience, and bring up wind. Here is partial confirmation for the limited assistance obtained from medication. For although most mothers tried medication, it is not high on their suggestion lists.

A second question in this set related to the possibility of other adults being available for helping. Just what would have been asked of them? About a fifth of the mothers answering said "nothing", and this was followed by around 10% for each of; take baby for walk, hold baby/nursing, do housework. In other words parents saw this as a difficulty which they would weather out.

Perhaps many mothers are still trying to manage with the idea that they should be able to cope, come hell or high water. For when asked about their own health just under half reported they were tired, exhausted, fatigued, rundown. Another third replied "good". Then why is it these mothers, worn out by their crying babies, don't seek assistance? A person who is at her wits' end trying to cope with a crying baby needs all the encouragement available; from husband, parents, in-laws, friends. Those who are trying to cope should not be shy to say "baby cries". Frankly, it's not likely this is their fault. And it isn't baby's either. Over 75% of colicky babies were reported to be in good health by their mothers.

Well, whose fault is it? Unfortunately the notion of "fault" is the wrong one. There may be a "family" trend. Over one-third of the mothers answering had a relation who had colic as a baby. Since most infants do "grow out" of their colicky spells, it seems there is a strong maturational component. From results colic seems to be fairly resistant to any environmental intervention and lasts longer than generally believed.

In a thorough review of infantile colic Asnes and Mones (1) present the table shown in Box 3.1 which shows that the diagnosis of colic and irritability can be extensive. In addition these authors relate points made by another writer (2) offered as a guide during counselling. These include sensible suggestions like; parents not being responsible, it will not harm the baby either physically or psychologically, and parental need for time away from the situation.

Further details concerning suggestions for dealing with colicky babies do not deserve a separate section. When presented with any crying baby, whether colicky or not, it is useful to proceed through the general plan provided for a first meeting. Otherwise, if one deals only with the presenting symptoms, it is possible essential items may be missed.

Medication

Of the numerous drugs available for babies some are helpful for soothing prolonged crying. Of these there are three main classes. First, there are home-made concoctions blended according to family traditions or local custom. At one time alcohol, and particularly gin, served this purpose. A second class includes medicines which can be purchased "over the counter", even at supermarkets. Once opiates were used, but now many contain alcohol and others a mild sedative. The final class is generally obtainable with a doctor's prescription.

Although many parents resort to some sort of medication to placate their crying babies there are few systematic research-based investigations about effectiveness. Given the current state of personal awareness with regard to drug taking; particularly of habit formation, unwanted side effects and unforseen long term consequences, this gap in the research literature is indicative of the low "political" status of babies.

Now for a note of caution. Whilst many parents do not exceed the stated dosage of "cry" medicines some administer several different ones at the same time. The point is simple: by combining separate doses, each of which may be within limits, there is really an additive effect. So

Box 3.1

Differential Diagnosis of the Irritable Young Infant

I. Psychoemotional factors
  A. Psychosocial deprivation
  B. Child abuse/neglect
II. Neurological disorders
  A. Subdural hematoma or effusion
  B. CNS infections
  C. CNS degenerative diseases
III. Cardiovascular disorders
  A. Paroxysmal supraventricular tachycardia
  B. Congestive heart failure
  C. Cardiomyopathies
IV. Gastrointestinal disorders
  A. Gastroesophageal reflux with esophagitis
  B. Pyloric stenosis
  C. Volvulus
  D. Intussusception
  E. Constipation
  F. Anal fissure
  G. Carbohydrate intolerance
  H. Milk allergy
V. Metabolic
  A. Hypoglycemia
  B. Hyperthyroidism
  C. Electrolyte imbalance
  D. Hypocalcemia
  E. Inherited disorders of metabolism (i.e., organic acidemias, amino acidopathies, etc.)
VI. Miscellaneous
  A. Underfeeding
  B. Narcotic withdrawal syndrome
  C. Fetal alcohol syndrome
  D. Incarcerated inguinal hernia
  E. Caffey's disease
  F. Anemia
  G. Colic
  H. Urinary tract infection
  I. Obstructive uropathy
  J. Congenital syphillis
  K. Glaucoma
  L. Deafness
  M. Osteomyelitis

Source: Asnes and Mones (1)

everything has to be totalled up. Although unintended, there may be some babies who are over dosed.

Merbentyl syrup contains the antispasmotic agent dicyclomine hydrochloride. Of three studies reporting on the effects of this drug on infantile colic one stands out (3). It was a prospective, double-blind, randomised clinical trial. Half of the 48 initial participants were given a placebo, which was a neutral solution. The others were given dicyclomine hydrochloride. Colic was defined as unexplainable irritability, agitation, fussiness or crying which matched or exceeded three hours per day for three days per week over a three-week period. In addition, babies had to be gaining at least 150 gm per week and not been given medication for their crankiness. Forty two families completed the two-week trial. Of the six who withdrew only one baby received the drug. Overall the results were quite striking; colic was eliminated in 15 out of 24 with the drug but for only six of 24 with the placebo. As a group those babies who responded (either to drug or placebo) had almost three hours less crying per day.

Of special interest here are the dosage instructions reported in this study (3). The main reason these are summarised here is that labels are often brief, and verbal instructions can be ambiguous. Note, for instance, there is reference only to time of day and not to meal times with the directions printed in Box 3.2. Consultants and parents may find these instructions helpful when using alternative mixtures or drugs which may have different dose rates. Always check dose amounts and concentrations before giving.

For many parents there is an important issue involved in deciding whether or not to use drugs to try and pacify a crying baby. Effective drugs can be a godsend. Often the disruptiveness of incessant crying is broken by the selective use of drugs. And once this cycle has been interrupted successfully parents can catch their breath, get some sleep, and face the future with a little more hope. Their new found hope may be short-lived.

A couple of days later things could seem to be back where they were previously. There are two options available if the crying continues when baby is on drugs. Either give up and try again at a later date, or increase the dose. If parents reach the maximum dose level without a break in the chaos then they can either switch to a stronger drug or back off from this approach altogether. There is no easy resolution to this issue.

Fortunately babies can be responsive. In the study cited above over 60% were pacified. For some there may be the secondary issue of weaning babies off drugs. Consultants may have to caution some parents about excessive and continual drug administration.

From my own experience with crying babies drugs can be very helpful. If they work then a respite from the onslought of vocal pollution is provided. Once the crying stops people can become more reasonable.

The stress level is lowered. So a major benefit from using drugs

Box 3.2

Dosage instructions for (Merbentyl) dicyclomine hydrochloride (10mg/5ml)

(Note: these are guidelines only. Always check printed label for dose amounts and do not exceed these).

1. Begin at the lowest dose listed for the age of your baby.
2. Start with three doses per day. One in the morning, one at midday, and one in the evening.
3. If needed, increase daily dose to a maximum of 2.5 cc (half teaspoon) four times daily. The extra dose should be in the afternoon.
4. Do not exceed this maximum of four daily doses (each of 2.5 cc).
5. If excessive drowsiness or infrequent urination (three or fewer wet nappies in 24 hours) occurs then reduce to next lowest dose according to the list below.
6. If a dose is mixed with a small amount of juice or formula all of this mixture must be finished.
7. If you have any questions or difficulties phone your doctor.

Doses

		Up to eight weeks of age	
1 cc	(quarter teaspoon)	three times daily	(lowest level)
1 cc	(quarter teaspoon)	four times daily	
2.5 cc	(half teaspoon)	three times daily	
2.5 cc	(half teaspoon)	four times daily	(highest level)
		At and over eight weeks of age	
2.5 cc	(half teaspoon)	three times daily	(low level)
2.5 cc	(half teaspoon)	four times daily	(high level)

Adapted from Weissbluth et al. (3)

according to directions is helping to create an altered state of existence. Once a change has occurred then make the most of it. Drugs can be a useful aid in the short-term. They can quieten a crying baby for just long enough to sustain hope. As well another intervention may introduce further opportunities for mutual and positive involvement.

Crying it out

Apart from this book few guidelines for the systematic assessment and presentation of interventions aimed directly at crying babies in family settings are available (4,5). By default many writers of baby manuals have adopted a position of virtually leaving a crying baby alone. Their comments are typically along the lines that a good cry a day never did a baby any harm. From a physiological point of view empirical evidence on this matter is not available. From another stance the data is to hand and the statement is clearly wrong. As noted already many abused babies are victimised precisely because of their continued crying.

On theoretical grounds both Freudians and Behaviourists would favour leaving a baby to cry it out. The former would accept this as one contribution toward ego development, a view which persists in those who believe babies ought to be hardened up. For Behaviourists a retrieved crying baby is reinforced for crying and will come to make this into a demanding routine. As mentioned already there are other theories which contradict these views.

Practically speaking there are occasions when babies have to be left to cry it out. For instance when a parent is so utterly exhausted that any further contact with a crying baby is likely to be explosive then it is in both of their interests to remain separated. Providing parents can be reassured, occasional episodes like this are unlikely to handicap baby's later development. There is no need for them to feel guilty.

Many parents will have experimented already with leaving their babies alone, especially at night time, in the hope the crying will stop. In doing so the parents have bowed to accepted ignorance of well-meaning friends or relatives. There are enough cases, even though these be few and far between, where someone knows someone who did this and it worked. Comments along the lines of "look at their children, nothing wrong there. And they were all left to cry it out. They soon learned what was best" are easily repeated.

A crying baby left alone at night and one left during the day when due for feeding, present two quite different situations to parents. Or, as another way of looking at these variations in family settings, contrast a baby which cries during feeding from one protesting when put down to sleep. Quite obviously there are indications which alert parents to one course of action rather than another. To treat all of these as the same and to make a blanket recommendation which covers them all is impossible. Babies are more likely to "grow it out" than "cry it out".

How long will the crying go on

For babies for whom no known cause may be identified and treated it is simply a matter of letting the crying take its course. Some researchers have noted a sharp decline in infantile colic at around twelve weeks, thus supporting the common phrase "three-month colic". There are some parents who anticipate the magical three month birthday with hope for a better tomorrow. From our own survey, as reported above, there was little support for a clear cut twelve-week boundary which limits colic attacks.

Nonetheless it is reported that for some infants the crying stops as if a radio had been turned off.

There are those for whom a known agent makes a direct contribution. In one report it was noted baby crying subsided when visiting mothers-in-law departed (6). For others a change in mother's diet, like the elimination of dairy products, or an alteration of infant formula have remarkable results.

Unfortunately, at present, for most crying babies a single cause is not likely to be found. It means that long range forecasts cannot be made with any degree of accuracy. Hence consultants need to adopt a flexible approach which can be adjusted to families. Sustaining hope through maintaining morale is one important role for consultants.

Is this a crying baby?

One of the biggest knocks new parents experience is the obvious challenge to their earlier misguided belief that babies sleep for long periods and in more or less regular patterns. Another shock is the amount of crying and how devastating this can be when having to cope with it all day, every day. With regard to crying all that really matters is the parents' views of what is going on. The actual amount of crying is not particularly relevant. If a parent feels under pressure from baby's crying then this needs attention and warrants action. The links between the amount of crying and feelings toward it are not simple.

That's not as obvious as it might appear. A parent might have a high flash-point and be upset by a little crying. Although baby is not crying excessively, these parents are not able to tolerate the noise. This is quite normal for many people. Others, equally normal, can have low flash-points, and seem to be immune to lots of baby crying. On the one hand then, there are parents who have little tolerance for baby crying and are easily upset by it. And on the other hand, there are those who are fairly resistant to noise disruption and carry on pretty well as if nothing is the matter. As a cautionary note, let me add, in rare cases ignoring baby's crying is a mark of abnormality on a parent's part. The main point here is that some people are more easily upset than are others.

Then there is the part played by the nature of the cry sound itself. Some infants have particularly grating and high pitched cries which are very uncomfortable. Others have cries that are more or less in an "acceptable" range. So it could be that the nature of baby's crying is itself an important contribution to any personal or family disruptions.

In addition, there are the beliefs parents may have about crying. These beliefs will influence how crying is viewed. For example if a parent believes something is physically "wrong" when baby cries then any action will be based on quite different criteria than those emerging from another belief like baby is just being "awkward". How we see situations influences what we take out of them and how we decide to act.

Sounds complicated enough? There is much more. For instance a parent's state of general health, baby's health, amount of fatigue, experience, loneliness, household routines, assistance from others, extra children about, and so on, all have a bearing on whether or not there is a "crying baby" around the place. Possibly the actual amount of crying is almost incidental.

It does not take much crying on the infant's part to remind a parent of how things were in the past. Let me relate an example by way of illustration. In several of our studies it is necessary to go into family homes to make tape recordings of babys' cry signals. An appointment is usually made and the equipment left with the family.

In several instances we have not obtained any lengthy cry recordings at all. When this first occurred I put it down to coincidence. That is, baby happened to stop crying at the same time as recordings were wanted. But when it happened in about 25% of the samples this looked like more than mere coincidence. In fact some parents pleaded with us to leave the equipment, even offering to purchase it on the spot.

When thinking about this my first thought was that the parents did not wish to participate. By telling me baby was not crying any longer it satisfied me without them losing face. But I knew these people. If they did not want to continue they would have made this clear. As an alternative possibility, perhaps now that the crying was wanted these parents were dealing with the babies differently and their babies "sensed" this change of attitude. Instead of being tense, were the parents now behaving in a more relaxed manner? We know babies are capable of picking up this sort of thing. So a mutually-interrupting spiral of anger could have been broken by the parent's mood change.

Some of these possibilities, and others, were appealing. It is my strong hunch that the recording request was the first time for a good while that parents stopped to look at the actual amount of disruptive crying going on.

Consider what might have happened. After mother and baby returned home following birth there may have been a few weeks of regular daily crying. During this period the parents would have coped as best they could, trying to pacify baby and maintain their own health. Since baby crying is such a terrible sound not much of it is needed to serve as a reminder of previous horrors. Even if the actual amount of daily crying was decreasing at a steady rate this could not be "seen" by parents who continued to imagine it as being excessive. Without any "objective" measure it is likely baby may be seen to be a "crier" for much longer than was actually the case. My intrusion into the family setting with the recording equipment required parents' co-operation. Now they had to look at crying episodes closely in order to capture these on tape.

A systems analysis was adopted by Evelyn Thoman and her co-workers in a study of infant crying and the stability of mother-baby relationships (7). By considering families as systems one can look at the effects each member has on the other. A dynamic framework accepts complex series of events occuring at the same time whilst stabilising about its own self-maintenance. Thoman's team observed 20 pairs of mothers and babies in their homes during four occasions; feeding, bathing or changing, social attention, and when baby was alone. Interactional stability was related to crying only for social occasions and was strongly negative. Although social crying occurred on an average of only five minutes during a seven-hour stretch it "... suggests that this small (crying) component of the system is a potent expression of the integrative processes involved in maintaining overall stability in the relationship" (p. 658). The authors speculate that if this social crying gets out of hand the system will become unstable and may lead to battered babies or those who fail to thrive.

It would seem that the actual amount of crying is not particularly important. What is of greater relevance is when this occurs, what effects it has on the family and what can be done about it. Even if a mother reports at a subsequent meeting that baby seems not to be crying a great deal do not dismiss the point lightly, for there may still be important repercussions.

Teething, wind, hunger and "getting at me"

There are dozens of explanations adults provide to account for continued baby crying. Those babies who draw their knees up, go rigid and utter shrill, piercing wails are obviously in pain. If these classic wind (colic) symptoms are less extreme they may then be attributed to teething or hunger, depending on the time of day and so forth. There is no doubt hungry babies cry. If this is the main cause then additional or alternative feeding patterns can be miraculous in relieving the presenting symptoms.

During the cutting of new teeth a baby may be more susceptible to certain foods, rashes may appear on the skin, in the mouth and around the crutch. In spite of these changes it is unlikely that teething itself is as devastating as it seems. One possible explanation is that increased irritability shown by a hungry, windy, or teething infant alters the entire family dynamics. What worked satisfactorily previously no longer holds any appeal for baby, for virtually everything fails. It doesn't take much of a knock for an already strained system to buckle under additional pressure. Hence, although current difficulties may stem from crying induced by teething, wind or hunger, the effects of this disruption ripple and reverberate to such an extent that simply "fixing" the teething problem is but a start in the right direction. Nonetheless, teething (like wind and excessive tiredness) are acceptable explanations. These are occurrences which happen to babies. If parents did not have these sorts of explanations available there would be many more babies victimised through their inexplicable crying. So these explanations have a place.

Technically speaking "attribution" is the word used to deal with the rules average people use when attempting to work out explanations for observed behaviours. Within the attribution domain it is assumed that people can think about what is happening. They search for causes of events and then do something based on the incomplete information available. Here are some important distinctions. "Causes" bring about change whereas "reasons" are the purposes or goals for which change is bought about. Unintended things which happen to a person are occurrences, and are explained as causes by others (8). In a practical application, things happen to babies. They suffer occurrences and do not go about deliberately upsetting people by continually crying. In short, these are causes and not reasons. Reasons can be found to serve as adequate explanations by adults of events which happen to babies. It is erroneous to consider that baby crying is done on purpose, for a deliberate reason.

Here is an illustration of what this means. Consider an older child on a morning when it approaches a parent fixing breakfast, wanting immediate help with this and that. "Mummy, help me do a drawing, get my cuddly blanket, pick me up", and so forth. Pressed to meet upcoming demands from other family members the reply is strongly negative, in spite of imploring whimpering. This parent has explained the child's action as a reason. There is something the child wants to do which is not convenient to provide help for at the moment. The consistent message from the parent is along the lines of designing a strategy so as to be left alone and get on with the breakfast schedule. Typically, something is done *to* the child. But timely reflection by the parent may place this child's clinging behaviour into another context. Last night she was wakeful. This morning she sneezed a couple of times and appears to have a nascent cold. Quite quickly the original attribution, a reason, is replaced by another, a cause. Notice change in a parent's behaviour this shift can produce. Instead of wondering what can be done *to* the child there is concern now about what can be done *for* her. "Come and have a cuddle".

Most babies do need cuddles, attention, warmth, love. These are needs, lack of which may be a cause of their crying. Just as appropriate food is a biological requirement for sustained infant health so too are these "softer" needs. When parents do not accept these needs as basic essentials then a crying baby can be dismissed with comments like "All she wants is cuddles" or "He always wants to be picked up" or "She is so demanding of my time" or "He drives me mad with his always wanting to be carried about". By calling these needs wants, it is presumed baby has made an active, intelligent decision from among a host of other possibilities and is simply being a nuisance, getting in the road of other plans (the wants but not the needs of adults). Gently, one way to go about unravelling this complicated business is to work out whose needs are being met or ignored and take it from there. This may be easier said than done.

PART II

DESIGNING PLANS FOR ACTION

4 ON ORGANISING SCHEMES

Getting into the maze

When a baby cries there are dozens of influences which may be affecting events.

Some parents who have lived some time already with a crying baby, without sympathy, guidance or assistance from other agencies, may be in a very bruised state. The last thing they want is to be knocked about by another disinterested consultant. A blend of tact and compassion as well as a plan of action are needed if progress is to be made.

Other parents are more than willing to participate and will practically leap at any chance to do anything at all. On these occasions their eagerness may be a handicap since it may lure a consultant into providing too much all at once. The obvious danger here is that parents may not do what they commit themselves to before the next meeting. I believe it is better to provide sufficient material to engage parents initially, to offer just enough to meet their immediate requests which will carry them on through the next week, without being an additional burden.

Educationally, this means meeting the parents and babies where they are, both physically (i.e. in the home) and psychologically. To do this satisfactorily one treads quietly, probing here and there gently and intentionally in order to uncover those areas which are presenting themselves as difficulties. Consultants, like most counsellors, are teachers too.

Finding the way

Consultants need to be familiar with the techniques of map making. They should become competent at surveying and marking out the contours of land, recording communication links, transport routes and obstacles. In addition they require skills at applying these techniques to construct maps which others may recognise and make use of as well. Ultimately, parents are expected to negotiate their own maps.

The analogies and examples drawn from map making are intented to illustrate in a graphic way an ongoing task of consultants. Parents and their crying babies are on unfamiliar terrain, they do not know the way and seem to be lost in a desert of uncertainty. Stranded in the wilderness and searching for an oasis to rest, recover, and replenish, these parents are often ready to grasp at any passing hope.

Consultants are more than mirages, they offer concrete advice which will make a difference to survival.

More than anecdotes

One distinction which may be drawn between a consultant and other untrained helpers is that the latter are not good at map making. Instead of plotting a course which does justice to predictable obstacles they rely entirely on the presenting symptoms. For example it is now well known that around seven months of age many babies will exhibit what has come to be known as "stranger anxiety". Quite suddenly it seems, the baby who was warm, cuddly and affectionate toward other adults shows an abrupt change. Only to very familiar adults does baby remain friendly. All others experience a rigid, tense, unhappy baby. This phase lasts about four months and seems to be characterised by an increase in night waking as well. Since these two behaviours occur in most babies, they appear to be maturational changes which emerge quite independently of how baby is reared. A consultant should be aware of these developmental themes and be able to plan accordingly. Other people, unaware of these natural changes, will tend to over-react and put the family under pressure it does not need to suffer.

Further, a consultant is able to justify a course of practical suggestions by associating this to a general plan. The plan forms the basis for decisions and is tailored from what is known about crying babies in families. Others tend to make suggestions based on anecdotal comment and may be supported personally by an effort to maintain "authoritative" status, throwing their weight around.

Another characteristic of consultants is their willingness to use the information which is being presented to them, of incorporating this into a general plan and of modifying it in the light of what is offered. The plans are flexible. Maps can be redrawn to suit individual needs. In time and with experience mapmaking skills will improve as consultants draft plans to suit different families.

Unfortunately in the training of many professionals old maps are handed down as if they are satisfactory. When this happens the training is closed, it serves only to make sure the characteristics of certain maps are retained without change. Since the community settings from which they were initially constructed have now changed, these old maps have little practical use. This is one way of thinking about the familiar expression "All very well in theory but useless in practice". Old maps are like anecdotes, they might apply but are unlikely to provide a workable plan which goes beyond obvious limitations.

Crying baby syndrome

In medical terms a "syndrome" refers to a number of symptoms occurring together which are characteristic of a particular disorder. I coined the phrase "crying baby syndrome" to describe the plight of many parents, trapped by their crying babies.

An analogy may be useful here. Crying serves as a lens which focusses numerous contributing features directly onto baby. According to a dictionary definition (1) one meaning given for "focus" is "the point

Box 4.1

The crying baby syndrome

Baby crying is like a lens, distorting events and creating the crying baby syndrome

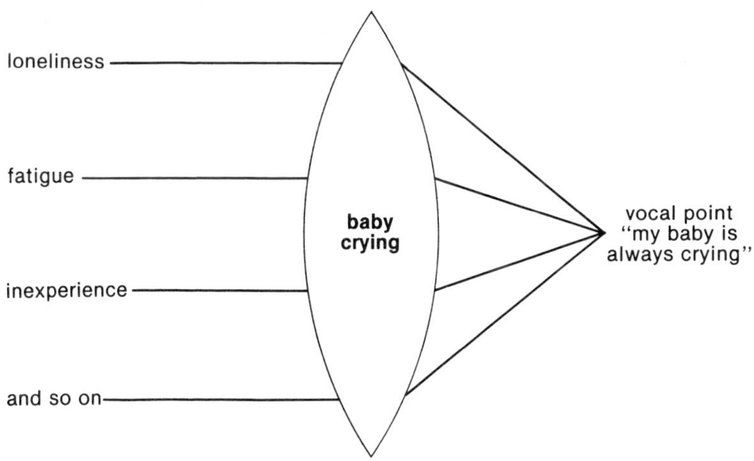

where rays of light, heat, etc. or waves of sound come together, or from which they spread ...". A slight change of wording alters "focal point" to "vocal point". Hence the vocal point is where significant contributing factors come together through the lens of baby's crying and are illuminated by a typical parent's comment "my baby is always crying". This is the crying baby syndrome (Box 4.1).

Fay Deane makes a useful distinction in her PhD dissertation (2) between a baby who cries and one who is described as a crying baby. On the one hand a baby who cries does many other things as well; it feeds, sleeps, plays, dribbles, and so on. Here the crying is part and parcel of babyhood. On the other hand a crying baby is one that seems to do little else; it is the vocal point of everything. Consultants, by knowing about this distinction can avoid making the crying into a problem. Since this book is itself focussed directly on crying then it is possible that all babies are seen as nothing but criers, an error which ought to be avoided.

Further, we may be dealing with a syndrome which, like a lens, focusses events in an unhealthy way. Thus one task is to identify contributing factors. But simply changing these will not be of much use since the lens itself will continue to draw together whatever is available. So switching attention from tiredness to inexperience or to hormonal disruptions will not in and of itself alter things. Change lies in redefining the shape or location or content of the "lens" now labelled as baby crying. In another crisis this lens has a different name, but calling things names does not help. One has to go beyond syndrome identification and offer practical advice and manageable suggestions.

Spinning out of control

The analogy of a focusing lens illustrated aptly what was meant by the phrase "crying baby syndrome". Another analogy may be useful to appreciate the downward spiralling which seems to occur with those ensnared by the crying baby syndrome. This one comes from piloting a light aircraft and came to my notice when a friend told me about learning to recover from deliberate spins. Subsequently he (3) kindly provided the following answers to three specific questions.

1. How do you get into a spin? A spin is caused by reducing the airflow over the wings of an aircraft to such a degree that insufficient lift is available to keep the plane in the air. In technical terms it means that weight and drag exceed thrust and lift so that the aircraft will no longer continue to fly. A spin is the final stage of a fully developed stall, a stall simply meaning that the airspeed of the plane is beginning to approach that point where insufficient thrust is being created to overcome drag and weight by developing lift. What that means is that the aircraft falls out of the sky and it does this by spinning downwards,

in a corkscrew motion. In order to get into a spin you have to reduce the speed of the plane at the same time raising the nose in order to try and maintain lift. As the power is reduced, the nose has to be raised further and further to keep the aircraft flying. Eventually vibration is felt over the tailplane of the aircraft as the airflow begins to break up over the wings creating turbulent air which causes the plane to shudder. The stall warning will be sounding continuously at this point with planes fitted with this device in the cockpit. If all these warnings are ignored, i.e. low airspeed, raised nose, vibration throughout the aircraft, and the continuous sound of the stall warning, together with increasingly sluggish controls, then eventually one wing will drop and the plane will begin to spin toward the ground losing height rapidly. In some aircraft this happens very quickly once this point is reached and a wing will drop quite violently. In other planes it occurs quite slowly since the plane is designed to return to a stable position if put out of balance. But when all the forces holding a aircraft in the air are destabilised it will not automatically return to a position of stability.

2. What happens in a spin? In a spin, the plane is literally out of control, falling to the ground in a corkscrew fashion which is caused by the airflow turning the aircraft around its longitudinal axis as it descends. The ground will appear to be rotating from the point of view of the pilot in the cockpit, either clockwise or anticlockwise. In fact however it is the plane which is rotating. Sometimes this can result in complete disorientation of the pilot because of the felt sensations induced by the spin and by the inability to perceive a fixed horizon. Likewise, the instruments will be behaving wildly (except for the turn indicator which will be angled toward the inside of the spin). However if the pilot is trying to fix a point of view outside the plane at the spinning ground the instruments cannot be read inside the plane anyway. In some aircraft the body sensations experienced in a spin may be quite severe i.e. the balance mechanism in the ear may be disturbed, the stomach may feel as if it is being pushed up, the face may feel flattened, and the body generally feel heavier as a result of the "g" forces which may be experienced. All these sensations may further interfere with the ability of the pilot to regain orientation.

3. How do you get out of a spin? In order to recover from a spin the pilot must apply full opposite rudder, check forward slightly on the control column, and apply full power. If the pilot is not sure of spin direction it may be ascertained by concentrating on the turn indicator inside the aircraft. Full rudder in the opposite direction to the spin is applied by the feet. There is a natural tendency to try to straighten up the wings by turning the control column in the spin direction, but this will simply cause the wings to stall even more and increase the violence of the spin. In addition there is a further tendency to want to bring the

nose of the aircraft up by pulling back on the control column but this will simply stall the aircraft more and make the spin even worse. Ideally all the movements have to be performed in a smooth co-ordinated fashion so that the wings are levelled, the wings unstalled, and full power applied in a synchronous way. If there is not sufficient height above the ground for this to be performed then the aircraft will crash, before recovery has been achieved. Significant points about recovery from a spin include; following the accepted procedure for recovery properly, preventing disorientation by concentrating on what is occurring inside the aircraft, not being distracted by some natural tendencies and to some extent doing the opposite of what one might feel. If the pilot is overwhelmed by the sensation and feelings experienced during the spin panic may arise, in which case there is little chance of recovery until a state of control and reasonable calm has been achieved, hopefully before colliding with the ground!

There are several parallels in this analogy to those who are not coping with their crying babies. For instance, although initially managing to cope at home quite satisfactorily with baby, the gradual accumulation of opposing forces upon a new parent may be likened to those which produce a stall. There is insufficient stamina to keep going at a manageable pace. If additional personal effort fails then collapse is inevitable. Of course there are individual differences; some parents are more susceptible than others.

Helping people recover from helplessness may mean encouraging them to do the opposite of what in their eyes is the only solution to these pressures. Although some parents have the personal resources to work at twice the pace in order to meet demands, others will need help in sorting out their priorities and thereby reduce the drag. This may mean sacrificing regular house-cleaning or bed-making for a brief period. A comment from one mother on this topic was: "so what if the beds don't get made as often as they ought. I am at last able to cope and that's the main thing."

Finally, it is each parent who has to recognise what is contributing to loss of stability. This may be due to any one, or combination, of the following possibilities; loss of sleep, in-laws, marital relationships, illness, and so forth. Above all else a crying baby both increases this plight and seems to prevent the possibility of accepting alternatives and doing anything constructive.

If flight recovery from spins was through "trial and error" one can only surmise how many aircraft were lost before survivors were able to persuade others that restoration was managed by actually going against what seemed to be the most obvious course of action. Applying this analogy to those who claim not to be coping may be productive, it helps consultants select relevant interventions.

Chaos and consistency

There are two opposing and deep-seated desires which we all have. The expression of these desires can be biased toward one or the other. For some the urge for order is uppermost. This is revealed by a mechanical precision. Here constituent parts are neatly ordered and connected in sequences which have predictable consequences. One example of this sort of activity may be observed in the logical tightness needed for computer programming. It is a bringing together of facets, of skills, of rules, in order to accomplish a definite task. There are many aspects of dealing with babies which can fit into this pattern, like the so-called "maintenance" tasks of washing or disposing of soiled linen or preparing food for those in the family. For some parents feeding, bathing, and socialising become mechanical due to energy, time or experience. In addition, consultants who personally endorse a mechanistic metaphor are biased toward this approach.

The other desire is one of exploration. For some there is an accumulated bias toward discovery, of a pushing into the unknown. The aim here is to find out what lies beyond known frontiers and to return, reporting discoveries using recognisable vehicles. Artists are the psychological explorers who offer alternate explanations through a wide variety of channels; poetry, painting, novels, music and so forth. So too are research scientists; yet, nonetheless, most science is aimed at "mopping up" in a mechanical sense. For others the discovery of the unknown is involuntary. Soldiers drafted into front line action are not unlike parents who, quite unexpectedly, are experiencing the full horror of what lies beyond the boundaries of reasonableness. An awareness of these intense illogical feelings is not uncommon for many parents at home with crying babies.

Consultants who ignore these intense feelings are dismissing significant events in the lives of parents. Nonetheless there are occasions when it is better to avoid becoming directly involved with these scorching emotions. This does not mean disregarding them. John Bowlby put this point aptly. "When the language of feeling becomes an obstacle to recognising that feeling entails action of particular sorts, it is best abandoned and replaced temporarily by a language of behaviour." (4,p.159).

Note his use of the word "temporarily". If omitted this quotation is quite acceptable to behaviourists, a group whom Bowlby is not aligned with.

Parents do have feelings and these can be very powerful forces. Having passionate feelings is quite distinct from going ahead and acting these out. We all have strong feelings, even destructive ones toward those we love. But we do not display these as physical outbursts of aggression. Most of us could take a stand to safeguard our own lives and the lives of our families if threatened. In spite of the sheer power of baby's constant demands these situations are seldom life-threatening for parents. The crying can be psychologically devastating. Maintaining a sense of balance on the tightrope of parenthood is an art learned on the job.

How interruptions are dealt with depends very much on what success one is having coping with present demands. When events are going smoothly and are more or less predictable then a niggling urge to expand horizons and seek novelty arises. For example, for a parent, when things are pretty well sorted out there is a pleasant desire to tackle something further; perhaps planning another baby,or a job outside the home can be considered, and so forth. The same sort of divergence out can be observed in baby too. It is when some mothers cannot or do not have the opportunity to explore these creative longings that they become trapped into a limiting service role. Playing is not only something that just happens, it emerges when safe conditions are established and maintained by foresight. This applies to parents as well as to babies. A desire for order emerges when things are confused. Confusion can be self-imposed, as when exploring something new. For some people this happens when they are taking part in a creative task, at the threshold of chaos. But for others chaos is not deliberately sought out; it is the upshot of not being able to recognise patterns in a consuming mess. Non-soothable babies are ideal agents for creating disorder. One source of strain on this need for order comes from parents who are not in full daily contact with baby, typically men, who possibly arrive back from a demanding day's work and require peace, quiet and regularity. Mothers too, caught in the bustle of family life, often need time to sort things out. When opportunities for having time out are not available the chances of spinning out of control are increased.

What is proposed here is the notion of a curious conflict. In essence it is that when things are going well people seek change and challenge. Contrariwise, when things are in a state of uncertainty then order is desired. While this idea may approximate what goes on generally we are left with some important and unresolved questions. What, for example, counts as ordered and disordered events? Do these alter for different people at different times? What is satisfying anyway? And, when does a person wish to (or need to) switch from taking part in extended explorations, discovery or play so as to get out of a comfortable rut? All these are relevant questions, the answers to which will depend on individuals in their unique situations.

The point of it all is that there are two opposing, deep seated, desires which we all have. One is for order and the other for exploration. It is the continual search for balance between these opposing forces which propels us onward into life. Both babies and their parents are influenced by these dual drives. The main difference between these participants is that parents are responsible for providing a safe family setting.

Harmony lies in understanding the subtle rhythms of the natural pendulum which swings between consistency and chaos. Curious conflicts occur at the end of each stroke when, with apparent hesitation, the pendulum pauses briefly prior to returning quickly through the familiar arc which pulses the dance of development. Crying babies accentuate the need for order and a demand for peace and quiet. When this need becomes a passion it must be met, and quickly. Nonetheless, it still needs to be recognised that the ongoing process of development has another pace.

Multi-axial schemes for assessment and intervention

In the late 1940's a useful distinction was made between symptom and aetiology which were then used as two separate ways for making psychiatric classifications (5). These axes appear in most subsequent systems. Symptoms typically include features such as duration, course, type, pattern and/or developmental disorders. Aetiology usually involves disposition, precipitation, abnormal psycho-social conditions and/or somatic diseases. The main thrust behind using two distinctive dimensions is to remove confusion which occurred with a single continuum.

In the assessment of crying babies several dimensions are available. These were designed from related literature as well as from clinical experience (6). The scheme itself is presented in the next section. It was created to provide a systematic approach to the specific question "What would you do if a parent presented a crying baby wanting practical guidance?". It is likely the scheme will be useful for handling the more general question as well, namely "What would you do if anybody sought assistance?"

Prior to documenting the scheme a dilemma should be introduced. Any scheme can become mechanical. For example if sets of check-lists are used these may be easy to apply, even computers can be programmed for this purpose, but have little meaning. The twin horns of this dilemma are first, a desire to have a tightly integrated scheme where known components are arranged logically, and second, a need to maintain sufficient looseness to be of practical use for accommodating individuals.

Two resolutions to this dilemma are available. One is to consider any scheme as an open system which "maintains itself in a continuous inflow and outflow, building up and breaking down of components ... maintained in a so called steady state ..." (7). Such a system would be evident in a scheme which interconnects contributions from several disciplines, orchestrated by developmental themes.

A complementary solution is offered by the developmental notion of transactional models for which the underlying assumptions "... are that the contact between organism and environment is a transaction in which each is altered by the other" (8). Actually, taking this a step further, since an assessment scheme is itself part of an environment then those who use it are engaging in a transaction. Although traditional test users would find this concept unsatisfactory, since reliability is hard to sustain, consultants ought to be aware that calls for greater objectivity are not just disguised pleas for increased mechanical rigidity. By and large consultants are comfortable with a transactional approach. However this can make any systematic instruction in its application very difficult. Another casualty of a transactional focus is "evaluation", but that's another story.

Why is this baby crying?

The organising scheme which underlies strategies adopted by consultants when choosing action plans is shown in Box 4.2. This scheme is an expanded and updated version of an earlier one (6). As before it is designed to integrate contributions from several disciplines and indicates to whom specific assistance may be directed. It enables those with specialist training to enter the scheme from their own positions of competence and extend these by linking them to related areas.

There are three assumptions. First, as the distinctions between the themes may be more apparent than real there is an ebb and flow amongst them. Second, theoretically it is possible for each theme to be connected to every other one thus producing a multi-dimensional spider's web. Practically this is most unlikely. As drawn the scheme itself is intended to orchestrate various themes by showing their more probable links. Third, the goings on within baby are presumed to be directed more by a biological/biochemical impetus which depends on the availability of an adequate structure for its realisation than it does on a social/cultural one. This is not intended to deny the significance of the latter which assumes greater importance with the lapse of time. Initially however, it implies that babies are guided by reflex-directed machine-like programming. In a responsive environment there are many transitions which gradually ease a growing infant into developmental routes for optimum health. These transitions are tailored to match an infant's unfolding maturational drives which occur in the order of crying, smiling, clinging, crawling, and walking (4).

In visual terms the proposed scheme may be considered as a series of concentric circles similar to the radiating ripples which spread out from a stone splash in a still pool. Assessments at a similar level are shown on the same circle. There are only three circles. The innermost shows genetic influences since, after all, genes control the whole organism's functioning throughout life. On the outer rim are those things we encounter; the actual behaviours are represented by the twin themes of developmental status and form. Hence, as a ripple expands its influence is more obviously affected by the impact of other people.

Except for those who have previous training in one of the middle-circle themes (wherein they will begin directly with a particular theme), most consultants will commence from the outside, with what is being observed

Box 4.2

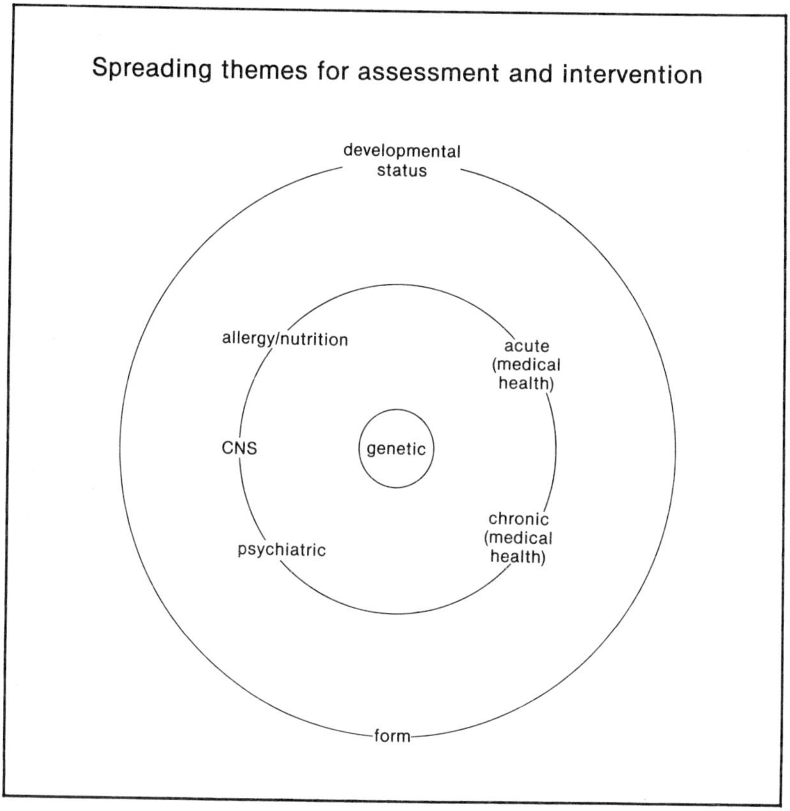

as behaviours. This will be with "form" and "developmental status". Then, whilst collecting information relevant to these two they will dip into others in order to check out different causes.

In the next part of this book each theme is dealt with separately. Different interventions are designed within these themes. They are called "interventions" since each can disrupt family functioning. Some involve parents more than do others. Throughout, the aim of this book is to provide practical tools which consultants may modify to suit their own conditions and interests, eventually producing variations on the themes.

There is no straightforward answer to the deceptively simple question posed at the outset; "Why is this baby crying?" By applying the general scheme offered and implementing relevant interventions, consultants will develop strategies to enable them to use them more skillfully. Relevant skills are acquired when economical procedures for selecting appropriate entry points and making the best use of what is available become self-evident. If you know what you are doing there is no need to be flustered and fall back on bluff. Consultants, once equipped, can make a significant difference in the delivery of preventative health care services, cheaply and with effect.

Why is this mother upset by baby crying?

This is another simple-looking question for which there are hundreds of answers. Already some indications have been provided in earlier sections, like the notion of different flash points. What is needed now is another scheme which will provide consultants with opportunities to assess different situations as well as to select and to implement relevant interventions.

As a starting point the same scheme presented for babies applies. This one is extended by an additional circle containing the three themes mentioned in the crying baby syndrome. Thus, within the single circle presented in Box 4.3 place the entire contents (of the three circles) shown in Box 4.2. These ideas are not dealt with systematically in the present book.

Boundaries of interaction

According to the two schemes outlined in Boxes 4.2 and 4.3, what goes on between parents and babies occurs at the places where their respective circles collide and/or overlap. Typically this is at the outer limits. This is what may be directly observed, the outcomes of contributing themes. These interactions are the regions of affective exchange. Applying the metaphor mentioned earlier, this area becomes the pooling of resources.

Incidently, the scheme designed for parents applies to other adults too. Even consultants are not immune from these themes. For instance without support, lack of training, inadequate experience, and a dullness from overwork professional effectiveness will be diminished.

When looking into the dynamics of parent-infant interactions these schemes provide consultants with purposeful courses of action. Instead of dismissing disruptive babies it is now possible to systematically assess each contributing member's themes and do something positive about the situation. Part III presents interventions aimed at babies and involving parents.

Box 4.3

An expanded scheme for assessment and intervention when involving adults

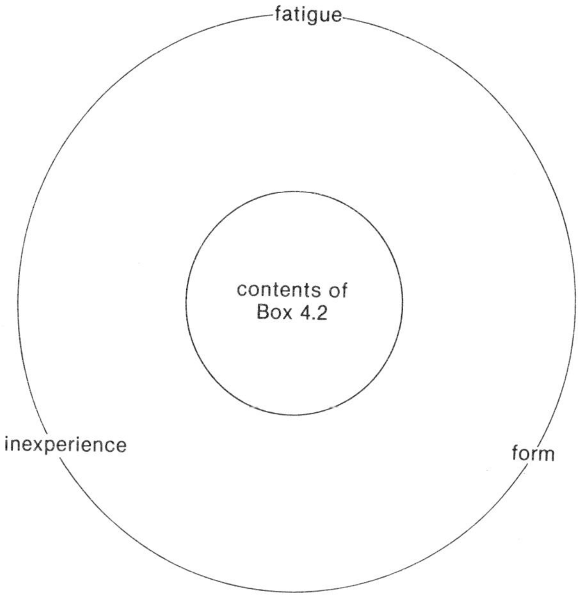

5 PUTTING SCHEMES INTO ACTION

Co-ordinating perspectives

The themes outlined in the previous chapter are designed to enable consultants to select from among several available interventions in order to maximise practical effectiveness. Simply applying an intervention without regard for any overall plan or selected strategy is unprofessional. Sometimes desired results can be obtained in this way. However, when interventions are considered in contexts they can be brought to bear in an integrated manner, beyond simply "making do". The outlined schemes offered one type of context.

In addition we have found it useful for consultants to be knowledgeable not only about these schemes but of broader frameworks. To be limited to mere application of procedures without an appreciation for and an understanding of related matters is to restrict any consultant's competencies. Thus a holistic approach aimed at guiding others to cope with and understand crying babies is endorsed. In part, it means going beyond the interventions and their co-ordinating schemes to grapple with those perspectives which spawned them.

There are five relevant perspectives which offer a broader set of contexts (1). The main headings for each one and a brief indication of their content areas outlined by sub-headings are offered below. An extended description of these is not provided since consultants will be better served by constructing their own sets of perspectives.

1. Philosophical: Consistent and deliberate attempts to conceptualise (through reading, discussion and writing) several structural themes upon which the clinic is designed and operates.

—theoretical positions
—rationale, justification
—considerations of worth, involvement, committment, purpose
—interdisciplinary couplings
—assumptions
—general orientation and purpose

2. Professional: That continuing involvement by consultants in the clinic is of a professional standard and is maintained, through "continuing education" type activities.

—links with other professionals, agencies
—supervision of consultants
—case study presentations
—ethics
—professional updating, e.g. by reading, discussion, and writing of relevant applied work
—certification, clearance, competence
—training sessions
—integrative network of activities

3. House-keeping "research": Although the clinic is not designed for carrying out research it can offer insights upon which research studies may be designed and carried out elsewhere. Nonetheless, there is be a prevailing "research" orientation which serves several convenient house-keeping functions.

—methodologies
—evaluation
—documenting (archiving) ideas, possibilities
—equipment, technology
—ongoing related studies and their integration
—raw data archives, e.g. cry signals
—funding possibilities and support
—bibliographies
—popular literature on crying and related topics

4. Dissemination: Concerned with the proper handling of any documentation prepared about the clinic.

—reports to agencies, e.g. other professionals
—academic papers in journals/books
—conferences
—seminars
—talks
—popular media (radio/TV press)
—reports to funding agencies
—correspondence with colleagues
—public relations
—scrapbook for archiving materials

5. General session guidelines: It is highly desirable for consultants to be friendly. The following guidelines are provided to help maintain a basic humanistic approach.

—fair and accurate descriptions
—bias toward future hope rather then past guilt
—"open-ended" sessions so as to accommodate individual participation

—supplying the conditions for parents to "discuss" their situations without fear of recrimination
—err without damage, learn by doing
—build upon parental strengths
—build upon what is available to parents but is not immediately visible
—make options available for parents to choose among. Note, one choice can be non-cooperation, so accept this gracefully.
—activities to make sense to all participants
—encourage parents to participate away from clinic, at home with baby
—have concrete activities; leave them something to do and report upon at next meeting
—encourage parental observations which may lead to other (desirable) outcomes
—promote manageable involvement; to enable parents to stay on top
—allow "natural" parent involvement without pressure
—work within parent/consultant range of practical possibilities
—keep open an opportunity for "natural" graduation and termination
—maintain a "professional" approach (no easy answers)
—aim at elegance and simplicity with your thinking, though this can be conveyed loosely (paradox)
—be "informal" but deliberate
—consultant to be "comfortable" (familiar and understand) applied interventions. Let this "rub off".
—be diverse in approach (one intervention can be presented in many different ways)
—suggest, don't direct
—know what you are doing

CrySOS — clinics for parents with crying babies

A general description of these clinics is provided in Box 2.3. In the present section attention is directed toward the practical workings of clinics.

In order to help develop and apply interventions which can be used simply and without confusion two approaches are adopted. One is to develop procedures which have general use and serve as strategy guidelines. The other is to consider each parent-infant pair as a unique couple and design unique plans within a broad strategy.

At the outset the task is to promote hope and foster survival tactics. There are numerous ways of accomplishing this objective. One is to participate actively with parents in a co-operative venture. Simply put, the challenge is to introduce parents to procedures which help them make sense of their complex situations, create and sustain a belief in being able to "make it".

In this setting a primary focus is upon infant crying and its effects in the family home. As could be anticipated, a good dose of crying coupled with sleep loss, fatigue, loneliness (the Crying Baby Syndrome) makes for a good introduction to many of other domestic issues. It seems that infant crying encourages scrutiny of all sorts of family dynamics. And as long as the crying continues to be irksome many family issues remain unanswered. Consultants ought not stray beyond their competencies; it is an easy lure for those in the helping professions to become involved in topics which are introduced but for which training has not been obtained. Consultants have quite enough to do with their primary target: crying babies in families.

Due to the novelty of the setting, the topic, and/or irritable behaviour on the baby's part, it is unlikely that mothers will be able to devote their full attention to the consultant. One way to overcome this difficulty is to make an ongoing record in note form. Taking time out to write case notes during a session enables parents to marshall their thoughts too. By adopting a considered pace during a session, the periods of silence which occur when taking notes is not disruptive. For a clinic's files the second, carbon, copy of these notes is quite adequate. With a top copy to take away parents can discuss with their partners what happened. The notes in and of themselves are an intervention since they can open doors for communication between co-operating adults. An example of first-session case notes is provided in Box 5.1.

An "open records" system is adopted. Most notes are held by the parent in a supplied envelope. An exception is the consent form (Box 2.2), yet, if requested, a copy is furnished. Since parents hold materials they are able to pursue these in their own time. For subsequent meetings additional materials are included.

A consistent pattern is typically adopted for the first meeting. Here the main task is to get into the "problem" and to optimise available time. To do so it is convenient to follow a procedure which is robust enough to catch most cases. Behind this approach are the twin schemes outlined in the previous chapter. What happens in subsequent meetings depends on the results of the initial one and so general guidelines are not available for these. The main point of entry is a review of the intervening period and following up suggestions to see how these may have been implemented. People graduate when they no longer participate, having weaned themselves toward independence.

An outline for the first meeting

Several of the items mentioned in the sections presented here are extended in Part III. There each of the interventions is considered in detail. One governing factor in the selection of relevant sections during an initial meeting is the age of the baby. For those who are older, details about the birth and pregnancy may be of less importance than feeding. Another factor is the opportunities taken by parents to discuss what seems

Box 5.1

A section taken from case-notes written by a consultant

Mrs Ruth Allen	SALLY	(14 May)
Dr. Hayfork	DOB: 10 Jan	Age: 17 weeks
7/49 Hewitts Road	258–635	At Clinic

- Until 4 weeks of age Sally was an ideal baby, sleeping and feeding well. Then "something" happened. Parents don't know what. From then until now Sally has been hard to handle.
- There are two main difficulties. One is with sleeping. Sally just will not go down to bed. If she has gone to sleep in parents arms then can be put down. Mostly she wants to be held and carried about. The second difficulty is with feeding. Now her motions are smelly, loose, pale and frequent. Often Sally seems to be in pain, as if wanting to pass a motion. Feedings are long and drawn out. (My hunch is these are related, made enquiries about mother's diet) Ice-cream, milk, chocolate are liked and eaten often.
- Daily family routine is: Up about 2am for first feed. Although Sally wakes crying this session is the best of the day. The next is around 3:30 when a loud, piercing cry breaks the night. This is not an easy feed. Mostly restless, lots of walking the floor. Typically settles when ....

Notes about case notes The top line is reserved for a parent's name, baby's name and consultation date. The next two lines are left blank initially and information about family doctor's name, date of birth, age, address, home phone and venue are entered during a session. Throughout I try to use both the words and sentences used by a parent. The case notes are written as the family story unfolds, prompted by questions from the consultant.

to be going on. This, in turn, will determine how much time is available.

From experience it is most helpful to get over the introductions and settle down as quickly as possible so as to get to the grist of the issues. Details about family members and other biographical comments will arise quite spontaneously. There is no need to adopt a cold formal approach at the beginning merely to complete detailed forms. There is no point in collecting information which is going to be of little use. Hence parents' ages, occupations, martital status, etc are generally omitted at this stage.

One copy of selected sections is given to participating parents so they can follow what is going to happen. Another is retained by the consultant and used as a working guide. These sections are shown in the boxes below.

A. General background (Box 5.2.) This serves to introduce participants, the clinic and to offer a cautionary note.

a. "greeting and personal introduction" is quite straightforward. Enter parent and baby's names onto the notes at this stage.

b. "time limits" are mentioned to indicate roughly the length of the session. A comfortable working period is around 45 minutes.

c. "baby OK ...." is an enquiry as to baby's whereabouts. Even if present find out if the parent is comfortable. Remind her baby comes first and to do as she would usually, pretending you are absent.

d. "my taking notes..." As this has begun already, indicate a copy of the notes will be given at the end of the session so these may be looked over at home. At the next meeting a consultant may begin by asking about any of the comments, whether clarification is wanted. (Try to write legibly. It

Box 5.2

General background

- —greeting and personal introduction
- —time limits
- —baby OK during this meeting
- —my taking notes, something to look over later if in place other than own residence:
  - — finding location all right
  - — any other problems getting here
  - — plans following this visit
- —some disruptions may by likely tonight
- —about changes in babies "quick to be upset, slow to calm"
- —overview of CrySOS clinic (introductory notes)

Box 5.3

Broad statement on CrySOS

Research findings agree with what many people feel when dealing with a crying baby. Some of these findings seem little more than what would be expected. But it is important to realise that several people from different countries are reaching similar conclusions in their research. The sort of things we are coming to accept with regard to understanding crying babies and the influences they have are:

—The baby crying usually makes people uncomfortable
—That many babies cry a good deal more often and for longer periods than is generally believed
—That many parents can be upset by a crying baby
—That parents should not be "blamed" for having a crying baby
—That many parents can be pushed into doing things they would not do usually by their crying baby

Then, there are some other general observations which may be noted. These are:

—That few professional people believe how difficult it is for parents to cope with a crying baby
—That little constructive assistance is available to parents coping with a crying baby.

A group at Massey University working with Dr Kirkland is aware of the research findings and of the limits to which parents will go in seeking assistance with a crying baby. Apart from research work, this group is offering a clinical service which is known at CrySOS. The main purpose of CrySOS is to provide parents with an opportunity to discuss their crying infants' demands and explore coping procedures.

CrySOS is not designed as a research setting but as a way of putting research findings to some use. However, since few CrySOS-like clinics exist some of the approaches will be exploratory. Any known limitations will be explained to participants.

It is possible that some ideas could be followed in a systematic research project. Unless it is made clear otherwise, participants may assume with safety that they are not part of a research project. There will be at least two meetings arranged. At the first meeting, the influences of the crying baby on the family will be discussed along with other topics, such as causes of crying and soothing remedies tried. A second meeting will be arranged within three weeks (where possible). Thereafter, meetings will be by mutual agreement.

No single remedy is available for soothing a crying baby. There are numerous "solutions". To help parents cope with their situation it will be necessary to try to identify sources of infant distress. Very broadly, parents will be invited to become partners in a joint search for mutual development.

is a useful exercise to go over these notes at the end of a session, reading them aloud whilst the parent follows so as to clear up ambiguities at that stage.)

e. "finding location". Sometimes unknown buildings are hard to find. It may be necessary to apologise for lack of signposting etc, even though this is not your fault.

f. "any other problems....", for instance general reluctance, partner hostility, lethargy, guilt.

g. "plans following..." If this is a "trip to town" then some parents may have overscheduled themselves. Enquire gently.

h. "some disruptions...." For a few parents this may be the very first time they have been out with baby. Maybe the general tension will interfere with what goes on typically. Indicate that if disruptions occur then these may be due to the trip. In spite of this try to encourage them to attend the following meeting, if one is planned.

i. "about changes in babies...." An analogy can be useful. It is as if a baby stumbled into a large hole, fell quickly and is taking quite some time to recover. Hence, some changes have sudden onsets and it may take much longer to help them overcome these by gentle, consistent, positive support. There's no need to dwell on this point as it will emerge again and again. At this stage make it and move on.

j. "overview...." This is a one-page written statement. A copy is handed to parents for retaining. Follow them through it by reading it aloud. The statement we use is shown in Box 5.3.

B. Session one (Box 5.4.) Following the general background an overview of topics which may be covered in the first session is provided.

a. "general background", has been covered already (Box 5.2).

b. "about your present situation" is in the next section (Box 5.5).

c. "consent form". Not until you have found out about the present situation, whether or not the Crying Baby Syndrome applies, can a decision be made to continue. If it appears that another agency would be better suited to handle the case then suggest a referral. When a decision is made to continue then complete a consent form, an example of which is shown in Box 2.2.

d-h. are discussed below as separate sections.

i. "daily diary record" as an intervention, see Part III. Since this is a straightforward and readily acceptable intervention it is almost always presented at the first meeting. By complying to complete it parents are involving themselves in a concrete activity and are producing a record which can be discussed at the next meeting. Additional blanks are offered in case the subsequent meeting is cancelled. This record is usually maintained throughout and may be continued independently after meetings have stopped.

j. "selecting another activity...." Depending on what happens at the

Box 5.4

Session one

—general background
—about your present situation
—consent form
—medical-health overview
—about motions
—about feeding
—about pregnancy
—about birth
—daily diary record
—selecting another activity to go with until next meeting
—cancellation procedure
—telephone contacts
—not alone

initial meeting a consultant may select another intervention or provide a choice of other activities.

k. "cancellation procedure" will be designed to fit in with agency policy. It may be necessary to remind parents they are free to withdraw (as per consent form).

l. "telephone contacts". It is helpful to phone the next day to re-establish contact. This can be repeated as often as necessary.

m. "not alone". A reminder that some reports have implicated over 20% of babies, and some over 80%, as crying for which there seems to be no underlying pathology (2). Parents ought not to feel guilty about seeking out sources of assistance.

C. About your present situation (Box 5.5) consists of a series of questions which are not unique to this topic. Indeed, whenever a person seeks a consultancy, these few questions can serve to release what is going on. There is no need to hurry, use the parent's own words in the case notes to describe what is happening.

There is no need to go into detail about these items, the answers will serve to guide a consultant's strategy for the remaining session and, possibly, future ones too. As another beginning for subsequent sessions ask how answers to these questions may have altered.

Box 5.5

> About your present situation
>
> —what is bothering you most at present
> —how has it been bothering you over the last few days
> —when did it start
> —was there anything which seemed to start it off
> —how long has it been going on

D. Medical-health overview (Box 5.6.) Since there is no point at all in implementing an intervention if baby has a raging infection, medical status needs to be checked out as soon as possible.

a. "limits of the clinic" Since clinics will have different amounts of medical support, limits should be made clear to participating parents. For instance if none is available directly then this should be pointed out.

b. A "check list" is one way to direct the attention of parents towards medical conditions. An expanded version of this approach is provided in Part III.

Box 5.6

> Medical-health overview
>
> —limits of the clinic
> —check list
> —recent doctor's visits
> —drugs baby is on at present

Box 5.7

About baby's
motions: —frequency —colour —smell —consistency *urine:* —frequency —staining —smell *feeding:* —what is given/rejected —how much —how often —night routines —changes tried

c. By asking about "recent doctor's visits" it is possible to ascertain not only reciprocal doctor/patient attitudes but also of immunisation records and standard check-ups. This item may be extended to include paramedical personnel.

d. An enquiry about "drugs baby is on at present" will reveal medically diagnosed issues. This is not always the case since many doctors are prone to prescribing antibiotics for viral infections, a useless exercise often justified under the guise of controlling any secondary infections. By checking with a local chemist/druggist it is possible to find out what the current vogue is with baby prescriptions. There will only be about a dozen popular ones so find out something about each one, like adverse reactions and how to spell the names for your notes. It may be useful to jot down these names along with common ailments inside the cover of your note pad if you tend to have trouble spelling correctly.

E. About baby's motions/urine/feeding (Box 5.7.) This is a probe inquiry at the first meeting. On the basis of information provided it may be necessary to make a referral. In and of themselves these items are not of much use it is how they fit into a broader picture which is important. For example with regard to feeding practices there are available excellent consultants in most localities. This book is not addressed to issues in feeding. There are available already many sources of information on this topic.

F. About the pregnancy (Box 5.8.) There is now emerging a respectable body of literature which indicates that parental attitudes toward the baby during pregnancy have important consequences for their subsequent and mutual development. Classes for parenthood are often designed now to cater for both the classical mechanical nature of pregnancy/birth as well as important emotional/organismic aspects. There are dozens of items which could be included in this section and the next one. Instead of making these into primary targets it is usually satisfactory for consultants to be aware of significant incidents which have been "carried forward" by parents and are reported to be influencing the current situation. One is the mistaken and popular belief in "instant bonding" rather than a gradual process of discovering love (3).

a. "shifting to a new residence" often characterises first-time expectant parents. Perhaps it is the belief that since in late pregnancy women typically give up regular daily employment, then there would be more time for setting up another home. There are other reasons too. Unfortunately the upshot of relocating during this time can result in extreme isolation. Cut off from a previously established local network, and too tired to socialise in the evenings, many women are left devoid of personal support.

b. "Other children" may be a source of annoyance since their needs still have to be met.

c. An enquiry about "general health" during this time may reveal whether a current issue has been ongoing. In addition, it provides an opportunity to explore consequences of early hospitalisation.

d. Meaningful "personal support", as expanded upon in an intervention discussion in Part III, is crucial to many people. This item will acquaint consultants with any contributions made by partner and serve to introduce friends.

Box 5.8

About the pregnancy

—shifting to new residence
—other children
—general health
—personal support
—working

e. An item on "working" is not aimed at establishing social class; it is designed to inquire in an oblique way about what sorts of preparations were made during pregnancy. As well, highly competent women often adopt a mechanical approach which helps them succeed in their paid work. Since this approach enables schedules to be made and appointments to be kept, the day is programmed to maximise accomplishments. As many babies cannot be scheduled a serious conflict of interests occurs. This is likely to be an obvious collision of metaphors; the mechanical pitted against the biological.

G. About birth (Box 5.9.) There is little doubt that events surrounding birth can be highly significant in the promotion of parent-infant well being. When birth experiences do not fulfill their expected promises parents can have misgivings about the whole episode. It is quite simple to point the finger and "accuse" those present of failing in their tasks and of upsetting a natural bonding process. My "battle" is not with birthing; this I leave to articulate, assertive parents who are committed to preventing others from experiencing similar horrors, or are aware that an optimum birthing experience is one of the best forms of preventative medicine, or are supporters of fully engaging a biological event with their families to welcome another member. Whatever the motivation of these birth-oriented parents I am impressed with their impact and the positive changes achieved. But this is not my topic. Instead, I'd like to encourage and support undertakings to alter current practices applied to infants in the three to thirty week zone.

Box 5.9

About birth

—birthweight
—conceptual age
—early physical contact with baby
—forceps
—drugs
—incubator
—personal support
—discharge/homecoming
—first impressions

For consultants it is those birth experiences to which parents now relate current difficulties which are important to consider. Although it is impossible to rectify these by changing the past, it is the present and the future which require attention. Even so, these earlier experiences cannot be dismissed, for they may offer the only threads of continuity and are the sole source of present existence. This is particularly so if a version of post-birth depression is now in full swing. Consultants are not intending that parents relive birth episodes, but enquire about those which seem to have initiated or appear to maintain infant irritability. Details about each item are omitted since, again, it is how replies fit into a broader picture which is relevant and to attempt to comments on every combination would be futile.

PART III

INTERVENTIONS AIMED AT BABIES

An overview of chapter arrangement

A similar format is adopted for each chapter. Following a general introduction relevant interventions are documented under broad headings. Of these the first few are aimed directly at consultants and provide specific information. The later ones offer a consultant guidelines to follow when implementing an intervention. These may be modified to make them more personal and/or fit a particular situation. So within this framework consultants can develop their own style, variations, relevant literature and case examples.

Following the intervention number and title a *rationale* provides a brief introduction. As well, a selected review of associated literature is offered. This is not intended to be exhaustive. Interested readers can find further information by checking out the references cited. The *projected outcomes* indicate some of the objectives established for each intervention. Next, and since it is possible to make an intervention far more general than it was designed for, some *limitations* are presented as a caution against unnecessary generalisation. A brief note on *assessment/monitoring* indicates how the intervention can be followed up at subsequent meetings. The next sections reiterate some of the points made already. These aim at providing a broader sweep of the topic in a more colloquial style. Some consultants may wish to give parents a copy of these sections, others may prepare notes for distribution, and others will be content to read out just what is written. From my own experience it is appropriate to provide something written on paper which can be taken away and considered elsewhere. Otherwise we always expect full comprehension during a single session. Remember, always provide enough room for non-compliance as well as reassurances concerning freedom from any guilt which may result from not doing as asked.

The *background* offers an overview of the particular intervention. Then, labelled as *activity* follows an outline of what is involved. Response forms onto which information may be recorded are provided in this section. Finally, where appropriate a *summary* concludes each intervention.

For some of the themes presented in the assessment/intervention scheme (Box 4.2) no specific interventions are offered. There are several reasons for these omissions. First, they may be areas about which I have not yet attained sufficient knowledge to justify designing or evaluating a particular course of action. As always, one important constraint is to avoid straying beyond spheres of competence. Second, there are already available excellent sources elsewhere which cover these grounds adequately. Finally, emphasis in this book is directed toward parent-infant interaction and the fostering of their mutual development; it is important to offer what is available now, other interventions will have to wait.

6 GENETIC INFLUENCES

Traditionally, one of two mutually exclusive views had been adopted by human development theorists. For one group development was predetermined by genetic disposition, for the other it was the different situations (environments) in which people found themselves that made them what they became. Acres of paper have been covered in small print by those advocating one or other of these two views. Now we understand each was correct in a way, a point put succinctly by one writer when she noted that development is 100% heredity and 100% environment (1).

The main reason for locating this section, on genetics, at the hub of the assessment/intervention model is that it is central (see Box 4.2). This is the core of one's existence. Our genes provide the basic equipment of life. Technically speaking the *genotype* consists of a person's potential. What is recognised or seen is known as a *phenotype*, the actuality. Further, the phenotype (what a person is in the flesh and in action) emerges from both the genotype as well as the various environments which contribute to personal, social and cultural experiences. There is a dual process here. As the phenotype is influenced by different environments it can alter in these environments.

As a significant and radical addition to this view it has been suggested that the genotype influences both the phenotype and the environments (2). These authors indicate that before the full phenotype is developed changes in the genetic programme can prompt new experiences. There is, as it were, a preliminary tuning up by the genotype of environmental influences. These then effect the emerging phenotype. This theory extends traditional views and provides a thrust for further research by its focus on *process*, a dynamic system.

It is not known to what extent a parent's information about genetic influences can itself moderate parental behaviours. Here are two examples. First, knowing that a particular child's continual vomiting is not in response to a positive dislike for the food it is being given but is attributable to a narrowing of the opening from the stomach to the gut, shifts "blame" from baby's personal whim to a possible genetic influence. Second, if a baby does have a strong reaction to foreign substances (for example cow's milk) then continual crying may be linked to a family trend on this matter rather than to sheer stubborness or straight out irritability.

It is my belief that the genetic net should be cast as wide as possible on these matters. The size of the mesh is important; not too fine so that it catches everything (which takes us back to genetic predetermination), nor too loose so that nothing is retained (environmentalism). The subtle interplay between the various influences will tease researchers for some time yet. In the meantime, for practical purposes, it is necessary to do what we can. One approach to this topic is through constructing family trees. These can show where some previous genetic trends may have revealed themselves. Of course there will be genetic influences which are unique to individual family members. It may well be that a particular baby does not appear to link with others in its biological heritage. Nonetheless, an awareness of what can occur through family members' expressions of particular genetic effects may ease any burden of guilt.

Intervention 6.1 Tracking patterns of genetic expression through construction of family trees.

Rationale By accepting an easily grasped but naive environmentalistic position with regard to human development it is possible to ignore important biological bases of behaviour. This is both restrictive and foolhardy. Restrictive because it fails to acknowledge many contributions which can influence genetic expression, and foolhardy because it allows a popular egalitarian bias to be maintained.

Hundreds of genetic disorders have been documented. In one report (3) it is noted that there are: 1,489 autosomal dominant, like Huntington's Chorea; 1,117 autosomal recessive, such as cystic fibrosis; and 205 sex-linked phenomena of which colour blindness is an obvious example. These exert continuing influences upon human behaviour. There are many other, multifactorial, disorders among which is pyloric stenosis (the narrowed or closed opening from the stomach to the small intestine producing projectile vomiting with every infant feeding session), which are involved too. It is likely cow's milk intolerance, and persistent crying (as an infant temperament characteristic) will be implicated as well. However, at present we do not have sufficient data on these less direct phenomena. By constructing a family tree parents will be able to see for themselves the expression of various genetic influences through successive generations.

Projected outcomes Over the short term a family tree provides an opportunity to enquire of other family members' (such as in-laws) network information. So a map of this kind can be useful to organise thinking about family members. Simultaneously, it provides a chance to become involved in a long term endeavour. Pieces of relevant data can be added as these come to hand. Thus, a family tree offers both short and long term involvement quite independently of noting genetic influences. This is the sort of thing genealogical societies encourage; mapping family members' ancestoral links across and through successive generations. However, for the present intervention other family characteristics are requested.

The main outcomes desired of this activity are two-fold. First, to involve parents in a task which can be built up over a period of time. Implicit in this time-locked involvement is a subtle pattern-construction; pieces make sense as they are organised systematically. This makes a nice analogy to what is occurring on the psychological plane; the emergence of meaning.

Second, there can be an important shift in attribution of responsibility. In short, baby may be crying a good deal because that is just the way it is, a characteristic which may be noted throughout the family. The effect of such a discovery can itself be support for a parent trying to cope with a familial trait, and of allaying any guilt arising from beliefs about the way baby is handled and so forth.

Limitations The negative aspects of stressing inheritance are obvious enough: sexism; racism; elitism; nationalism and selective breeding, among others. In addition an awareness of unpleasant characteristics in a particular familial line can give rise to awkward questions about responsibility and blame. None of these outcomes is sought in the present intervention. However we do need to be aware of these "twists of inheritance".

An obvious shortcoming applies to adopted babies whose biological family is, perhaps, unknown to its "parents". Additionally, a similar difficulty would arise when dealing with surrogate parents. Finally, there can be marked communication blocks between family members, for geographical and/or for psychological reasons. Consultants should be alert when these shortcomings exist and make appropriate modifications when implementing this intervention.

Another shortcoming is that people may believe genetic effects are immutable, unaffected by different environmental settings; a position as naive as that expressed by ardent environmentalists. If they did so, a likely upshot would be along the lines: "It is genetic, nothing can be done so I'll do nothing". An awareness of a probabilistic epigenetic theory (4) makes this statement unacceptable. Of course there are important genetic influences, but all of these are not resolved absolutely at conception.

Assessment/monitoring Consultants introduce the intervention only if baby's biological parents are willing to participate. If there are no ongoing family "problems" then verbal reporting at subsequent clinic meetings will cover the relevance of the exercise.

Constructing your baby's family tree

Background or parents)

The best time to begin creating a family tree is when baby is young. As your child grows the number of older family members declines. So catch the information while you can.

Somebody else in your family may have constructed a family tree already, showing names and relationships between different members. If so then your task is half completed (assuming you can borrow a copy). The other half (for self or partner) still needs to be drawn up.

There is no doubt that collecting together relevant family information and arranging this into a manageable form is a very demanding task. But, in spite of a slow start, many people are more than willing to contribute if they know it is being done seriously. Some will want to have copies as well. Then there is the chance that an interest is awakened and a hobby flourishes. In some places, genealogical society members comb graveyards, marriage registers and so forth in an attempt to extend their family's documentation.

For the present there are two main purposes for taking on a family tree exercise. First, for the challenge of simply seeing where various people occur in the two biological contributing lines. Accordingly, it will be possible to show your partner where cousins link in with various aunts and uncles. Besides family names, marriages and places of residence can be seen at a glance. Secondly, it makes possible the tracing of some characteristics from generation to generation, member to member. Although the general guidelines provided below serve both purposes our main focus will be on the second, genetic inheritance.

Apart from noting each person's sex, there are thousands of genetically primed characteristics which show up in family lineage. Some of these are called dominant, because it only needs one partner to transmit these to offspring. Examples include: brown eye colour; wavy hair; normal colour vision; long eyelashes; and so on. Other characteristics are recessive (both parents need to make a similar contribution before an effect is seen). Some examples include the opposites of those mentioned above: blue hazel eyes; straight hair; colour blindness; short eyelashes; etc. Then there are some characteristics which are sex-linked, carried typically by females and expressed in males. In the family tree illustrated below haemophilia is shown. Another group of genetically-linked characteristics cannot be traced to a single beginning and are the outcome of many influences, genetic as well as environmental. Genes continue to have an influence for as long as a person lives, and longer (if they contributed biologically to offspring).

It is becoming apparent that certain trends tend to run in families. The members of these families are said to have a "genetic predisposition" toward a particular display. This means a person can be genetically primed (much like loading a bullet into a gun) and environmentally released (pulling the trigger). We do not know what many of these triggers are; some could be food intolerances brought about by an unknown combination of certain foods offered in certain (like extremely stressful) environments. Some suspected genetic predispositions include a bias toward obesity; alcoholism; allergies; schizophrenia, and so on.

Perhaps persistent infant crying is another behaviour which has a genetic basis. We do not know what cry triggers are. There will be lots of different ones. But the way some crying can just go on and on regardless of what a parent does, seems to suggest a certain perseverence which has other than a direct relation to a particular family setting or parental handling style.

Box 6.1

Symbols to use when constructing family trees

Here are the notations:

□ male

○ female

• carrier

? possible

■ affected

| siblings

┌┐ generation

/ deceased (diagonal stroke through symbol)

= marriage (or biological union)

Shade in symbols to show which members affected by condition

Activity (for parents)

The easiest way to construct a family tree is to have some acceptable shorthand ways of showing what has been found out. It may take sheets of paper, note books or reference cards to hold the snippets of information. This needs to be arranged in a form which can be read off quite easily.

Start off by limiting enquiries to biologically close family members. Locate a person who would be likely to have much of the information you lack; this could be the person who maintains regular correspondence. A basic family tree will show: baby; baby's siblings (brothers and sisters); parents; siblings of each parent; grandparents. From these your tree can go up, down and out.

The symbols in Box 6.1 will help to condense your documentation. If there is not enough space on your chart, simply number people and keep a separate record of names; birth (death) dates; sex; and so on.

As far as is possible it is helpful to keep similar generations on the same level. Older generations can be arranged above more recent ones.

An example of a family tree is shown in Box 6.2. It is part of Queen Victoria's line. The darkened squares show males affected by haemophilia, the dot-centered circles indicate carrier females. You can see that for each sex there is about a 50% transmission (female) or display (male).

This gives you a good idea of how to set out your family members. Once you have done so, make discreet inquiries about the following behavioural displays. You may wish to use different coloured pens (though, remember,colours do not photocopy well) or shading tones to represent each selected characteristic.

Of course you may like to consider additional displays. The ones which could be worth noting to begin with are:

—excessive crying as a baby
—asthma (all year, or certain times each year)
—hives (and what brings these out)
—excema (and what prompts this)
—known food intolerances (this could be for selected years only, like between 7–11 for cow's milk)
—pyloric stenosis (narrowed or closed opening from stomach to small intestine which causes vomiting, even projectile vomiting, with every feed)

Outcomes (for parents)

The main point of tackling this task, apart from getting to know baby's lines of descent, is to show that certain features do make regular appearances in some families. Coping with a crying baby is not an isolated event. Regardless of any possible genetic influence it is possible someone else in your family (or that of your partner) has been involved with one in the past. The idea of a family tree is that something more than "cold comfort" is available.

Remember, unlike colour-blindness, baby's crying will become responsive to handling. Just because there is a family link is no reason to give up hope. At least you can see trends and take some of the load (and possible guilt) off yourselves.

Box 6.2

Part of pedigree of Queen Victoria, showing transmission route of haemophilia (deceased not shown).

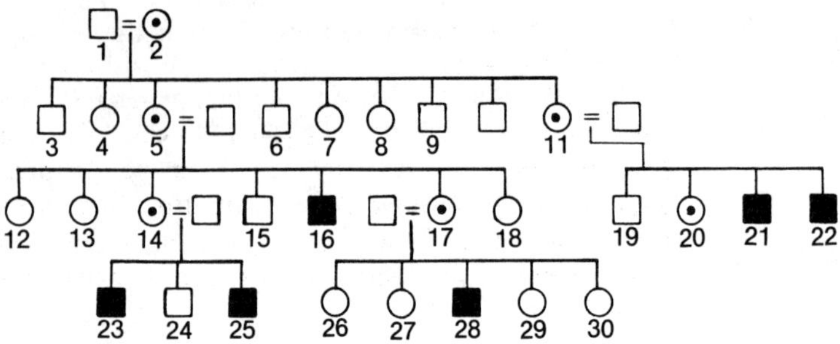

Key:

1. Albert Guelph
2. Queen Victoria
3. Edward VII
4. Victoria
5. Alice
6. George
7. Helena
8. Louise
9. Arthur
10. Leopold
11. Beatrice
12. Victoria
13. Elizabeth
14. Irene
15. Duke of Hesse
16. Frederick William
17. Alexandra*
18. Maria Victoria
19. Alexander
20. Victoria Eugene
21. Leopold
22. Maurice
23. Waldemar
24. Sigismund
25. Henry
26. Marie
27. Anastasia
28. Alexis
29. Olga
30. Tatiana

* married Czar Nicholas II

7 THE SECOND RING

Four of the topics for the second ring of the assessment/intervention scheme (Box 4.2) are introduced in the present chapter. These include intolerance/nutrition, chronic- and acute-medical health, and psychiatric factors. Since a whole group of interventions have been designed to address the topic labelled as Central Nervous System, which is the remaining member of this group, it is presented in the next chapter.

In the present chapter few specific interventions are provided, mainly because these topics fall within the precincts of established professional disciplines. This being so, a consultant's role here is more likely to be as an adjunct, making referrals to others. Indeed, if consultants attempted to become involved in areas for which training or experience had not prepared them, serious repercussions would be a highly probable outcome. To avoid this keep a tight rein on your own competencies and maintain communication with other professionals. All the same, to assume other consultants will be as accommodating as you are yourself is another error which is easy to make. Even though your referral notes are of an impeccable standard there will be some who object just as a matter of principle. Personal whims are distinct from a professional approach and they can be quite damaging when trying to build confidence.

The delicate path of a consultant lies between the quagmire of doing more than one ought and the haughty dismissal from those to whom a referral has been made but are unwilling to help. With experience and patience one can establish a role which is not threatening to others. Word will eventually get around that what you have to offer is worthwhile and serves to complement other services.

Intervention 7.1 Intolerance/nutrition

Some babies cry simply because they are continually hungry, they are not getting enough food. If babies' insides were transparent this would save a lot of agony by breast feeding mothers. Not only could they see how much baby was getting at each feeding session but they would also notice what was happening once the food was swallowed. There are available elsewhere excellent books on this topic. And, as well, it is so complex that a few pages of summary notes here cannot be of much help. My reluctance to deal with these matters is two fold. First, it lies beyond my own training and, second, most consultants will already have a working knowledge of what is involved or have located a contact who can offer appropriate guidance. Nonetheless one or two comments are provided.

Feeding, like crying, can be one of the crises of infancy. There is more to feeding than simply topping up a baby and removing its remains. Food is essential for survival. Yet, and especially for babies, there are the added dimensions of social contact, personal involvement and the building of a sense of trust; these are foundations which remain throughout life. Each society has its own rules about how a baby's demands are to be met. Even during infancy there is a bias towards grooming the next generation to take its place in the broader group of adult members. As implied in this book with regard to handling infant crying, the processes surrounding the routines of feeding reflects where parents fit into society through the metaphors which direct their actions. Those twin metaphors of machine and plant are quite obvious; schedule the baby to fit in with your plans or adapt yourselves to gratify the demands of a species. Each of these positions can be legitimised and is evident in different societies.

When an infant's energy requirements are adequately met this is reflected in changes of length and weight over time. One way to monitor these is by plotting them against established norms. The familiar growth curves are printed in many places. Through regular assessments a profile indicating an infant's growth changes may be drawn. The main point to note here is that hungry babies do cry.

So too do those who seem to be overfed. Here the mechanical apparatus is malfunctioning, there is interference in the system. There are many ways in which an infant's digestive system can react unfavourably. One is by regurgitating. This can be the result of pyloric stenosis (a physical blockage of the stomach outlet) in which case projectile vomiting is typical. In severe cases the force behind the propulsion is strong enough to splatter the stomach's contents against a wall some distance away. In moderate forms this handicap shows itself by less forceful eruptions. There are three ways of handling pyloric stenosis. One is by surgical means, which is not performed on young babies except on rare occasions. Another is by drugs, attempting to relax muscles around the stomach. The third is to wait it out until the baby grows old enough to handle the food satisfactorily. It does help to know there is a good, sound, organic reason for this continued sicking-up. Otherwise parents are hard-pressed not to blame the baby, an error which can have tragic consequences.

Another type of malfunction occurs, when the body cannot handle what is being offered. For instance, some people's skin bursts out in red itchy spots when they brush against certain things. Others are susceptible to "hay fever" and display an adverse reaction to breathing in minute particles carried in the air. Although most people call these allergies, professionals tend to prefer a more general term like hypersensitivity or intolerance.

An excellent and highly readable book on this subject is Maureen Minchin's *Food for Thought* (1). Her book is divided into three parts. The first provides a discussion of food intolerance and indicates how the immune system interacts with both personal and situational factors. A list of common symptoms of allergy or intolerance in infancy is provided and reproduced in Box 7.1. The second part provides a wide range of practical aids, guiding a reader to make appropriate decisions and offering suggestions about what can be done about these. In the final part there is a smorgasbord which includes case histories, a range of practical resources and a list of support groups in different countries.

One criticism levelled by many people against the notion of food allergy and intolerance is that it does not account for every occasion. The argument goes like this; if a person is allergic or intolerant then the relevant symptoms will be shown each time without fail. Although some people do exhibit an extreme reaction every time an adverse encounter occurs, there are others for whom a sort of "stacking up" occurs. For those who only occasionally show an intolerance there seems to be a certain amount which can be accepted without reaction. There may well be sub-clinical effects about which nothing is known until they erupt. But if different stressors occur at the same time they seem to add together and break through the sub-clinical barrier. For example family discord and certain pollens and inappropriate food and tiredness can combine to overload the body's management control system.

There are two analogies which may help to illustrate these points. One is of a balloon, the other of a lock.

Consider first an inflated balloon, in which additional pressure will cause it to explode. Pressure can be supplied from inside, inflation, or from the outside, by squeezing. Now let the balloon stand for a particular occasion and its rupturing for an adverse reaction.

Internal pressure is determined by a person's genetic make-up and the strength of the balloon's skin by previous experiences. Hence the more susceptible a person is, the greater the pressure. If there is a string of recent bad experiences its surface will be weak. An allergy is like a sharpened point to the balloon, an explosion is inevitable.

For others the internal pressure is not so great and the skin is tougher. All the same, if pressure can be brought to bear this stress will squash the balloon. Initially dull pressure can be sustained, and if increased further will cause bulging. The bulge is like a genetic susceptibility. Clinically, any adverse reactions are still unclear. Where and when an explosion occurs

Box 7.1

Common symptoms of allergy or intolerance in infancy

Gastro-Intestinal Tract

- frequent possetting or regurgitation
- vomiting, projectile vomiting
- frequent loose stools-mucus
- windiness, excessive flatus
- diarrhoea
- constipation (uncommon in the fully breastfed)
- stomach pains, bloating
- colic
- blood in stools
- poor appetite and weight gain
- feeding difficulties (breastfed babe often refuses breast after couple of minutes and screams despite obvious hunger. Also rejects bottles.)

Respiratory Tract

- nasal stuffiness, mucus
- sneezing
- coughing
- nose-rubbing
- unusual breathing
- sniffing, snorting, etc.
- noisy breathing
- hiccoughs
- recurrent croup
- recurrent bronchitis
- frequent ear infections (or any in the fully breastfed)
- runny nose (clear at first)
- frequent "colds"
- bad breath

Genito-Urinary Tract

- cystitis
- vulvo-vaginitis
- haematuria
- nephrosis

Skin

- dry patches of skin, cracks
- cradle cap
- 'spots'; rashes
- eczema
- hives, welts, swelling (eyes)
- purpura
- scratching or rubbing indicating itchiness
- sweatiness
- redness around mouth, anus, or on cheeks
- easy bruising
- cold hands and feet

Circulation

- changes in pulse rate and regularity, palpitations
- changes in temperature (usually slight fever)
- changes in skin colour, especially around lips
- anemia, haemolysis
- cold hands and feet

Source: Minchin (1)

depends both on the type of stressor applied as well as its sharpness.

The lock analogy is slightly different. It is aimed at illustrating why for some people there are unmistakable outcomes and for others a less predictable association between cause and effect. Let a key-opened lock stand for an "allergic" reaction. Not all keys fit and fewer still will release a lock's mechanism. An allergin is a special kind of key which unlocks reactions. A master key will open many locks; some people are susceptible to a wide range of allergens, each of which may be slightly different.

An alternative is a combination lock. Here different dials have to be set to match a predetermined pattern before the lock will open. A cumulative effect from several different stressors will result in a reaction. The reason these can be hard to track down is that one or two dials of the combination lock appear to be self-setting. When you think you have it, the lock seems to change just enough to open at another setting.

Many other analogies can be provided to illustrate the main points. First that for some individuals there is a strong genetically based pre-disposition toward adverse reactions. It is apparent these dispositions change with age. For example many babies appear to display immediate and at times long-lasting responses to the early introduction of cows' milk to their diets. Second, the causes of many reactions are difficult to isolate since there are cumulative effects which include interpersonal stressors as well as chemical ones. Finally, some effects are "masked"; they appear at some times but not at others. Clearly, there are far more substances which influence human behaviour than is generally believed. Until further research has been carried out on this matter consultants should be aware of what common symptoms are, the current state of knowledge about the underlying mechanisms, and practical courses of action which can be put into effect quite quickly and cheaply. Minchin's book goes a good way toward meeting these requirements, and is strongly recommended.

Intervention 7.2 Chronic medical health

The persistent high activity and intensity of reactions exhibited by some babies may prompt a doctor to apply the label "hyperactive". Once a label of this sort has been applied it can be very difficult to remove. One reason is that subsequent behaviours are viewed with a bias which serves only to confirm the existence of the original label. So if a baby is diagnosed as "difficult" then parents tend only to see extreme and disruptive behaviours. There is a sub-conscious spiral of affirmation which creates a distorting pattern. This is hard to replace.

Even though a baby may be showing every sign of not conforming to the label, research has shown repeatedly that these disconfirming actions are simply not attended to at all. Although initially intended to describe something in the present setting, a label can be extended and not only become an explanation of how that phenomenon came about but will be a constraining force directing future activities. One way to prevent the contaminating effect of labels is frequently to reappraise the situation as objectively as possible in order to introduce contemporary observations which offer positive alternatives.

At one time it was believed there was absolutely no hope at all for babies born with a chromosomal aberation, like Down's syndrome. Now, fortunately, through the diligent and systematic work of many caring researchers it is quite obvious education can make an important difference to the unfolding capabilities of these children. A point made by many who are victims of these sorts of accidents is that "we are people first". So too with crying babies. These are babies first. To think otherwise is to believe in and be trapped by the crying baby syndrome (Box 4.1).

There are many chronic conditions which affect babies' development. Many of these would have been identified at birth. Included are the hundreds of chromosomal disorders, as well as and including heart and respiratory dysfunction, diabetes, sensory impairment and the like. Many babies affected in these ways will already be under the care of personnel in other agencies. In these instances a crying consultant may be requested to assist. A team approach will be adopted. These cases present a challenge as the interventions need to adapted and tailored to the situation at hand.

An extensive examination of this topic is beyond the confines of this present book. Good readable sources are available elsewhere. One of the better books which introduces these and other medically-related topics in a thorough yet understandable manner is entitled *The First Year of Life* (2).

One question which can be almost answered by parents themselves concerns an infant's hearing. The following is modified from a brochure prepared by New Zealand Federation for Deaf Children Inc., (Reprinted by permission).

> Of course it is important to detect deafness at the earliest possible age, so proper help can be given. But how do you tell? What signs can parents look for during the development of their child? Many mothers have suspicions at some stage, and often they are groundless, but check; always check with a doctor. A child with a hearing problem needs help. The sooner, the better.

A hearing defect is not obvious, and normal hearing is an assumption. It is not a test — merely a check list for you and your doctor to assess your child's hearing abilities.

Some children are born with a higher risk of significant hearing loss. Risk factors include the following:

—Maternal Rubella (German Measles). This is an infectious disease, but the symptoms are mild and complications are rare. However, if a pregnant woman catches Rubella, her child may be born deaf, blind, mentally retarded or with heart defects.

Check with your doctor before pregnancy to eliminate risk

—A family history of hearing impairment, not counting normal loss through old age.
—Defects of ear, nose and throat.
—Birthweight less than 1500 grams (3lb 5oz).
—Rh-incompatability in the parents.

A child exposed to or exhibiting one or more of the above factors will not necessarily have a hearing loss, but is definitely more at risk than other children.

What to do if you suspect hearing problems

Stay in regular touch with your doctor, keeping a check on your child's development on the check list in this brochure. A doctor can refer you to an Ear, Nose and Throat Specialist for further diagnosis or treatment.

If you still have doubts or queries, there are other avenues open to parents of children possible hearing disabilities.

Importance of observation

The following is intended to serve the parents and the doctor as a means of observation, not a test. If the parent will observe and check the items mentioned in the normal environment of the home, then take the check list to the doctor at the infant's regular examination, it will provide a fuller report than that which is possible in the curtailed time of an office visit. The doctor can then assess the infant's response to sound, and along with professional observations, counsel the mother if the child's response is not entirely normal. A checklist is provided in Box 7.2.

Intervention 7.3 Acute medical health

As already mentioned many causes of a baby's crying can be traced to something being medically "wrong". The body's machinery is not working as it ought due to malfunction brought about by an infection of one sort or another. This section refers to baby's general level of health at the time of referral. It includes both observation by a consultant as well as parental reporting about effects of ailments which are sudden and typically of short duration. Included are colds, as well as gastric and respiratory disorders, among others.

The whole point about classifying different interventions in the overall scheme is that these may then be selected to match presenting symptoms. Although many of the interventions are complementary, there is no point at all in recommending one which ignores another topic which has greater urgency. For example, if a baby has a raging ear ache this needs immediate attention. If this is not treated it will interfere with any attempts to override it through trying to apply another intervention. A medical clearance is very important.

Rationale Several interventions depend upon baby's healthy co-operation. Since emphasis in the clinic is toward providing educational self-help for

Box 7.2

Checklist for parents

A = Always, F = Frequently, S = Sometimes, N = Never
(Circle the letter to show your answer, enter the date you made the observation)

	From birth to 2 weeks old does your baby:				
1.	Jump when there is a sudden loud sound	A	F	S	N
2.	Blink when there is a sudden loud sound	A	F	S	N
3.	Stop crying when you start to talk	A	F	S	N
4.	Seem aware of your voice	A	F	S	N
5.	Stir in its sleep when there is continuous noise close by	A	F	S	N
6.	Jump or blink when there is a sudden soft click, such as a light switch or a camera click when the room is otherwise quiet	A	F	S	N
7.	Stop sucking momentarily when there is a noise or you start to talk	A	F	S	N
8.	Look up from sucking or try to open eyes when there is a sudden noise	A	F	S	N
	From 2 weeks to 10 weeks old does your baby:				
9.	Stop crying when you talk to it	A	F	S	N
10.	Stop its movements when you enter the room	A	F	S	N
11.	Seem aware of your voice	A	F	S	N
12.	Sleep regardless of noise	A	F	S	N
13.	Waken when the crib or bassinet is touched	A	F	S	N
14.	Respond to comforting only when held against mother	A	F	S	N
15.	Cry at sudden loud noises	A	F	S	N
16.	Blink or jerk at sudden loud noises	A	F	S	N
	From 10 weeks to 6 months old does your baby:				
17.	Always coo with pleasure when you start to talk	A	F	S	N
18.	Turn its eyes to the speaker	A	F	S	N
19.	Know when its Daddy comes home and wriggles in welcome (if it is awake)	A	F	S	N
20.	Startle when you bend over the crib after it wakes up	A	F	S	N
21.	Seem to enjoy a soft musical toy: like a crib musical toy	A	F	S	N

22.	Cry when exposed to sudden, loud unexpected noise	A	F	S	N
23.	Stop movements when a new sound is introduced	A	F	S	N
24.	Try to turn in the direction of a new sound or a person who starts to talk	A	F	S	N
25.	Make many different babbling sounds when alone	A	F	S	N
26.	Try to "talk back" when you talk to it	A	F	S	N
27.	Start wriggling in anticipation of a bottle when you start preparing it (if the baby is awake and preparation is out of sight; e.g. refrigerator door opening, etc.)	A	F	S	N
28.	Know its own name (smiles, turns or otherwise gives an indication)	A	F	S	N

Source: New Zealand Federation for Deaf Children Inc.

infant-trapped families, it is assumed babies are well to begin with.

There are numerous sources of information about educational aid to different infant handicaps. Most early infant intervention programmes are designed around clearly identifiable handicaps, such as Down's syndrome, blindness and so forth (3). Practically none is aimed at "softer" handicaps like allergies, infant crying or sleeping difficulties. It is important that babies are checked over by a doctor since there is little use asking parents to take part in activities if the crying is caused by an infection or organic disorder. Thus parents are encouraged to have a regular medical check up for their infants. To help them in this process the list prepared by the New Zealand Department of Health is provided (Box 7.3).

Projected outcomes To have baby checked over by a family doctor or other medically qualified person.

Parental action on this matter depends upon their interpretation of an infant's presenting symptoms. Nonetheless, if there is any doubt at all then medical advice should be sought.

Limitations Three main limitations are evident. First, that the list is clear, understandable and comprehensive enough to prompt somebody into doing something when an ailment is present. Second, that people using the list can make relevant observations. And, finally, that doctors are able to make an accurate diagnosis and will not leave a parent in doubt as to baby's distress from a medical point of view.

Assessment/monitoring This could apply to each of the points raised in the above section on *limitations*. Only the latter two affect the clinic. At the initial meeting, parents will be presented with the Checklist to take home for reference purposes. During this meeting each item is read out and parental comments requested. Even though there may not be direct involvement with medical personnel, it is important to support parents who have not had a fruitful interaction with their own doctors. At the same time it is important for consultants to maintain professional contact with doctors, even where there is a distinct lack of co-operation. This situation can become difficult for consultants who can work only to the best of their professional capabilities. Some consultants are able to foster direct access to local Paediatricians who will then assess infants independently.

A screening procedure for baby's acute medical health status.

Background (for parents)

There are dozens of different reasons why babies cry a good deal. Some of these have to do with medical causes. For this reason you are strongly encouraged to have baby checked over by a medical Doctor. Even if you have been to your Doctor recenty and nothing was found, but you now think there is likely to be a medically linked cause then make another appointment and go again. Although busy, most Doctors are quite willing to investigate baby. This is especially true if parents can make and do take some notes which would help guide a medical diagnosis. Remember to let your Doctor make the diagnosis; but present enough additional information which can help in the decision-making process.

Activity (for parents)

As soon as a baby (or child too) shows signs of sickness take a blank sheet of paper. Put baby's name at the top and down the left side print the date and time. After each date/time entry print a few words to describe what went on. For example, describe symptoms (some of which are listed below) and say what you did about these. Be sure to mention any medications offered, and baby's reaction to them. Take these notes with you on your visit to your doctor, and either use them to refresh your memory or hand them over. (If you do plan to hand them over, give them to the doctor, not a nurse. And, if they go onto baby's file, you might like to keep a copy at home for your own use.)

Box 7.3

DANGER SIGNALS FOR YOUNG CHILDREN

Get help from a doctor if your child

—breathes quickly or grunts, or breathes with difficulty, has a raspy cough or wheezes
—has more than two runny, smelly diapers (motions)
—cries with a different cry for one hour or more, is difficult to wake up and refuses her feed
—has a convulsion or fit
—feels limp or floppy, looks pale and feels too cold or too hot
—cries, grizzles and touches her ear again and again or has a wet discharge coming out of her ear.

If your child is ill, do not blame it on teething.
—If you cannot find any doctor, wrap your child in a blanket and take her to the hospital.
—Ask when the child's condition should improve.
—If this improvement doesn't happen, or the child gets worse, have seen again.

Source: New Zealand Department of Health

Summary (for parents)

There are many lists available that are designed to alert parents about health related matters. One such list is provided in Box 7.3. However, remember that no list can offer a complete and fool-proof diagnosis. In the end you will need to rely on your own judgement and act accordingly. The above mentioned check list is provided as a guide in this matter.

Intervention 7.4 Psychiatric disorder

Since it is unlikely consultants will have professional training to treat any of the conditions described below it is advisable to make referrals to relevant professionals. One scheme for providing "clear descriptions of diagnostic categories in order to enable clinicians and investigators to diagnose, communicate about, study, and treat various mental disorders" (4,p.12) is offered in the *Diagnostic and Statistical Manual of Mental Disorders*, third edition (DSM-III) published by the American Psychiatric Association (4). This manual adopts a multi-axial approach. This means individuals are assessed on each of several axes and these refer to different classes of information. The first three axes are used for official diagnoses. These are supplemented by two others which are available for applications to special research and clinical settings.

The present section is not aimed at Axis II (specific developmental disorders) nor at Axis III (physical disorders and conditions). However, on Axis I there are four groups of disorder which are relevant to infants. Broadly, these are the intellectual, physical (eating), developmental, and emotional domains.

In the *intellectual* group, mental retardation is known to interfere with an individual's adaptation to the environment. This may be implicated in other mental disorders too. In about a quarter of cases it is associated with known biological abnormalities, such as chromosomal ones, and affects twice as many males as females.

There are two eating disorders which belong within the *physical* group. One is pica, the continued eating of non-nutritive materials, which has its onset between one- and two-years of age. The second is called rumination disorder of infancy. This begins between 3 and 12 months and is the repetitive regurgitation of food for at least a month after a period of quite normal behaviour.

A *developmental* phenomenon of this period is known as infantile autism. As pointed out in DSM-III any relationship to schizophrenia is controversial; some authors believe it is a precursor and others a completely independent entity. It is quite rare (about 2–4 cases per 1000) and is more common in boys and upper socio-economic classes. In babies it is typified with lack of warmth and a general distancing by the baby.

A "rejecting" baby once came to our attention. An interview with the parents has been published and offers a useful description of what occurred in the first few months following birth (5). The affected baby was a member of a twin set and had an older brother. For the first few weeks the parents did not notice anything unusual. However at three months of age it was quite apparent something was "unusual". The most characteristic behaviour was complete avoidance of eye contact. Even if one rotated her little baby body in an attempt to align heads, front on, she would quickly flip away to avoid looking. Once sensory handicap had been ruled out the parents began to attend to her other preferences; she disliked cuddling and would lay awake but quiet in bed. Indeed, if crying lustily she would quieten down when put into bed and left alone. In addition she was a tense baby who jumped with the slightest of interruptions. Once this was recognised as a general rejection of people the parents began to design means of establishing contact and maintaining communication. One way was for the father to lie down on his back and hold her around the chest and under the arms in a vertical position whilst allowing her to stand up on his chest. Playing games like this led her gently to accept interaction with other family members.

The final class considered here is the *emotional* and in particular a phenomenon labelled in DSM-III as "Reactive attachment disorder in infancy". It will not be unusual for consultants to come across babies who

Box 7.4

Diagnostic criteria for Reactive Attachment Disorder of Infancy

A. Age at onset before eight months.
B. Lack of the type of care that ordinarily leads to the development of affectional bonds to others, e.g., gross emotional neglect, imposed social isolation in an institution.
C. Lack of developmentally appropriate signs of social responsivity, as indicated by at least several of the following (the total number of behaviors looked for will depend on the chronological age of the child, corrected for prematurity):
(1) lack of visual tracking of eyes and faces by an infant more than two months of age
(2) lack of smiling in response to faces by an infant more than two months of age
(3) lack of visual reciprocity in an infant of more than two months; lack of vocal reciprocity with caretaker in an infant of more than five months
(4) lack of alerting and turning toward caretaker's voice by an infant of more than four months
(5) lack of spontaneous reaching for the mother by an infant of more than four months
(6) lack of anticipatory reaching when approached to be picked up, by an infant more than five months of age
(7) lack of participation in playful games with caretaker by an infant of more than five months
D. At least three of the following:
(1) weak cry
(2) excessive sleep
(3) lack of interest in the environment
(4) hypomotility
(5) poor muscle tone
(6) weak rooting and grasping in response to feeding attempts
E. Weight loss or failure to gain appropriate amount of weight for age unexplainable by any physical disorder. In these cases usually the failure to gain weight (falling weight percentile) is disproportionately greater than failure to gain length; head circumference is normal.
F. Not due to a physical disorder, mental retardation, or infantile autism.
G. The diagnosis is confirmed if the clinical picture is reversed shortly after institution of adequate caretaking, which frequently includes short-term hospitalization.

Source: American Psychiatric Association (4)

may be diagnosed thus. According to DSM-III predisposing factors from baby include "difficultness", lethagy and lack of body-to-body contact during the first few weeks of life (for example incubator isolation). From parents and other caretakers predisposing factors include severe depression, inexperience, loneliness, neglect and indifference as well as a extreme deprivation during mothers' own childhood. Further information regarding diagnosis is offered in Box 7.4. (Reproduced with permission from American Psychiatric Association)

To date there is not a great deal of information available about this phenomenon. However, *reactive attachment disorder in infancy* has specific diagnostic criteria. Through being aware of these, consultants can assist affected families by making referral or, when this is not possible, engage in selected interventions themselves.

8 PRACTICES RELATED TO THE CENTRAL NERVOUS SYSTEM

In this context the phrase "Central Nervous System" (CNS) is interpreted broadly. The CNS can be likened to the classical idea of a switchboard in the head. Although out of date it still serves as a useful analogy. Messages come in from the outside world via the senses (of taste, touch, smell, sight and hearing), are switched about in the brain, linked up with memories and so forth. Finally a return message is sorted out and sent down the line as an order for a particular action. The CNS is concerned with integrating incoming messages and for directing behaviour and thinking.

A malfunctioning CNS is likely to impair regular development. Handicap can range anywhere from mild to extreme. In one study the "pain" cries obtained by snapping a rubber band on the infant's foot were recorded from two groups of babies and compared (1). One group of babies had suffered mild trauma during pregnancy or birth but were otherwise quite healthy. The higher complications group included pregnancy conditions like infection, edema, toxemia, previous C-section, etc., and birth events such as induced delivery, drugs, forceps, knot in cord and so forth. The lower complications group of babies had fewer of these "backgrounds". According to the researchers, cries from the higher complications group, taken as a whole, were different. Not only were more band snaps needed to produce the cries, but the first cry was generally shorter, shriller and shorter. As well, the cries from this group were reported by listeners as being more grating, sick, urgent, distressing, piercing, etc. The point here is that even rather "mild" variations among otherwise normal babies can produce cries which may be indicative of CNS impairment.

Then there are some babies who are "jumpy". They seem to be very highly strung and react vigorously to any disturbances. Even internal disturbances seem to upset these babies. For instance they can be sleeping peacefully then give a sudden start, throw out their arms in a Moro-like response (see Intervention 8.1 for description of Moro) and wake crying strongly.

It is not yet known what causes babies to be like this. For some it may be have been due to their mothers who smoked, or to those who worked hard well into their pregnancies, or it could be a stressful shock during pregnancy such as the death of a friend. Then, for others, it may have been a long slow birth, or their reaction to drugs during delivery, or the absence of close physical contact following birth. And so it goes on, and on.

The business of tracking down possible contributing causes and doing something constructive about these lies outside the realms of this book. This is the task of others whose involvement is often sparked by personal experience or the political pressure from those who have been unwilling "victims"; namely, parents of inconsolable babies. For consultants and parents the damage has been done. Their coordination now needs to be directed towards doing something constructive with the product, a jumpy baby.

One way to think about active babies is that they are under internal stress. They cannot calm themselves easily. Hence a parent is faced with the task of discovering ways to soothe them without inflicting damage. It is as if these babies are always on the brink of being highly active even when calmed down. So it takes only a little disturbance to start the whole business off again. Others are typically well below this ceiling level and it takes quite a bit of irregularity to push them through. Of course hunger, temperature change and lack of physical comfort are disturbing. But for the jumpy babies it is as if they are either always beyond the limits of calm or poised to shoot through the boundaries of internal control. It is a mistake for adults to think these disruptive babies are reacting on purpose, to "get at" their parents. No, this is just the way these babies now are. Parents should not think that helping these babies to help themselves is spoiling them. Far from it. These babies need quiet consistent comfort from those who can gently encourage them to take on the world without alarm.

It is as if these babies have only limited ways of settling down. These ways of settling are like windows, the openings which allow others to influence their actions. Some of these windows are built into developing babies. For instance sucking is one such window. It is often reported that "colicky" babies are soothed by feeding, yet, at the same time, it is the food which appears to cause their pain, a fact which is confirmed by the loud crying a few minutes later. There are other windows and these are discussed as separate interventions in the remainder of this chapter, following "reflexes".

The idea of testing reflexes is to see just how jumpy a baby is at present. This procedure also helps a consultant to decide whether or not to seek other professional help. Hence this is dealt with first. Anecdotal comments from the parents about sudden startles, shaking or twitching will help ascertain the jumpyness of a particular baby and will provide clues about CNS integrity. It is not "brain damage" but rather a certain immaturity which is the main focus of attention. To talk in terms of brain damage is to imply permanence and irreversibility. This ought to be avoided.

Intervention 8.1 A screening procedure for baby's Central Nervous System.

Rationale People living with crying and/or difficult babies are often frought by the question "Is there anything wrong with my baby?". There are various ways of going about offering relevant answers. The present approach is an outline of a screening procedure which is designed to focus on the integrity of baby's Central Nervous System (CNS).

Involvement in this instance is limited to providing an initial screening service, it is not intended as a 100% assessment procedure. Hence if there are any doubts at all about the results make a referral to a medically qualified person. Results will need to be presented in a way that makes sense to medical personnel.

The 11 reflexes (or elicited responses) outlined below are not intended to be a full range. These have been selected on the basis of low intrusion (not making baby cry), ease of administration and acceptable results. As well they are mostly quite straight forward to apply; can be understood without elaborating training; can be applied in a brief time period; and do not demand any sophisticated equipment. Their focus is on screening for neuro-epileptic impairment (above the brain stem).

Additional documentation is available from numerous sources. Interested readers are encouraged to read further in any of the references listed (2,3,4,5,6).

Since an infant's parent is most likely to be present at the meeting some results will be known immediately. Good news will be quite obvious. If there is any doubt ask the parents to repeat selected tests in their own time at home and let you know of the outcome. Then further action may be taken. In any case some parents will pursue these activities at home, making them into games.

Limitations In the clinic we are interested only in screening for possible neurological handicaps, not a full assessment. There are two likely areas for making errors.

The first is in regard to consultants, whether they can conduct a screening test reliably. That is to say, go about applying the procedures in a similar way on different occasions.

The second limitation is related to the first. It may be summarized as the likelihood of committing, what in statistical terms are known as, Type I and Type II errors. A Type I error arises when, on the basis of looking over results obtained from the screening test, it is suspected there is something wrong with baby when, in fact, there is not. An alternative descriptive phrase for this error is "false positives". Type II errors emerge when an infant is "cleared", but does actually have something wrong with it.

Both of these major sources of error can be lessened by training, practice, and discussion among colleagues.

Of course the extent to which medical personnel accept your results will depend on their familiarity with elicited responses, the accuracy of reports, and their respect for our professional judgement.

Assessment/monitoring Doubts about any results which are raised by parents on subsequent occasions will be dealt with as they come to attention. They will be reminded that consultants are screening only and that a full assessment must be obtained elsewhere.

Vigilence both toward the application of techniques for eliciting infant responses as well as the presentation of results will be maintained. When in doubt medical guidance should be sought.

A Screening procedure to check Central Nervous System

Background (for parents)

Clinic participants will be introduced to the proposed screening test with a verbal statement along the following lines:

"The activities which I plan to do in the next few minutes involve baby. Please watch what happens and feel free to ask any questions.

This is a quick check to see if things are all right in baby's brain. Please note that this is nothing more than a basic screening test. If there is anything unusual at all you will be asked to take baby and my report to your family Doctor or Paediatrician who can check further and perhaps carry out a full examination.

Let me remind you then, that while baby's general state of health is important this is not my concern with this screening test. Instead, I am trying to find out if baby's brain is all right, and likely to function as it should. The way this is done is by providing baby with certain well-known and acceptable things to which it will react. Most of these reactions are known as reflexes and are quite automatic on baby's part.

Do you have any questions at this stage?"

Of course these comments would be modified if, for example, the test was conducted without parent's presence. Furthermore, any questions would be dealt with as clearly as possible.

Activities (for parents)

The screening test is made up of items selected from the following set. In part, selection will depend upon baby's age, its state, its co-operation, and the time when offered during a clinical session. A quick guide showing the optimum age range for each reflex is provided as Box 8.1.

A blank scoring sheet is provided as Box 8.2. The superscript following some item descriptions indicates the maximum possible score. Except for items 1,3 and 11, with the remainding items each side (left/right) is assessed separately and results are entered under the appropriate columns. The column headed "Symm" refers to symmetry, and either "O.K." or "?" is entered, depending on the outcome. Since baby's best performance

Box 8.1

Quick guide for showing typical age range for reflexes described

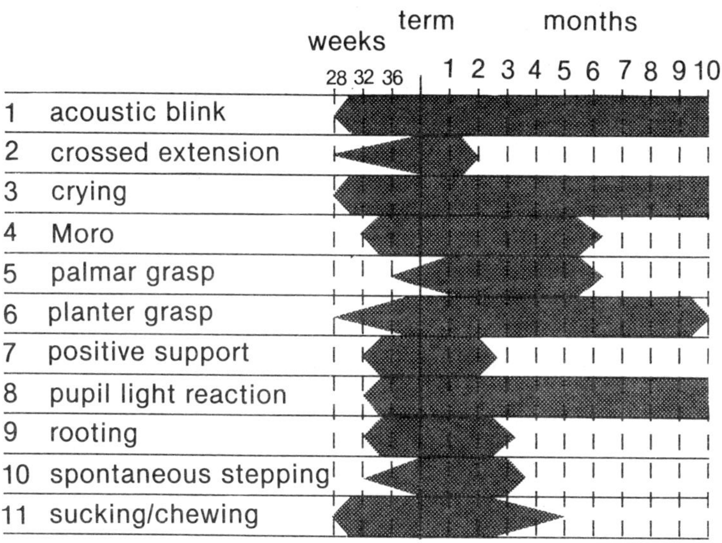

Adapted from Wilson (6)

Box 8.2

Blank scoring sheet for reflex results

Infant's name ____________ Date ______ Consultant ____________

number *item* *Left:Right:Symm*

1 acoustic blink = = = = ______ = = = =
2 crossed extension =:____:____:____:
3 crying intensity: L M H pitch: L M H
rhythm: L M H pacify: F M S
4 Moro abduction (out) =:____:____:____:
threshold: L M H adduction =:____:____:____:
5 palmar grasp =:____:____:____:
6 planter grasp =:____:____:____:
7 positive support (weight bearing) =:____:____:____:
8 (eye) pupil light reaction /head turning =:____:____:____:
9 rooting =:____:____:____:
10 spontaneous stepping (toe-heel; heel-toe) =:____:____:____:
11 sucking /chewing = = = = ______ = = = =

Notes:

is desired it is permissible to repeat items. It is helpful to indicate on the response sheet which items were not presented (one way to do this is to circle item numbers which are offered). Finally, for items 8 and 11 the alternative responses may be circled if these are obtained.

Remember to provide a warm environment, wash your hands and warm them up before starting. For each of the 11 elicited responses nine headings are provided. Here is a brief explanation of these. The first two, *from* and *until*, indicate the period during which the response is most likely to be evident. The comment on *positioning* indicates how the baby is placed. An *intrusiveness* scale extends from a low of 1 through to a high of 7 and shows how disruptive a procedure is likely to be. An extended discussion on *states* is available elsewhere (Intervention 10.4). In the present context optimum states for observing the elicited responses are listed. What one actually does is described under *procedure* and what the baby may do to show evidence of the reflex is offered under the heading of *response*. To *record* the response use the number which most closely matches the observations. These distinctions may not be clear cut, so score on the conservative side (use lower numbers). Finally, a brief comment about *relevance* is offered. Each of these is a possible implication and is not necessarily definitive. Hence, there ought to be a question mark following every item in under this heading. If in any doubt seek the opinion of others and/or make a referral with a note about your own findings.

1. Acoustic blink

From	28 weeks gestation and less likely on birth day
Until	Remainder of life.
Positioning	Typically lying on back, although may be held
Intrusiveness	2.
States	Any awake state, excluding crying (C,D,E).
Procedure	Make a sudden sharp, but moderate noise such as from hand clapping about 30 cm (1 ft) from an infant's ear. Avoid possible air blasts to ensure it is the sound baby will react to. For another approach to this topic if deafness is suspected see Intervention 7.2 (Box 7.2).
Response	Rapid closure of eyelids.
Record	1 absent 2 a single weak blink which cannot be obtained again by repeated stimulations 3 strong blink that can be reproduced after a lapse of 2 seconds
Relevance	absent : hearing impairment

2. Crossed extension

From	28 weeks gestation and less likely on first few days after birth.
Until	1–2 months.
Positioning	On back.
Intrusiveness	2 when using fingers, or 5 when using a pin.
States	Any waking state.
Procedure	Hold one knee so as to straighten the leg and then stimulate the sole of the foot. Either apply firm steady pressure with your fingers or prick slightly with a pin.
Response	Watch the non-stimulated leg. There should be a pulling back and then a pushing out. Premature babies show both a drawing up of the leg and a spreading of their toes. Repeat for both sides.
Record	Record only the extension (pushing down) of the unstimulated leg: 1 absent 2 short, rapid push 3 persistent, clear extension 4 long and sustained with rapid extension
Relevance	absent : spinal cord lesion asymmetrical : peripheral nerve injury : muscle weakness

3. Crying

From	28 weeks gestation.
Until	Throughout life.
Positioning	Any at all.
Intrusiveness	7.
States	Any waking state but displayed as F.
Procedure	Crying is likely in some phase of a session (for example when taking part in the Moro — see below). If crying does not erupt spontaneously then omit, or ask a parent what tends to happen in a home setting. As soon as crying begins simply pass baby to a parent. Observe comforting procedures and its effects. For further details and a more elaborate technique see Intervention 10.1.
Response	intensity (or force) — low, medium, high pitch (shrillness) — low, medium, high rhythm (continuous pattern) — low, medium, high pacification (soothing) — fast, medium, slow
Relevance	alert : shrill, piercing, intense : weak : harsh and rasping : non-rhythmical

4. Moro

From 28 weeks and less likely on birth day.
Until Around 6 months.
Positioning Held on back.
Intrusiveness 7 (Perhaps indicate to parents before hand that the procedure may be upsetting to baby).
States Any waking.
Procedure Of the many ways to elicit a Moro response two methods are described below. For each of these hold the baby on its back so the feet are toward your midline and the body on a slight upward angle. Support the head from underneath using one hand and begin with baby's hands in a midline position. For one method when baby is quiet with a relaxed neck, drop the head a short distance by quickly lowering your head-supporting fingers. Prevent baby's head from falling right down. An alternative method can be used for a more vigorous, crying, baby. Begin in much the same manner as before. This time "drop" the whole infant; from a standing position lower your arms rapidly and at the same time bend over to get the maximum "fall" distance. Be careful to "catch" baby close to the floor. For either method repeat three times after a brief recovery rest and record the best performance.
Response A startled flinging out of the arms as if to "break the fall". There are several aspects which are deserving of attention with this display.

a. The threshold, how easily the response is elicited on each attempt.
b. The amount of outward movement of the upper arms from baby's body.
c. The fling of the lower arms, pivoted at the elbow.
d. The amount of recovery (adduction) after each trial.
e. Any asymmetrical reactions where one side has more extreme responses than the other.

Record Indicate degree of both outward (abduction) and inward recovery of the upper arm from baby's body. In addition note the threshold of the response (low, medium, high). A high threshold means much difficulty in getting the response.

abduction (fling)		*adduction* (recovery)	
1.	none	1	none
2.	slight on most trials	2.	half range of abduction
3.	most trials 45 degrees from truck	3.	full range on most trials
4.	most trials over 90 degrees from trunk	4.	back to original position (perhaps even crossing over in chest)

Relevance asymmetrical : insult to a brain hemisphere
: peripheral nerve injury
: muscle weakness
: upper limb injury
beyond 6 months : CNS
alert : if adduction exceeds abduction
: there is a high threshold (only one response on many trials)

5. Palmar grasp

From Term (40 weeks) gradually increasing with age.

Until Around 6 months.

Positioning On back or may be held by another; hands free.

Intrusiveness 1.

States Any awake, excluding crying (C,D,E).

Procedure Slide your index finger into an infant's hand from its little finger side and press gently against the palmar surface. Remember to repeat for both hands.

Response Can be quite different between babies or on different occasions with the same infant. Less likely to occur following feeding.

Record
1 absent
2 short, weak tightening
3 strong and consistent for 10 seconds
4 hard grip with finger tips going white

Relevance absent : not significant (individual variation)
asymmetrical : CNS
: primary muscle weakness
: peripheral nerve injury

6. Planter grasp

From	28 weeks gestation.
Until	Around 9 months.
Positioning	On back with head in midline and legs relaxed.
Intrusiveness	1.
States	Any.
Procedure	Holding a foot (most easily by hooking second finger under baby's heel and placing the index finger over the ankle) press with thumb against the ball. Remember to repeat for each side.
Response	Curling down of toes.
Record	1 absent 2 weak and brief 3 good and continued (about 10 sec) 4 very strong and elicited with light touch to foot
Relevance	absent : not significant asymmetrical : insult to a brain hemisphere beyond 9 months : alert, check developmental status

7. Positive support (weight bearing)

From	Around 32 weeks gestation.
Until	About 2 months of age.
Positioning	Held around chest, under arms.
Intrusiveness	3.
States	Any waking, except crying (C,D,E).
Procedure	Hold baby around the chest and under the arms facing away from you. Lower onto a flat solid surface, such as a table top. Allow feet to make firm contact and don't let baby go.
Response	Upon contact baby will attempt to support its own body weight by leg stiffening.
Record	For each leg note whether or not self-support is evident by tension applied: 1 absent 2 present, stiffening
Relevance	absent : primary muscle weakness : spinal cord injury : low muscle tone

8. Pupil light reaction

From 28 weeks gestation.
Until Throughout life.
Positioning On back, but doesn't matter.
Intrusiveness 2.
States Easiest during quiet alert (D).
Procedure Cover one eye, say with palm of hand, for a few seconds and then uncover. Remember to test each eye.
Response During shading the pupil will enlarge. As soon as shade is withdrawn the pupil on the covered side will constrict (shrink in diameter).
Record
1 absent
2 just noticeable change
3 marked change
(Note, some infants will not allow their eyes to be covered and turn heads vigorously to avoid this. In these cases circle the response "head turning" on the recording sheet.)
Relevance absent : CNS
asymmetrical : CNS

9. Rooting

From 28 weeks gestation, less likely on first few days following birth.
Until Around 3 months.
Positioning On back, but not critical. Can be helped by adopting feeding position.
Intrusiveness 1.
States Any waking, but not crying. There is some individual variation and the response is influenced by baby's state, time since last feed and so on.
Procedure Moving toward the cheek stroke the skin at mouth corners using a finger. Repeat for each side.
Response Turning of the head toward the stimulated side. As well the head will tilt to track the stimulus for upper-or lower-lip cheek stroking and the mouth will open.
Record
1 absent
2 weak incomplete turn
3 full turn for at least 3 seconds with lip-grasping of finger
4 keen head-turning and firm lip-grasping
Relevance absent : depressed, drugs
asymmetrical : insult to a brain hemisphere
: facial injury
turning away : just fed

10. Spontaneous stepping

From	From 37 weeks gestation, changes depending on age.
Until	Around 3–4 months.
Positioning	Held.
Intrusiveness	3.
States	Any waking, though easier to manage if in D or E.
Procedure	Hold around chest under arms in upright position facing away from you. Approach a flat firm edge such as a table top and brush the top of a foot against the lower edge. Lean baby's body forward and move gently along so as to follow any stepping movements. Repeat for each foot.
Response	Baby will make rhythmical stepping movements which alternate as in walking.
Record	1 no stepping 2 1 or 2 slow steps, and other limb movements 3 at least 3 steps but delays between each 4 at least 3 steps in quick succession
Relevance	asymmetrical : CNS : muscle weakness : peripheral nerve injury toe-heel : premature heel-toe : term

11. Sucking/chewing

From	About 28 weeks gestation, less likely on first few days following birth.
Until	Around 4–5 months.
Positioning	On back, but may be held on feeding position.
Intrusiveness	1.
States	Any waking.
Procedure	(Wash your hands) Slide your index finger into baby's mouth about 3 cm (1 inch).
Response	Rhythmical sucking of the finger pushing tongue against finger to roof of mouth. Older infants will chew on finger rather than suck it. (Circle on response sheet for chewing).
Record	1 absent 2 for short burst (1–6 sucks), weak 3 for long periods (15–30 sucks), strong 4 practically uninterrupted, strong sucking.
Relevance	absent : just fed : CNS : drugs : apathetic beyond 5 months : check developmental status.

Summary (for parents) It is possible to repeat these different reflexes at any time, so long as baby is not upset unnecessarily. The point is that since the reactions are reflexes there is little baby can do but to comply. At the outset it was stressed that these reflexes do not comprise a full neurological screening. If you have any doubts at all about the results then seek another opinion. Nonetheless, do not get alarmed about any "failures". These need to be understood in a broader context, and this is what a trained person can offer.

In this section several different reflexes were described. These have been selected to provide the most information for the least interruption. For parents who are reluctant to try these activities, watch somebody else demonstrate what happens.

Intervention 8.2 Carrying/rocking

Rationale As already mentioned humans belong among those species who have evolved to have continuous contact between adult and infant. We differ from the "drop and leave, feed after long intervals" species. There are numerous consequences arising from this sort of evolutionary design. Besides needing many short feeds, human infants are primed for being carried about. This point is more than obvious to those parents whose babies protest when not being ferried, even in the middle of the night. For some a brief rest is not tolerated by the infant.

From the late 1960's a whole series of studies were reported on the effects of different rocking strategies. Several factors were systematically altered and their effects noted. For example Ambrose (7) found with 5-day old babies a vertical movement of 3 inches (7.5cm) paced at a rate of one per second corresponded to slower heart rate, more regular breathing and increased relaxation. A ceiling hung spring device which mimics these features is available commercially. For details write to: LULLABABY, Pembridge, Leominster HR6 9HB England. The device is distributed both by mail order, at the address mentioned, or through branches of John Lewis Partnership in U.K. Alternatively, from: Schlummerbaby, Mozartstrasse 1, Postfach 3, D – 6957, Elztal-N (in West Germany), or Universal Imports 11975 St. Germain Boulvd., Montreal, Quebec H4J 2A3, Canada (in North America), or Ubimex, J.F. Willemsstreat 69, 2530 Boechout (in Belgium). Overseas posting weight is 1.1 kilo, either Mastercard or VISA is accepted by LULLABABY.

In another study (8) a marked distinction was noted between vertical and horizontal rocking, and whether the movements were continuous or intermittent. The general results indicated that horizontal and intermittent rocking was a good way to make baby more alert. However, vertical and continuous rocking tended to induce drowsiness.

Finally, in a nicely designed investigation 2-month old babies were rocked vertically at different speeds with groups of low-and medium-active infants in each condition (9). During the first minute the babies were observed and their states determined. Each was then rocked for 15 minutes at one of four speeds (0,30,60,90 per minute) and observed for a further 10 minutes. Regardless of babies' sex or state those rocked at the faster speed slept more and cried less when compared with the other rocking speeds.

Overall it seems; vertical rocking is better than horizontal movement for inducing rest, continuous movement is better than intermittent, and that a rate of greater than 60 per minute is preferable.

Numerous reasons have been provided to account for the lulling effect of rocking. Most refer to a link between fetal experiences and later rhythmical rocking. One hypothesis is that repetitive stimulation of sense organs influences those centres which control sleep and wakefulness and/or influences reflex systems (9). There is another view which is mentioned below (Intervention 8.3).

Limitations From both experimental results and anecdotal comments it is clear that small babies can be soothed by continuous rocking. Yet surprisingly, few people have designed mechanical aids which do this automatically. Of course there are several dangers associated with any equipment. One is that a machine could malfunction. Another is that without adequate safety features people may get hurt. And, finally, a machine could interfere with the subtle rhythms of development which emerge during parent-infant interaction, if used extensively. Some people may strap baby in, turn the machine on and just walk away.

Assessment/monitoring Apart from watching a parent calm an infant by rocking, consultants can enquire about the effectiveness of different approaches to this technique. Are there some times of the day when it is more effective than others? Are there some movements or speeds which are better suited to particular babies?

Carrying/rocking

Background (for parents)

It has been known for a long time that rocking babies can be very soothing. More recently it has been demonstrated in laboratory studies that both the type and the speed of rocking play important parts. For example rocking a baby from side to side seems to make it more alert whereas bouncing it up and down will soothe it more easily. A baby who is rocked vertically dozes sooner and stays quiet for longer periods.

The speed of rocking appears to be important too. There appears to be a critical speed beyond which rocking is more effective. Anything less than about 60 rocks per minute is of marginal use. So the faster the better.

Finally, a difference has been noted with regard to steadiness of rocking. For the best results rocking should be continuous. Don't give up.

In summary then, the research findings indicate that the ideal

Box 8.3

A simple sling

Fabric needed A piece of soft non-stretch natural fibre (like cotton or denim) measuring about 1.7m (6ft.) long and 0.6m (2ft.) wide.
Pattern Use a full-open sheet of newspaper and trim to about 80cm (32 inches) by 60cm (24 inches). Around the one end of a shorter side draw the symmetrical arc of a circle. This arc will touch the shorter edge mid-way across the page and dip at each side about 13cm down from the corners. Cut along this arc line. This gives a shape with a squared bottom and rounded top (where you cut along the arc).
To cut and sew Fold the material to halve the overall length. Place the newspaper pattern on top. Pin and cut only along the arc line. Sew only along this arc to join the halves, and then hem. The result is now a wide loop with a bulge at the arc end.
To fold the sling for use This is tricky, but once done correctly is easy to manage. The aim is to fold the whole loop lengthwise across the shorter sides, to halve the width. Fold by pushing an edge through the middle as if to turn the "loop" inside out. When the folding is completed correctly each of the longer sides will be alongside the opposite one so the arc will be halved. Now shake the sling briskly to align all the corners. If placed flat on the floor the sling will look a bit like a child's drawing of a boat, with a curved bow (which is the arc) and a straight stern (which is the original fold from halving the length before putting the newspaper pattern on).
Wearing the sling In its final position the sling will be positioned like a sash, the straight fold at the shoulder and the arc at the hips. If right-handed slip your right arm through so the sling lies diagonally across the body. Make sure the open edges of the sling are uppermost as baby will lie between these, snuggled against you and resting on the folded line created when the loop was turned inside out during folding to make the sling.
For baby With the left hand separate the top edges of the sling. Lean forward so the sling hangs loose in front then put baby in using the right hand. Check that the sling is flat along your back. Baby's legs will be toward your hips and the whole body lying comfortably along the fold line. Dress baby according to the surrounding temperature. Sling length is important. If baby seems too low then pin up the straight shoulder fold and sew this later. A comfortable height is with baby's head at breast level. Feeding can be accomplished with baby in the sling too. Don't cut off any extra from the straight edge at the shoulder as the sling may need to be lengthened when baby grows.

It may take time to get used to the sling. Try it first when baby is happy. Go for a walk, the motion may work wonders. Experiment to find out what is the most suitable position. If baby goes to sleep and you wish to empty out then simply roll baby out on top of the bed by leaning forward and release by folding back the sling edge.

Source: New Zealand Federation of Parents Centres

combination is to have continuous up and down movements at a rate of more than 60 per minute.

Activities (for parents)

Given that the ideal mixture is of continuous fast vertical bouncing, then people can design for themselves ways to achieve this combination. It can be very tiring. Some people have devised mechanical aids to help them. But, if you do use a mechanical helper remember to keep an eye on what is happening because all machines can fail.

One practical illustration of regular vertical rocking is with "jiggling", the bouncing action which some people use. A variation on this procedure is to jiggle quickly using your whole body. Hold the baby facing outwards with one hand under the bottom and the other secure around the infant's chest so its back is against your chest. For parents it becomes a matter of finding a jiggling position which works and is the least tiring.

Many parents have found carrying aids very helpful. There is now on the market a whole range of products designed for this purpose. For smaller babies a simple sling can be made quite easily and baby carried about. Some infants are soothed by the parent's movement and the firm contact.The general instructions for a sling are provided below (by courtesy of Helen Clarke and New Zealand Parents' Centre Bulletin where the article upon which this description is based first appeared) are provided in Box 8.3.

Summary (for parents)

For small babies fast, continuous, vertical rocking is soothing. For older babies movement is still important but they tend to want more social activity too. Rocking can be used along with sounds (Intervention 8.3) and swaddling (Intervention 8.6). A simple sling is described which is easy to make and straightforward to use.

Intervention 8.3 Sounds

Rationale When the popular media latches onto techniques which are reported as soothing crying babies these become instant international news items.

An early instance was a loud clock sound; ticking steadily and rhythmically, apparently mimicking heart beats. Although subsequent laboratory research has cast doubts on the efficacy of heartbeat-like sounds (10), many parents report their young babies are soothed when a clock is placed near the crib. Following a similar trend a long-playing record called *Sleep gently in the womb* is available and has various interuterine sounds, like a mother's blood pulsing through the aorta. Some of these recordings are not unlike an old-fashioned steam train huffing and puffing. The record jacket indicates that interuterine sounds played back at moderate intensities will placate fretful babies, but there is little published research on this matter. As with the heart beat studies there is a belief that uterine life was bliss and babies will settle if reminded of that calm, peaceful world; a matter which is open to doubt as much as to speculation.

Another news item reported an English paediatrician who could quieten crying babies by yelling at them. Apparently he begins with a resonant boom which is louder than baby's own wailing. Then, as a baby quietens he lowers his voice steadily until both are quiet.

A final example reported about the effects of playing back to a fretting baby its own previously recorded cry sounds. Although several mothers I know have tried this method at home, of their own choice, none has been successful.

As far as I am aware there have been no controlled studies investigating the last two methods. Although it would not be hard to design experiments to investigate systematically either yelling at or playing back recorded cry sounds there is, as yet, no scientific research on these topics. Given that many babies do cry this does seem surprising. Perhaps part of the reluctance of the research community to commit themselves to projects of this sort stems from the low status infant crying and its effects has in the broader world, in spite of the news worthiness of techniques which seem to work.

For very young infants continuous sound will decrease their arousal level (11). Yet, by itself, a tape recording of heart beats replayed at moderate intensity (85 dB) is not as effective as other types of continuous stimulation for month-old babies (12). A general dampening of arousal is proportional to the number of senses stimulated. This is a case of stacks on the mill. Or, to coin a phrase, "peace is wholly consistent", meaning that continuous stimulation of several senses produces a peaceful baby.

In a subsequent study Yvonne Brackbill (13) tested one-month old babies in a two hour session. This time she applied stimulation to four senses continuously. Each baby took part under two conditions, experimental and control. In the experimental setting she provided to the ears white noise (sounding like steam escaping under pressure at 85 dB), to the eyes light at about 100 watts, and to the body both swaddling and 31 degrees C temperature. All babies began when in the quiet alert state, a point worth noting since many babies are not often in this state. The general upshot of Brackbill's study was that both behavioural and physiological indices of arousal were reduced, an effect which happened quickly and continued throughout the two-hour sessions. For a possible explanation Brackbill suggests involvement of the CNS structure. Specifically, that continuous sensory stimulation has a role in suppressing the arousal system of an immature organism.

Another example of multiple stimulation is reported by Sandy Jones in her book *Crying Baby and Sleepless Nights (14)*. After picking up a screaming baby Sandy Jones describes what one mother did:

> "She planted the tiny baby against her shoulder, holding it firmly by the buttocks in one hand and gently cupping its head in the other.
>
> Then she began a dance that looked like an ancient mothering minuet. She took eight or ten rhythmical paces forward, turned around and took eight or ten paces back to where she had started from: step ... pause ... step ... pause. Her hand slipped down to the baby's back, patting with each pause, and his toes uncurled.
>
> Sensing that the baby was still wound up, she continued her walk, adding sounds that I had never heard used with a baby before. She produced deep guttural groans; kind of groans that people make when they're having orgasm. The groans welled forth each time she came to a pause in her rhythmical stepping. Groan-pat-pause-walk, groan-pat-pause-walk, the dance went on. The baby's hands uncurled and he let out a huge, chin-quivering sigh that racked his tiny body.
>
> Ellen continued the dance, firmly holding the baby in place, refusing to move him from her chest even to check on his expression. After another deep sigh from the baby, as if to say "Home at last!" his eyes fluttered to half-mast. Within ten minutes of her mothering performance the baby fell into a profound sleep that left his body limp. "(p100–101).

Limitations Some parents are embarrassed to talk to their babies. Some are not aware that although babies cannot talk back they are still influenced by and receptive to continuous sounds. Besides natural sounds, like speaking and singing, parents can be afraid of damaging their babies' ears by exposing them to other sounds. Certainly consistent loud sounds do affect children, as shown by those studies comparing the school performance of those on noisy airport flight paths and those who are not. But these are much louder sounds than parents would use intentionally at home with babies and go on for much longer periods.

Another limitation is the reluctance of parents to sing to their babies. Some mothers I know would sing only when alone with their infants in the middle of the night. Others, however, are uninhibited and willing to engage with their babies musically in spite of personal limitations.

Then, there are babies for whom sounds will be ineffective and others who may react strongly to try avoid unnecessary noises. A particular infant's sensitivity can only be ascertained by careful parent monitoring as different levels of sound are tried out.

Finally, it seems that the younger the baby, the more effective continuious stimulation is likely to be for soothing. Those who have older babies should not expect the immediate effects reported for younger ones.

Assessment/monitoring If prompted, parents are willing to demonstrate how babies may be soothed by continuous stimulation. Alternatively a consultant can ask about what was effective in the home setting and take the matter from there.

Sounds

Background (for parents)

It seems that the younger the baby the more easily soothing can result from providing constant sounds. Although there is little experimental evidence about when sounds lose their effectiveness in soothing babies it seems that after about four months of age there is little success.

To provide steady sounds some parents have relied on loud ticking clocks. Others have resorted to a commercially available recording of a mother's inter-uterine sounds, what baby hears when in the womb. Others have found common household sounds work wonders, like a fan whirring, the buzz of a vacuum cleaner, the monotonous pulsing of a washing machine, the drone of a clothes drier, or the regular beat of a metronome. It seems the only restriction is the limit of a parent's imagination.

One consistent finding reported in the research literature is that the sound has to be moderately loud and it has to be continuous. Another finding is that sound has its best soothing effects when combined with other types of constant stimulation, like rocking.

Activities (for parents)

Once parents are aware that constant, monotonous sounds of moderate intensity can soothe fretful baby and have found this out for themselves, then the "magic" is quite apparent. There are many household noises which work satisfactorily. To find out which ones soothe the best it is largely a matter of trial and error.

One age-old technique which combines the essential ingredients for soothing young babies is the singing of lullabies. "Hush songs" are usually sung with a slow regular beat. The singing of lullabies to babies is an art rapidly disappearing. In its simplest form a lullaby is a vocal sound accompanied by regular breathing whilst holding or rocking. It can be as simple and basic as vocal "snoring", or as sophisticated as Brahms' familiar melody. Some parents find traditional Christmas tunes are very helpful. One father told me he first used a deep vibrating monotone to sing or hum. Later he dropped his voice into heavy and exaggerated breathing which then led to snoring-like sounds as he cuddled baby close to his chest.

Research findings indicate that a combination of different sorts of stimulation applied at the same time is most effective in lulling babies to sleep. So it is quite obvious why so many parents report car rides settle fretting babies. As soon as baby is taken out in the moving car sleep takes over. One mother found she was out in the car a good deal and then realised baby slept best while travelling so this habit was strengthened.

A word of caution should be mentioned. If you do find a particular combination of sensory stimulation which works for your baby then do not rely on this all the time, on every occasion and throughout the day. Babies need more than just sleep for they are designed to take an active part in their own development too. Give them room to become people.

Summary (for parents)

Research findings and experience from many parents are in agreement; constant sounds at moderate intensity seem to quieten young babies. And when sounds are combined with other types of continuous stimulation like movement the effect is even more striking. As babies grow older the effectiveness of these lulling techniques is lessened. But by then other procedures will have been developed. It is most important in the early weeks to achieve success at quietening crying babies in healthy ways since it is well known that non-soothable infants place families under extreme stress, sometimes with violent consequences.

Intervention 8.4 Non-nutritive sucking

Rationale During non-nutritive sucking no food is provided. Sucking of this sort can be on fingers, wrists, cuddly objects, toys, or commercial aids like teats or dummies/pacifiers. Older infants seem to use their mouths to explore many objects. As soon as something is picked up it goes straight to the mouth. This is why parents need to be alert and keep away small objects which can puncture the mouth or be swallowed, or inhaled into the lungs.

The mouth area is highly sensitised in babies. The mouth zone gradually loses its impact as an infant grows older. We do not yet know when or how these transitions from one zone to another take place.

For many young babies it is as if there is a biologically based sucking need. This is quite independent of hunger, so much so that offered food may not even be taken. There is often an unsatisfied need which can only be met by providing opportunities for non-nutritive sucking.

There is a persistent myth about using any aids to meet this need. Even in popular books (15) parents are told to use a dummy/pacifier only as a last resort, after having tried everything else. Several disadvantages are mentioned by authors biased against their use; they can be unhygenic, become habit forming, prevent other mouth explorations and may be constantly demanded if lost. The first point applies to young babies for whom cleanliness is important. But as babies grow older and test many objects in their mouths strict cleanliness is less relevant.

As for the twin notions of habit formation and restricted explorations, quite frankly we do not have available any empirical data on these matters. Casual observation indicates that indeed for some babies, long term sucking can result. Parents of these infants are quite willing to "plug it in" at every opportunity. However, by and large, babies will give up non-nutritive sucking when they are ready. It may be a bit like thumb sucking of older children; the more parents tend to fuss about it the longer it continues. When left to their own devices children will give up sucking of their own accord. Certainly, the ambivalence of some parents makes it awkward for a baby/child to establish consistency. For example when at home and out of sight of other adults parents may not mind sucking. But when in the presence of others adults they will reprimand and physically pull out sucking objects. Being inconsistent tends to make things worse. And since sucking can occur during times of stress, these parental inconsistencies may help to create a problem.

Finally, the belief of some authors that babies may demand their sucking objects if lost in the night is quite true; replacing it will soothe and resettle a baby. A simple experiment will confirm this observation. If a baby is in a light sleep state and sucking intermittently then ease out the object. Notice the gradual increase in activity. This activity is arrested quite easily by popping the dummy/pacifier back in and moving it around to encourage latching on once again. The corresponding soothing effect is obvious. As babies grow older they can be encouraged to find and use their own hands, fingers or thumbs for sucking on and self-comforting.

Selma Fraiberg (16) makes an interesting point on this matter when she writes

> "The problem of unsatisfied sucking need and the use of the pacifier for supplementary sucking is a good demonstration of the relationship of theory to practice.
>
> As long as the cause of this infant disturbance was unknown, or misconstrued, we could find no workable solutions. If we are right, if this distress is unsatisfied sucking need, then the provision of additional sucking should alleviate the discomfort" (P.70).

In a whole series of studies investigating newborns Gene Anderson and her colleagues in Florida have made some interesting discoveries. For example with preterm infants it has been reported that those provided with non-nutritive sucking opportunities showed readiness for the bottle earlier (27 less tube feedings for each) and were discharged four days earlier than the untreated group of babies (17). Thus sucking opportunities were clearly related to improved growth and maturation.

Dr. Anderson's group also makes the important distinction between "demand" and "cue" when offering non-nutritive sucking opportunities. On "cue" means when the infant is showing signs of wanting to suck. Cues include activities like putting hand-to-mouth, or whimpering, or rooting, or yawning, or sucking of tongue, hand and/or fingers. These cues are different for each baby. Hence self-regulatory non-nutritive sucking means sucking offered on cue. The phrase "on demand" means that the chance to suck is provided after the crying has begun. Alas, this may be too late. A modification of a familiar proverb captures the point: "A suck in time saves crying".

Commenting on an observation under the heading "Infantile colic: a possible solution", Dr. Anderson noted what happened with an extremely fussy two-day old baby when offered self-regulatory non-nutritive sucking (SNS) for as long as required (to satiety) after a feeding. "The effect was striking. The infant settled down immediately, sucked almost steadily for approximately 30 minutes, and fell into a deep sleep" (p. 185). The baby slept for four hours. When awakened the infant remained calm and fed well. After each feeding the baby had SNS. An enquiry six months later revealed that unlike an older sibling who had been colicky, this one had only few fussy days. Gene Anderson suggests, upon reflection, that SNS may alleviate colic since it does not compromise breast feeding and babies do not swallow air when "dry sucking" (18).

Limitations For young babies emphasis ought to be placed upon cleanliness of mouthing objects. Parents of infants up until about four months of age should be encouraged to consider and use self-regulatory non-nutritive sucking. For infants beyond six months initiating SNS is likely to be less beneficial. Do not put any substances (like honey or other sweeteners) on the sucked object.

Assessment/monitoring At subsequent meetings parents can be encouraged to report on their involvement with SNS. Apart from reassurance that no harm will befall the young baby given extra sucking opportunities and overcoming general community bias, most parents will be quite aware of the positive effects.

Non-food sucking

Background/Activity (for parents)

For young babies one important window they have to the outside world is through their mouths. It is now known that many small babies like to have extra sucking without food. It seems likely that colicky babies can be helped when given the chance to suck, especially following feedings. As some parents have found in the past, colicky babies like to suck and suck. If extra food is given at these times then the crying gets worse. One way to break this cycle is to offer non-nutritive sucking on a dummy/pacifier for as long as baby likes it.

However, it is not just a matter of plugging baby in whenever the crying begins. Generally there are tell-tale signs which a baby makes first. It could be yawning, sucking, or putting a hand to the mouth. When these signs are provided then ease the dummy/pacifier in to the mouth and wiggle it about for a little. You will notice when any vigorous sucking begins, the dummy/pacifier will bob about and be hard to pull out. Simply leave it in and put it back again if it drops out. Some babies have to learn how to suck. Lack of sucking can be an indication things are not as they should be. So if the sucking stays poor seek help from a doctor.

By providing opportunities to suck for as long as baby wants on each occasion greater settling should occur. For young babies, up until about six months of age, there is no need to worry about bad habits forming from too much sucking. Babies tend to give up on a dummy/pacifier and soon begin to suck other things, like hands, toys and so on. This is generally quite acceptable, so long as the parents are not overly concerned. When a baby's urgent sucking needs are finished with at around five months then it will tend to simply give up.

If you do decide to provide non-feeding sucking opportunities then be consistent. Do it at home as well as when out visiting. There is no need to be embarrassed or offer apologies. Just do it and enjoy the benefits.

Summary (for parents)

Non-food sucking is quite natural for many babies. They just seem to need it. Offer a pacifier/dummy when baby shows a need to suck. Sucking can be very soothing for small babies. It is rarely habit forming.

Intervention 8.5 Baby massage

Rationale People cannot have opposing feelings at the same time. From this straight forward observation a whole branch of clinical psychology grew. For example in the treatment of phobia, using what has become known as *systematic desensitisation*, phobics are gradually brought face to face with their fears. According to this view a phobia is a conditioned response so the whole process begins with relaxation. When a phobic is relaxed the clinician asks the person to make a mental picture of the feared object/situation. The clinician's skill lies in adjusting fear so that it does not swamp any relaxation. Sometimes additional conditioning is provided; when fully relaxed a gentle squeeze of one hand with the fingers of the other is one means by which a person can associate feelings of ease, patience, relaxation and peace. If faced with a phobic threat in the future then hand squeezing serves as a reminder that things are all right. Over a period of weeks a phobia can be regulated as the fear is lessened. To achieve this objective the clinician aims at maintaining a relaxed state. At first mental images are introduced. When these are managed satisfactorily the object/situation itself is presented, first at a distance and then closer and closer. Finally the distance is eliminated altogether, contact occurs and the phobia is broken.

People can be broken too. One illustration of how men are broken is offered in films about military training. It seems that recruits are forced to submit to authority figures and obey orders without question. The methods used to achieve this end are often nasty, brutal and merciless. In short, the means justifies the end. One tragedy of this process is the wastage; it is impossible to ignore the psychological costs for those who do not make the grade.

The phrase "broken in" is used to describe what occurs when a wild animal is domesticated. Noting what happens when a horse is broken in can be instructive. It is not uncommon for observers to note a kind of special bond between a horse and its rider; something more than each of them offers to the other. This is the result of a long process. At the outset a wild horse is very wary of anybody. It will attack those who come too close. In one method to begin with the horse is tied to a long rope. By speaking in soft tones throughout a trainer can encourage an animal to relax. As with the clinician dealing with a phobia, the trainer adjusts the physical distance to match an animal's wariness. Some say there is a sixth sense required here; it is a subtle craft of doing what is right at the right time, anticipating moves and countering these by stepping forward or back. When this magic works the spirit remains intact. A horse in fear is a subdued one. And a person whose will is broken is left without trust or hope, there is nothing but obedience.

There is a simple truth here. Namely, relaxed babies do not cry.

Massage involves more than touch. It is an opening of the channel of communication between those who wish to share what is important. It is a vehicle by which people can feel the sense of trust and the enveloping of self within a broader sphere beyond individuality.

The "evidence" offered in support of massaging is diverse. It is known that movement is essential for a developing infant (see Intervention 8.2). But beyond clinical reports there is a philosophy about our origins as a species. Those who and endorse massage not only draw upon illustrations from many different cultural groups to show how universal it is, but also dip into their own personal experiences and satisfaction obtained from physical contact.

There are some people who do not enjoy physical contact. They will shy away from suggestions that massage is a "cure" all. As always, a consultant's task is to be receptive to differences and to work positively with what is available. All the same, it is practically always possible to demonstrate the benefits of massaging, even to the strongest skeptics. The point is, don't go against the grain.

Try to emulate the horse-trainer and avoid the service model of a sergeant major. Begin at arm's length. Then, as a family situation allows, follow the relaxed trend to introduce alternative points of view. These are aimed at fostering health and the positive development of participants. Capture the energy and use that for working material.

There are available some excellent books on baby massaging. Two deserve special mention. One is written by Tina Heinl (19). Dr. Heinl is a biologist with extensive professional training in physiology and neuropharmacology who, since the birth of her own children, developed an active interest in baby massage. As she notes on the first page. "It seems to me that by doing the massage I also gained a better understanding of my children as persons in their own right, with their own bodies and identities, different from myself. At the same time the massage led to a very deep attachment between us". One chapter presents a step by step procedure and is illustrated by watercolours.

The second book is smaller in size and includes photographs in the chapter on technique. This one is written by Amelia Auckett (20). Written by an Australian the book deals with nurturing aspects of massaging. The author says "Family massage incorporates a positive interaction of the whole family through a shared learning experience, resulting in improved communication, enjoyment, relaxation, awareness and honesty" (P.6). Then, later, when citing a Melbourne paediatrician (Dr. David Bannister) the following points are made:

> "Sometimes mothers and babies don't 'click' or bond automatically, and if the baby is a difficult or 'colicky', irritable, non-responsive baby, then the mother may have difficulty coping, adjusting or understanding her baby, and angry negative feelings can develop. The mother may draw away from her child, rather than towards him, and the interaction around this crying baby may sometimes engender hostile, aggressive feelings. The interjection of a positive, touching caressing approach may be invaluable in altering the mother's negative reaction to a positive, tender, warm response. This can only be a good thing for mother and baby. I consider baby massage to be beneficial to baby from a very early age. It gives the mother something positive to do for her screaming 'colicky' baby, and if it calms the baby down without the use of drugs, then this is a good thing." (p.14).

Limitations Adverse effects of massaging are not known. It would be helpful to know if the baby's hips are not "clicky" and that there is no congital hip dislocation. If there is persistent pain-like crying when baby is touched and/or moved then seek a medical opinion. Some parents report successful outcomes from infant manipulations carried out by chiropractors. In my view this ought to be treated with caution since babies' necks are very delicate and their spines are still undergoing development.

Assessment/monitoring Parental self-reports are the main ways of keeping an eye on what is going on. Once parents have gained confidence in participating in baby massaging they are generally more than willing to demonstrate their skills. It is a lot of fun.

Baby Massage

Background (for parents)

There are some babies who just don't seem to like close physical contact. They wiggle about and prefer to be left alone. There are two groups of babies, cuddlers and non-cuddlers. In a similar way there are two groups of parents; some cannot show any warmth toward their infants. There are many reasons for babies and their parents not getting along with one another. These reasons are too complex to be discussed further here.

Even for the most "distant" baby, the ones who don't want to be touched fondly, there are occasions when they tend to relax. One place where babies do thaw out is in the bath. I don't mean a hot bath which burns them. In a "deep" family bath or in a warm shower it is as if all the tensions are soaked away or washed off.

Other babies experience the joy of being close to people in other settings. For some it may be during the very act of feeding, since feeding is itself a very intense massage. Not only is the mouth a particularly sensitive area (Intervention 8.4) but it can serve as a door to the broader world. It is through the mouth that comfort is spread.

When parents are involved with their babies they can begin to notice which things are enjoyable. It is possible to massage each of the senses. The gentle sounds of a soft lullaby soothe, as does rocking and touching. By and large however massage refers to the gentle physical touching which makes a pattern of love.

Massage is not new, although it is being "rediscovered" by many parents. In places where workshops are held parents are not only shown what massaging is about but are encouraged to apply these actions to their own infants. Once people realise what is involved, how pleasurable a massage can be, they are generally keen to carry it on by themselves and explore different possibilities. This is good news. By taking part in activities which are positive and calming we can be encouraged to do more for one another. It is an ongoing process of discovery which has benefits for the whole family.

Simply put, massaging is the systematic deep physical stroking of another which both relaxes and tones the muscles. At the same time it seems to make the other more receptive, comfortable and peaceful. Massaging is the physical parallel of trust.

Activities (for parents)

The best state (Intervention 10.4) in which to apply massaging is the quiet alert one. You will know already ways of encouraging this state. It may be upon waking, or by a small feeding, or by bathing, or by rocking. Of the whole range of possibilities available note how the quiet alert state can be brought about (Intervention 10.5): Some people have been successful at calming a crying baby through massage. At the outset however, you may be better advised to focus on the quiet alert state and apply massage during this period. If your baby begins to cry then offer comfort in the usual way. It is unhelpful to force a massage as tension gets in the way of trying to encourage relaxation.

Begin with a light gentle touch. Touching can get "deeper" as you both gain confidence. As some babies are very sensitive to their head and region begin with the chest or the extremities, the fingers and toes. Although oil is not necessary a cold-pressed vegetable oil moistens the skin. Warm the oil first and then put it onto your own hands. Let your hands transfer the oil. This way you know it is the right temperature.

Since you'll need an undressed baby for massaging make sure the room is warm enough. As a rule of thumb, would you be comfortable without clothes on? Although a certain amount of heat can be generated by the friction of your hands on baby's surfaces this is unlikely to be enough in cold weather.

So, in a warm room, without undue noise or other interruptions (like bright lights glaring down, or children rushing about, or immediate household demands on the horizon) begin your massage. The whole process can take from 10 to 20 minutes. Start with a small but meaningful amount and be sure to finish before either of you loses interest or gets too tense. Gradually extend the massage each time and gather confidence. Some people massage daily, others a few times each week. The timetable is of your own making; the only constraint is that the pair of you agree.

Beyond these simple, basic guidelines there are two things to do if you are unsure. One is to put a notice up on a local noticeboard (like at a supermarket) to advertise "help wanted for baby massage". You may get some crank callers. But, more importantly, there could be others who would like to form a support group. The second option is to buy a book on the subject which outlines procedures. There are some very good ones about.

Summary (for parents)

Baby massaging is a gentle art which can be learnt by parents. Begin with those activities you can manage when baby is in a quiet alert state. From gentle stroking of the limbs gradually increase the time available and with patience, understand the magic of touching.

The rhythmical patterns of the hands on a small body can open doors of understanding. Not only will each baby's individuality become more noticeable but the peace arising out of doing something together will radiate to all those involved.

Intervention 8.6 Swaddling

Rationale In many different cultures babies are still swaddled to prevent big, free limb movements. The trend to swaddle or not fluctuates in other cultures, depending on what is fashionable. It has been noted for instance that some parents have much difficulty swaddling their babies, having been brought up themselves in a culture which gives a lot of weight to personal freedom (21). Consequently the binding up of babies runs counter to societal beliefs about individual freedom.

Yet laboratory-based studies carried out on small babies indicates definite soothing effects for the irritable. Yvonne Brackbill (12) examined the consequences of applying different sorts of constant stimulation to one-month olds. One condition included swaddling infants tightly from neck to toes using long narrow strips of flannel. Compared to the other conditions, of constant sound or light or temperature, the swaddled babies cried less, slept more, had slower heart rate and breathed more regularly. In Brackbill's report participating babies began sessions after feeding and in the quiet awake state. The author makes an additional comment with regard to non-experimental observations. On many occasions it was the very act of swaddling which produced a dramatic change in baby's state. It seems the crying was arrested by the handling itself.

Following a thorough and extensive historical review of swaddling, Lipton et al. (21) report several studies on the swaddling of neonates. The age of these infants was between 2 to 8 days, much younger than most consultants will encounter. Hence specific experimental results are of lesser importance than general conclusions. Three conditions were examined, no swaddling, legs only, full body. Curiously, the authors omitted swaddling of upper body only and leaving the legs free. Overall, it appears physical restraint is the main contributor to effective swaddling. Thus an infant's own intermittent movements serve as ongoing stimulation and keep it alert. If these movements can be limited in younger babies then relaxation is encouraged. The authors note that swaddling may once again return to Western societies and be quite acceptable in the early weeks and months of life. Yet, in spite of the difficulties faced by researchers probing this area, societal changes should be data based. But as so few studies are now available most popular authors can rely only upon current practices and observation.

Limitations Since small babies cannot regulate their own body temperatures it is important to make sure they do not get too cold or hot. A small hat can help conserve body heat. Skin rashes may appear if baby gets too hot.

A second limitation concerns those few babies who adopted other than one of the common interuterine positions. From X-rays it has been observed some infants are bent over backwards, others have one or both legs up against their chins, and some lie at odd angles. Forcing these infants into a conventional swaddling mould after birth runs counter to their positions of comfort and is painful.

Another limitation applies to babies who may have congenital hip dislocation. In these cases leg straightening is not beneficial.

Finally, babies ought not to be left alone for long periods of time just because they are kept quiet and their parents want to get on with other things. In any case swaddling will be less effective with older babies.

Assessment/monitoring A consultant can demonstrate how to swaddle an infant and encourage a parent to follow suit. Thereafter assurance from a consultant will alleviate fears of possible damage. Swaddling ought to be tight enough to restrict movements but not binding.

Swaddling

Background (for parents)

In many countries of the world babies are still wrapped up, or swaddled, to prevent them from moving about too much. Although the idea of restricting babies may be distasteful there is some laboratory-based evidence which suggests this may not be as bad as many people think.

For example in one study with month-old babies swaddling was the most effective method of preventing crying and helping them to sleep. It seems that many babies will keep themselves awake in the early weeks through jerks and random movements. By limiting these actions they nestle down more readily.

Although there are many different methods of restricting infant movement it seems that the very act of doing the swaddling can be soothing too. So instead of simply tucking a crying baby down, pick it up in order to wrap firmly.

When lying on their backs some fretting babies are soothed by the gentle firm pressure of a warm hand placed on their tummies. When accompanied by continuous talking this can be sufficient to bring about calming. Other babies are soothed by firm holding. And others seem to prefer being carried about face out, with their backs right up against an adult's front, held securely. Essentially each of these actions limit a baby's movements.

However, swaddling usually applies to the binding of babies using a cloth or strips of material to stop or limit movement. Provided baby does not have congenital hip dislocation (which can be clinically checked for "clicks") or is too old there is no reason, other than parental aversion, not to try it out with infants up until about three months of age.

Activities (for parents)

There are many ways to restrict a baby's movements. Some parents simply tuck infants down firmly with a blanket. In his popular book *Baby and Child Care* Dr. Spock writes that a fretful or tense baby can be much happier sleeping in a small space like a small bassinet, a car bed or even a cardboard box with a folded blanket for a mattress and lining. Since the aim is to limit movement without doing any damage it matters not how this is accomplished. Penelope Leach in her very readable book *Baby and Child* (15) says the aim of wrapping is to encase completely the baby so the limbs are in a preferred position. There is no need to straighten out limbs before swaddling. Dr. Leach suggests using a technique where the baby's own weight serves as an anchor, leaving a hand out for sucking.

One method is to lie the infant down on a soft light shawl or cellular baby-blanket. The material can be selected to match the surrounding temperature, soft gauze is quite adequate if it is very hot. Leach suggests taking one of the top corners of the blanket and bringing this down diagonally across baby's body, enclosing the shoulder, and tucking in under the knees. Then, without moving baby keep tension on the other side of the cloth to bring it straight over, under the chin, and right around the body so the end comes out underneath the other side.

Although a single blanket can be wrapped in such a way as to limit movements, traditionally strips of material were used. Typically the body was first covered with a cloth. Then with arms raised the trunk was bound by three or four windings using strips about 7cm (3 inches) wide. Another band of several windings secured the arms to the sides, gently but firmly. Finally the hips and legs were bound by more windings. If necessary the cocoon could then be covered by additional insulation, like furs or skins.

Summary (for parents)

Many small babies are comforted by having their movements restricted. Although there is not a lot of systematic research on this topic it has been found that swaddled babies cry less and sleep more. Part of this success seems to be in physically moving the baby about during binding with cloth strips. Although many parents believe swaddling prevents free expression there are times when this can be beneficial to all involved. Since binding is designed to be temporary the relief provided to a cry-trapped family by the peace and quiet is worthwhile.

9 DEVELOPMENTAL STATUS

As human adults we can reflect upon a whole host of factors which may have shaped our pasts to make us what we now are. There are at least two ways of considering our own histories. One is to look at how things happened as they ran together over a period of time. An analogy which captures this process is a T.V. documentary; main events are arranged into a chronological order and a cause-effect sequence may emerge. Another way is to look back on single episodes which occurred within a limited period of time. An analogy here could be a photograph, or a series of snapshots taken of a particular event — for instance a class picture or an outing with friends or family.

Often it seems to parents that crying babies have no sense of history at all. They exist entirely for the moment and consume every hour with their demands. There is no past and no future. It is *now* which dominates everything. An early task for consultants is to disentangle this web which has as its centre a crying baby. One way to do this is to introduce a time frame against which changes may be checked. Time can help provide an essential baseline. It offers a benchmark for recognising patterns of meaning which can emerge if signposts are noticed.

The snapshot approach, of attending to what is happening at the present, is handled in the next chapter on "form". Various interventions are provided there to help parents begin to make sense of their immediate chaos. Focus is directly upon a baby's day-to-day behaviours.

Recognition of an infant's developmental status is more long term. Although an assessment may take place on a single occasion, it is how these observations fit into a broader plan which gives them a developmental flavour. It is a knowledge of how general ground plans shape an infant's present activities that enables a consultant to tune into broader systems of evolving competencies. Developmental status refers to the present position of an individual within these systems. Typically, assessment is directed toward examining those facets which emerge in an orderly sequence. Included are the domains of thinking, socialising, and doing things. Technically speaking these are referred to as cognitive (memory and attention), social (language and listening), and motor skills (gross and fine).

In my opinion it matters little which scheme a consultant makes use of to check developmental status. A cry clinic does not offer a full assessment. Rather, it can introduce several screening procedures. We are looking for any marked deviation from the typical range of actions which are acceptable for a given age. Further, assessments are not aimed at a research audience. If they were then careful training would be provided consultants so as to make sure identical procedures were being used.

A brief list of available scales for assessment of infant developmental status includes; Alperon-Boll(1), Bayley (2), Denver (3), DISC (4), Uzgiris and Hunt (5), Vineland (6), Vulpe (7). An interested reader can check out any of these sources for details.

In the remainder of the present chapter four developmental domains are mentioned. Particular activities are included for each of cognitive, fine motor, gross motor, and social. Since my aim is to present an introductory scheme which may be modified according to particular consultant-baby relationships, this is not intended as an exhaustive or thorough treatment of these topics.

Although several interventions are outlined below they share parallel content under some headings. This being the case, a general overview of these common sections is presented first.

Rationale In each of the following interventions it is desirable to observe baby's best performance. To do so consultants and parents ought to be aware of the concept of infant state which is outlined in Intervention 10.4. Otherwise a lot of time may be spent fruitlessly attempting to work with a non-cooperative baby. (It may be helpful and useful to attend to Interventions 10.4, 10.5 and 10.6 first.)

The present interventions are aimed directly at achieving a greater understanding of baby's developmental status. Two sets of background information are required. First, an understanding of the steady progression which occurs as baby grows older. And, second, an appreciation of how particular events can be used as indices of underlying dynamics. This means any particular action can be recognised as part of a steady unfolding set of infant capabilites.

Projected outcomes Consistent with most of the interventions proposed, the present ones are designed both to involve parents with their babies as well as to provide information which can be discussed at subsequent meetings. In addition there is a strong possibility parents may detect changes in their babies and notice for themselves the apparent sudden shifts in performance which correspond to growth spurts. There is a rhythm to the pulse of development and these interventions are designed to assist people in identifying them.

A further use is as an aid to the identification of either sluggish or accelerated development. With a crying baby there is always the possibility that there may be a handicap of one kind or another. To help clear up this question the following interventions are designed as a do-it-yourself screening battery. If applied with care a parent will be better able to judge whether further assistance ought to be sought for a full developmental assessment and a tailored programme of personal assistance.

Limitations Some parents will fail to see the point of doing any of these things. Others may not, or be unwilling to, follow the rather elaborate instructions. This can be overcome by omitting direct reference to any underlying explanation and of simply going ahead and doing these things with baby while parents watch. Often, just by watching what goes on, many parents will do it themselves. Two minor cautions ought to be mentioned. First, don't do too much. And, second, don't show off your own skills and thereby threaten a parent by revealing their incompetencies. This is as much an educational forum for sharing as it is a clinical setting for making impartial observations. Go gentle into that good night.

Assessment/monitoring At subsequent meetings parents can talk about what happened. But, as well, it will be possible for them to demonstrate how they incorporated the various activities into home settings. Difficulties, as well as ambiguous results, can be sorted out by direct participation. Suggestions about referrals can be made at this time too.

Intervention 9.1 Cognitive development

Rationale This intervention is a deliberate introduction to understanding an infant's cognitive capabilites. Activities are designed around the *object concept*, a notion of Piaget's which, it has been suggested, is the most important of all his discoveries (8). The activities are modified from suggestions originally put forward by Piaget and later discussed by Bower (9) as well as by Uzgiris and Hunt (5).

In this context Piaget's ideas are hinted at but not elaborated upon since in our clinical settings it is better to stick with what may be observed rather than getting involved with detailed explanations. And in any case, most people are quite capable of creating for themselves explanations for what seems to be going on. There are quite adequate formal presentations of Piaget's notions elsewhere. One of the better treatments of this view of infant development is offered by Tom Bower in a highly readable book entitled *A Primer on Infant Development* (10).

Projected outcomes Descriptions about and observations of changes which occur as infants grow older provide ample opportunities for consultants to involve parents in understanding some of the dynamics behind cognitive development. As well, some basic developmental data will be obtained and these can offer insights into delay or precocity.

Limitations In addition to those indicated in Intervention 10.6, parents ought not make unnecessary comparisons between their own infant's capabilities and the performance of other babies.

Assessment/monitoring With the addition of an awareness regarding normative or peer comparisons, the same as for Intervention 10.6.

Cognitive development — thinking

Background (for parents)

As baby grows older there are natural changes which are going on within it. Some of these changes occur in baby's brain. More and more "thinking" activities can be observed at different times. But because baby looks human is no reason for you to make the mistake of imagining baby actually thinks like an adult. This should not need to be said, though I'll say it just the same: baby is a baby. By this it is meant that baby's thinking skills are only beginning to emerge gradually. These take time to unfold.

In part, this point is spelled out a little more fully in another intervention (10.6). There are two dangers. One is of expecting too much from baby and demanding impossible performances. The second danger is to refrain from comparing your baby's capabilities with those of other babies.

Baby brings to a situation its age, past experiences and present state. A parent brings a capability for monitoring baby's state, memories of previous achievements, certain expectations about what can be done at the present, and a plan for involving baby in certain activities. Outlined in the notes which follow are activities concerned with an infant's capabilities at searching and finding.

The best state for baby is once again D, the quiet alert one (see Intervention 10.4 for details on state). Remember, there are no hard and fast ways of carrying out any of the activities described below. Make up your own variations and offer baby many chances to show best behaviours. First, read over the notes and get a broad idea of what is going on. Then gather up the odds and ends needed for playing. If you wish make up a record of your observations on a separate piece of paper (showing date, item number, number of tries and baby's best performance). So you'll need some paper and a pencil too.

The list of activities is arranged in order of increasing difficulty. It might be useful to begin with the first one shown. Do not be put off with an initial "failure", an inability of baby to complete an activity satisfactorily. Simply go on to the next one and try once again. If that doesn't interest baby then go back to the previous one for another attempt. The next time you start off on these activities your written notes will be useful as a reminder of where you got to. Of course you'd always begin with things baby can do first, and then gradually move onto the more "difficult" activities.

The person who pioneered these activities was Piaget (say that name as "Pee-ar-jae"). That's one name you'll hear and which most infant psychologists know. Briefly, his idea was that as a baby grows older there is less of a reliance on immediate happenings. As a baby ages there is a gradual emergence of baby's thinking, of things being done deliberately. Remember, this only occurs with some tasks, on some occasions, and in tranquil moods. It's no wonder many people fail to notice such small beginnings. As baby starts to think about what it is doing, plans seem to be designed in its head and then put into action. Piaget made many discoveries. The one which the following activities are planned around is known as the object concept. With it we observe baby's reactions to an object which "disappears" or is hidden from view.

As some of the following activities involve watching baby's eyes it is helpful to see these. One way to manage this is to have another person hold baby. Alternatively, you hold baby sitting on your knee with the chest near to a table edge and have your helper sitting on the other side watching the eyes. Another option which works quite satisfactorily for an older infant is to use a baby chair. The main advantage with a holding-on-knee position is that body comfort or feeding can be offered quite quickly if baby gets upset.

Activities (for parents)

1. A disappearing act. (about 2–4 months)

equipment:
- — small bright object or toy
- — a screen, like a thick book stood on its end with the flat, broad cover-side facing towards baby

Place the book screen on the table top just beyond baby's reach. Support baby on your knees and grasp around the chest so baby is facing the screen. Have your partner sit opposite. Capture baby's visual attention with an object such as a small bell or rattle. As baby watches, shift the object slowly, keeping it just off the table top to place it behind the screen. It may be necessary to wave the object in front of baby's face for a few times initially to capture attention.Then, as soon as baby fixes on, move the object to the start position (about 30 cm off to one side of the screen) and then begin the slow steady sideways movement which finishes with the hand-held object behind the screen where baby cannot see it. After a few seconds repeat the entire procedure once again. Do this for a few times and note what happened.

What did baby do? (Enter a letter to show the best performance.)

a. did not look at object at all
b. followed object with eyes to start position only

c. kept following the line of movement out the other side of the screen (even though object was held behind the screen)
d. eyes lingered at point of disappearance then continued moving on, across screen
e. (after several presentations) baby's eyes glanced to start position and then to screen
f. eyes activity searched about the edge of the screen where object disappeared.
g. (other).

2. Finding a partly covered object (2–6 months)

equipment: — an object small enough to be held but too big to be swallowed
— a napkin, or piece of cloth, or a tea towel

Hold baby as in 1. above behind the edge of a table. Place the cloth on the table and close enough for baby to reach. Capture baby's attention with the object and then slowly move under the cloth with just part of it still sticking out and visible to baby. Do this a few times and make a note of the baby's best action. The change from the third (c) to the fifth (e) action occurs at about 4 months of age.

a. didn't look at object at all.
b. followed the object briefly with the eyes.
c. followed object to table top but lost interest soon after it was partly covered by the cloth.
d. reached out briefly but did not take object.
e. reached out and picked up object (and, commonly puts it to mouth).
f. (other).

3. Finding a fully hidden object (6–10 months)

Proceed as in 2 above, but this time cover the object completely with the cloth instead of leaving it partly visible. Although your observations are similar to those noted previously there is a marked difference in baby's thinking capability when the fully hidden object is reached for and picked up. Try this a few times and make a note of what happened.

a. didn't look at object at all.
b. followed object briefly.
c. followed object to table top and then lost interest.
d. reached out briefly but did not pull cloth.
e. reached out, pulled cloth and picked up object.
f. (other).

4. Finds an object which as been moved (10–12 months)

equipment: — an object which is favoured by baby (it can be fairly large).
— two cloths (which will completely cover object)

When baby can successfully find the completely hidden object (3. above) introduce a little variation to the task. Place two cloths on the table top. Then on two or more occasions hide the object under one of these two cloths, say always the one on the left side. Then, in full view of baby, place the object under the other cloth, the one on baby's right. As younger infants seem to think hidden objects can always be found in the same place, what happened?

a. lost interest in whole thing.
b. looked under the previously successful hiding location, but now is just a flat cloth, and gave up.
c. looked and found object under "correct" cloth.
d. (other).

Summary (for parents)

That's a brief and manageable overview of different things babies can do as they grow older. Remember that baby's successful participation emerges gradually. So it's no use your getting upset if what you think should occur does not (even within the rough time limits provided). There are lots of variations you can make to these activities. Besides creating variations would you like to think about possible underlying reasons for these different infant capabilities?

After taking part in these activities you will:

— be aware of baby's capabilities
— at different times, week-by-week, see changes
— understand the unfolding nature of baby's thinking
— see that what is obvious to adults is really a major discovery for baby.

Intervention 9.2 Fine motor skills, changes during development

Rationale There are many published sources which offer guidelines and examples for several domains of fine motor skill activity. The present intervention focuses exclusively on what is happening to the hands. The simple reason for this decision is that the hands offer a sound illustration of developmental changes with increasing age. Further, by limiting observations to a single domain, consultants will be less confused. This should not be interpreted as meaning the other areas are of lesser importance. The point is that by beginning with the hands it is anticipated other domains will be integrated into the general developmental sequence as additional experience is gained.

My own favourite source book is *HELP*, published in the United States (11). This is a rich mine of information on infant and child developmental activities, spanning the age range birth to three years. It contains excellent guidelines as to what may be expected at different ages in the areas of; cognitive, language, gross motor, fine motor, socio-emotional and self-help. Within each one there is an age-graded presentation. As well as providing a very readable description, there are several excellent line drawings. Finally, and of great importance to readers, there is a list of things which can be done. The clarity and use of this book can be appreciated in the examples provided below. There are many more items mentioned in HELP.

Projected outcomes Changes in hand grasping are the only aspects followed systematically in the present intervention. There are many changes, apart from those occurring with the hands, going on during development. By focusing on one set of changes it is anticipated parents will make other observations about related developmental shifts.

Further, there are so many uses for the hands. Toys of different weights, textures and shapes can be tried out. For example there are rings. One simple set of interlocking rings can be made from toothbrush handles. Snap off the bristles. Boil the handles and when soft use tongs to bend into the required shapes, interlocking these with others to make a short chain. Other rings have soft sounding rattles attached. Softer toys with graspable "prongs" are popular in the younger months. Through knowing what can be managed with the hands developmentally appropriate toys can be supplied.

Limitations There is more to fine motor skill development than watching the hands unfold and grapple with the world at large. This point can be made clearer as parents are encouraged to report other changes, like eye-tracking and head turning.

Some parents may be overly concerned about whether their babies are "brighter" than others. These issues cannot be resolved through this intervention. The role of the clinic is in guiding and screening, not in carrying out full infant assessments. Thus overtures regarding comparisons ought to be minimised. Even if these occur, remind people of individual variations.

Assessment/monitoring With a co-operative baby at a meeting it is easy enough to observe what is happening. Parents are usually more than willing to show what can be done.

Remember to clean any toys etc. thoroughly between babies. Since many will put things straight into their mouths, limit the chances of spreading infectious diseases by washing in a safe disinfectant. Even if a baby is not showing clinical symptoms of any disease, make washing a standard routine.

Clearly, any consistent limited performance ought to be monitored. If there is no steady change with age, or if one hand is clearly less advanced than the other, seek further advice and/or make a referral to a person medically-trained.

Fine hand movements

Background (for parents)

A section dealing with fine motor skills is included in most infant assessment schemes. The word "motor" simply means action or movement. The ones dealt with here are called "fine", meaning refined or small in scale. These are distinguished from "gross" (or large) ones. Finally, a "skill" is something done deliberately. So, putting this all together, a "fine motor skill" is a small action done as baby tunes into the outside world. Examples include head turning (to look around to locate the source of a noise), or following an object with the eyes (which is slowly moving in front of the face), and so on. Some of the earliest fine motor actions babies show are described elsewhere (Intervention 10.6).

For this occasion all of the activities involve the hands. As baby grows older more and more things, can be done with the hands. There are many other fine motor skills which emerge during development. For the present case, examples are chosen which illustrate how the hands become more useable.

A preference for right or left handedness does not emerge until around two years of age. So provide opportunities for your baby to use both hands. In fact if you notice one hand is not being used for some things then bring this to the attention of your doctor or health nurse during one of the regular check ups. It may be an early sign that something is not working as it ought.

Activities (for parents)

The different activities are shown in the following boxes. These are just some of the things mentioned in *HELP*. The original item numbers are shown too. For further activities get a copy of the source books (HELP). It includes the whole age range birth to five years and has six different domains (cognitive, language, gross motor, fine motor, socio-emotional, and self help).

Box 9.1

4.12 INDWELLING THUMB NO LONGER PRESENT (2–3 mo.)

The child's thumb is no longer held in his hand.

1. Shake the child's hand gently if his hand is fisted with thumb indwelling.
2. Tap or stroke the back side of the child's fingers and thumb.
3. Bring the child's hands together at midline and rub them together.
4. Open the child's hand by bringing his fingers and thumb out gently.
5. Let the child grasp your finger or a rattle with a comfortably sized handle, placing his thumb and fingers around your finger or the rattle.
6. For the older delayed child:
   a. Let him bear weight on his open hand with his thumb and fingers extended while in prone, on hands and knees, or in sitting. Refer to 3.43 (Holds weight on one hand in prone), 3.54 (Assumes hand-knee position).
   b. Let him grasp the handle of a musical or percussion type instrument.
   c. Let him grasp the handles of a rolling pin with the thumbs out and his hand around the handle. Let him roll out play dough or clay. Let him press down or bear weight on the dough with open hands.
   d. Let him grasp and pull play dough or clay with both hands. Let him roll out the dough between his hands or on the table.
   e. Let him make thumb prints on the dough. (Theraplast, a putty for hand exercises, can be used instead of play dough or clay).
   f. Let him grasp cones to stack and unstack. Offer empty cone-shaped thread spools.
   g. Let him feel different textures, such as fabric, sand, uncooked beans, uncooked macaroni.

Box 9.2

4.20 GRASP REFLEX INHIBITED (3-4 mo.)

The child's grasp reflex is a response which occurs when pressure or stimulation is applied to the palm; The fingers close into a tight grasp. This reflex begins to diminish from about three months of age.

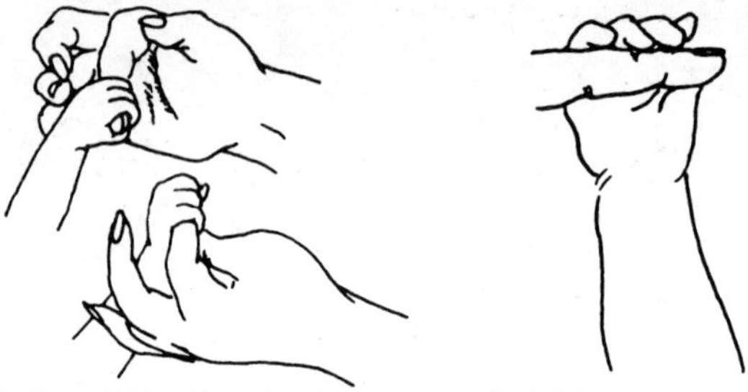

1. Provide the child with a toy he can comfortably grasp.
2. Let the child grasp hard toys and soft toys.
3. Let the child feel different textures with open hands, such as toweling, burlap, flannel, velvet.

Box 9.3

4.22 USES ULNAR PALMAR GRASP (3 1/2 — 4 1/2 mo.)

The child grasps an object which is placed in his hand. He uses an ulnar palmar grasp, that is, he grasps the object with the ring finger and little finger against his palm.

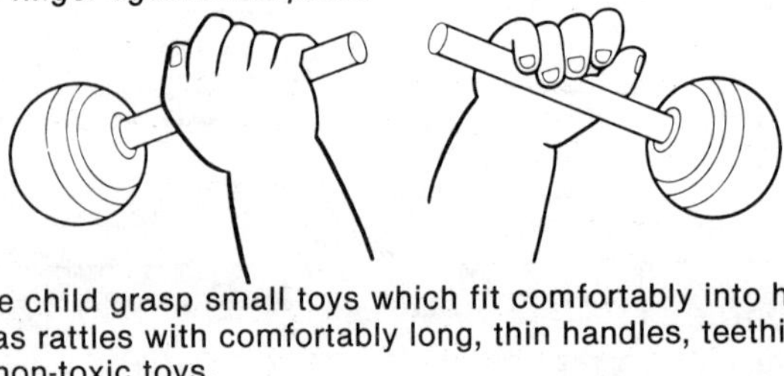

1. Let the child grasp small toys which fit comfortably into his hand such as rattles with comfortably long, thin handles, teething rings, safe, non-toxic toys.
2. Let the child grasp your finger from the ulnar side of his hand.
3. Let the child grasp a cone shaped toy with the small end of the cone on the ulnar side of the hand.

Box 9.4

4.28 USES PALMAR GRASP (4-5 mo.)

The child grasps an object against the palm without use of the thumb.

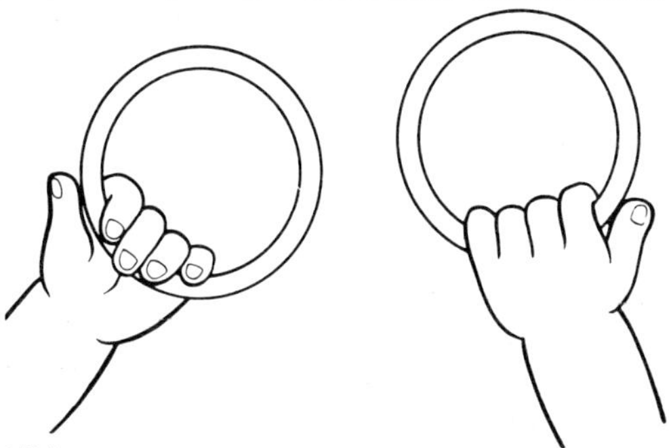

1. Let the child grasp small toys, such as a block, a spool, a squeeze toy, a teething ring, a bean bag, a peg, a spoon, a teething biscuit, a slice of hard toast.
2. Position the child in supported sitting, in prone with weight on forearms, in side-lying or in supine.
3. For the older delayed child:
   a. Position him in prone over a roll or a wedge, in sidelying or in sitting. If the child is sitting on the floor, use a low bench for a table.
   b. Let the child grasp the handle of a musical percussion percussion instrument.
   c. Let the child grasp a toy hammer or a xylophone stick.
   d. Let the child grasp a rolling pin to roll out dough.

Box 9.5

4.30 USES RADIAL PALMAR GRASP (4 1/2 — 6 mo.)

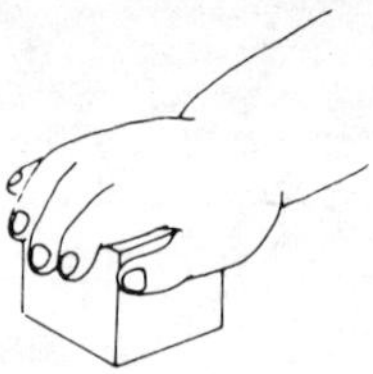

The child uses a radial palmar grasp, that is, he grasps an object with his thumb, index and middle fingers against his palm.

1. Provide the child with objects she can grasp with one hand.
2. Offer the toy toward the index finger side of the child's hand.
3. Place a cube or block in a box or container to encourage the child to grasp with the index and middle fingers side of the hand.
4. For the older delayed child: Let her squeeze play dough or theraplat (exercise putty) with the index and middle fingers side of the hand.

Box 9.6

4.43 USES RADIAL DIGITAL GRASP (7-9 mo.)

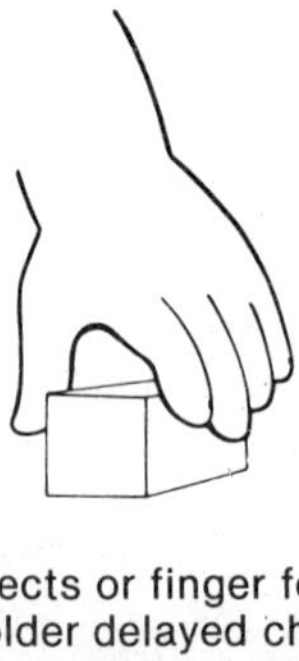

The child grasps an object with the thumb, index and middle fingers without the use of the palm.

1. Let the child grasp a block, peg, or other toy which encourages the use of his thumb, index and middle fingers.
2. Place the object in a cup, muffin tin or egg carton to encourage radial digital grasp.
3. Offer objects or finger foods at the thumb side of the hand.
4. For the older delayed child:
   a. Let him grasp and pull at play dough with his thumb and fingers.
   b. Let him use small castanets or clappers with his thumb and fingers.
   c. Let him use hand puppets, moving his thumb and fingers.

Box 9.7

4.44 RAKES TINY OBJECT (7-8 mo.)

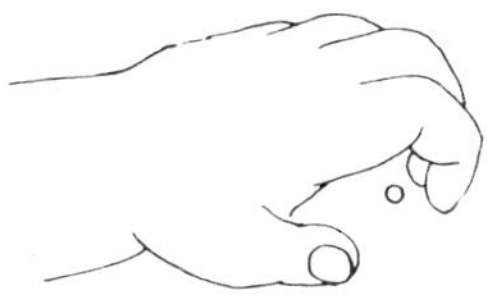

The child grasps at a pallet sized object such as a raisin by using a raking motion. The child flexes the fingers toward the palm without using the thumb.

1. Refer to 4.40 (Attempts to secure tiny object).
2. Encourage the child to grasp small objects placed on a surface within easy reach. Use a bell, a bean, dry cereal.
3. Position the child in prone with weight on his forearms, in side-lying or in sitting.
4. Caution: Be sure the child does not put small, unsafe objects into his mouth.

Box 9.8

4.49 EXTENDS WRIST (9–10 mo.)

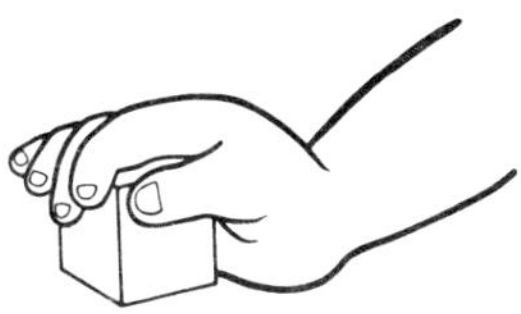

The child extends his wrist during play or during the manipulation of objects.

1. Encourage the child to wave bye-bye.
2. Position a toy above the child's wrist level to encourage wrist extension.
3. Place textured pictures on the wall which the child can feel with fingers and wrist extended.
4. Finger paint by placing the paper on the table, slant board or wall.
5. Let the child press down on a squeeze toy.
6. Let the child push against a large ball.
7. For the older delayed child:
   a. Let him turn pages in a book. Place the book on a flat surface or on a slanted bookstand.
   b. Let him press down on play dough with his hand or roll out the play dough with a rolling pin.
   c. Let him bear weight on his hands with wrist and fingers extended. Position him in prone with weight on his hands and with elbows extended, in hands and knees position, in side sitting with one hand flat and to the side, and long let sitting with hands flat toward the back.
   d. Position the child in prone over a wedge, roll or large ball and let the child bear weight on his hands with wrist and fingers extended.

Box 9.9

4.52 USES NEAT PINCER GRASP (10–12 mo.)

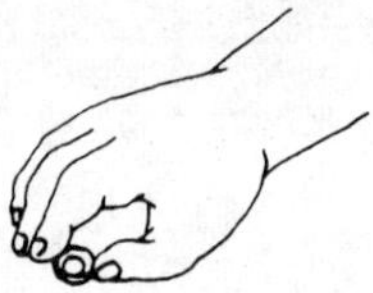

The child grasps a tiny object the size of a raisin with precise thumb and index finger opposition.

1. Place a tiny object on the table or any surface for the child to grasp one at a time. Use a raisin, dry cereal, other bits of food, a tiny bell, a pellet, a button, or narrow pegs. Be sure the child does not put unsafe objects in her mouth.
2. Use tiny objects which do not easily roll away when the child tries to grasp them.
3. Place a tiny object in a cup or egg carton cup to encourage the child to grasp the object with his thumb and index finger.
4. Place a short, colorful piece of string on the carpet, on the table, or even on the child where she can easily see and reach for it by grasping with her thumb and index finger.
5. Provide bits of food at snack time to encourage finger feeding as well as neat pincer grasp.
6. For the older delayed child:
   a. Let her make a collage using various items, such as shells, sticks, macaroni, beads, twigs, leaves, string.
   b. Let the child pinch and pull play dough with her thumb and index fingertips.
   c. Let the child pinch clothes pins. Let her remove the pins placed on the rim of a can. Let her drop them into the can. Then let her pinch and place the pins on the rim of the can herself. Tactfully provide assistance, if necessary.

Summary (for parents)

As babies grow older the sorts of things they can do change. In this section a brief overview of fine hand movements is provided. Once a broad developmental pattern is recognised then parents can use the activities described to help them decide what baby is capable of doing. These activities are "marker" items. Once the "level" of accomplishment is found then many other, similar, things can be introduced for variety and enjoyment.

Intervention 9.3 Gross motor skills, changes during development

Rationale In the previous intervention an outline of fine motor skills was provided. These referred to activities involving small muscle groups and the age-related changes which occur as a growing infant adapts its behaviours — for instance, when following an object with the eyes and then curling the fingers to grab hold of it.

The topic of this section is gross motor skills. These are the big movements involving large muscle groups. Not only does this include being able to co-ordinate movements but also carrying them out in a sequence. Both the coordinations and the sequences change as an infant grows older.

In some cases gross motor skills are called developmental milestones and include: head lifting, sitting, crawling, standing and walking. Many parents fail to realise there is a gradual unfolding of greater competencies; that the execution of later activities depends to a large extent on mastering of previous ones. Indeed, it has been observed by one person (12) that abusing parents tend to have unrealistic expectations for their children's development. To tease this matter out further parents were asked at what ages they would expect certain actions to be managed by their babies. Surprisingly, and quite contrary to any documented reports of what actually happens, it was noted that fathers believed babies could sit alone at 6 weeks whereas, in fact, this is seldom accomplished before 28 weeks. Further both parents believed toilet training ought to be managed by 6 months whereas this is seldom the case before about two years of age. Hence it is important consultants are aware of some age-related changes in gross motor skills. Of the many sources of information available readers are directed to sets of *Audiotape-slide programmes on paediatrics* which are available from Graves Medical Audiovisual Library (13).

Limitations These activities are not intended to be a full examination. They offer guidelines as to the regular appearance of specific behaviours which emerge during development. There are many other activities babies can do other than those listed here for each age.

Assessment/Monitoring Any doubts about developmental delays or unusual outcomes should become the basis for making a referral to somebody who is trained to take matters further.

On most occasions the results from carrying out these activities will be quite clear cut. Although there is likely to be some variation in how the activities are initiated by adults this should not interfere with what is observed in the baby. As matters of age, mood, state and familiarity with the setting can influence the results a co-operative setting is desirable.

Large muscle control during development

Background (for parents)

As babies grow older there are marked changes in the sorts of things they can do. Of all these changes some relate to how the big muscles of neck, back, legs, and arms grow. These are linked to the steady increase of control an infant has over its balance.

Good balance is important for getting around safely. Without balance people are clumsy and damage themselves or others. For example an obvious indication of lack of balance occurs when people have had too much alcohol to drink, they stagger about out of control.

The activities planned in this section are aimed at observing changes in the control of balance. These can be first noticed in what happens to the head, and later of how sitting and standing are managed. There is a steady but regulated change as greater balance is achieved by the growing baby.

Many of these changes seem to depend on the lapse of time before they can be seen. This means it is hard to speed them up. Even though we might like babies to be more co-operative they are imprisoned by the bonds of time. If their muscles have not developed then they can only wait. When their bodies have grown then it is possible to show greater capability.

This is an important point for two reasons. First, from the positive side, there are many things which lead up to a particular action. This means that parents who play with their babies can help boost development. Second, from the negative side, there are some parents who are unaware of the limits they imposed on babies simply because the physical equipment to handle a particular task has not yet matured. Some of these parents have quite unrealistic expectations. For example one researcher noted abusing parents expected their babies to sit alone and unaided without toppling over at the age of six weeks. In fact this is something which is rarely managed before six months of age.

You are quite welcome to try some of these activities at home. Remember though that there are many things which may get in the way of having a baby who will participate. If baby is in the "quiet alert" state (see 10.4 for details about infant states) then greater co-operation is likely. You may even like to think about ways to improve on these activities by making your own alterations.

Finally, the activities listed below are examples. Babies can do much more than it would appear from this brief outline. One challenge of any parent is to see where else the observations made in one setting will also apply. Although ages are shown these are approximate only. An individual baby may perform differently from the ages suggested and in most cases this is quite all right.

Activities (for parents)

Two sets of control are followed up in the following sets of activities. One involves head control. This will be checked from three different approaches; horizontal hold, vertical hold, and pull-to-sit/sitting. The other involves leg control and is dealt with in two sections; horizontal hold and vertical hold. (This may seem like making adjustments to a T.V. picture.)

1. Head control

A. Horizontal hold

i. Procedure When baby is lying on its tummy on a flat surface, like floor or table, notice what happens to its head. You may encourage head raising by calling softly or capturing attention with a toy.

Responses — can lift head raised and chin cleared from surface for very brief periods (0–1 month).
— head raised straight up for around 5 seconds (1–2 months).
— head raised and held up for 10 seconds (2–3 months).

ii. Procedure Hold baby horizontally, face downwards. (One way to do this is by placing a hand under its chest.)

Responses — head hung down no attempt to lift.
— weak lifting but still below body line (0–1 months).
— head raised and held in body line for at least 5 seconds (1–2 months).
— continued head lifting, even higher than body line (3–4 months).

B. Vertical hold

Procedure When baby is supported in an upright position held under arms and around chest notice what happens to the head.

Responses — head hung down, not supported at all.
— short periods of head lifting to alignment with body (0–1 month).
— head held erect and steady for longer periods (1–2 months).
— head held upright and in body line for several minutes (3–4 months).
— head mostly held in upright position without wobble if body slowly tilted (5–6 months).

C. Pull-to-sit (sometimes called "traction" response)

Procedure Slide your thumbs into baby's hands and grasp wrists with your fingers. Then gently pull the arms forward to raise baby into a sitting position. (There may be times when the legs will lock and baby will pull straight up to a standing position.)

Responses For each side note balanced bracing of shoulders, elbows, wrists and fingers. If the response is unbalanced this may be an early indication of an insult to a brain hemisphere or injury to shoulder muscles. As well as bracing we are interested in head lag during the pull up and how stable the head is when baby is in the sitting position.
— head falls back during rise, very brief support when sitting (0–1 months).

— head lag during rise but better control when sitting (1–2 months).
— slight head lag during pull up but steady control when sitting for few minutes (3–4 months).
— baby may attempt to pull by itself to sitting position and may reach out arms in anticipation of this activity. Excellent head control (4–5 months).
— strong attempt to get self to sitting position with steady head lifting, body stiffening, shoulder bracing and arm pulling (5–6 months).

D. Sitting

Procedure Observe what baby does when placed in a sitting position. (Remember to offer support to prevent baby falling.)

Responses — sits briefly on a persons' lap after supporting hands are removed (4–5 months).
— sits alone for a few seconds (5–6 months).
— without support of own hands remains sitting for a few minutes. It may be helpful to provide a toy to play with. The typical pose is with legs straight out in front (7–8 months).
— with legs out in front or cross legged (7–8 months).

2. Leg control

A. Horizontal hold (crawling)

Procedure When babys is face down on a flat surface observe what occurs.

Responses — supports the weight of upper body on both hands, raising chest (6–7 months).
— whole body supported on hands and knees in a crawling position with rocking movements (7–8 months).
— crawling, body off the floor (9–10 months).

B. Vertical hold (walking)

Procedure/responses

— when holding baby upright with feet on a flat surface it will briefly carry whole weight. There may be some bouncing movements without locked knees (6–7 months).
— active bending and straightening of knees when supported on flat surface. An increased amount of weight bearing (7–8 months).
— when standing with support makes stepping movements (9–10 months).
— Stands holding on to one hand of an adult with good balance and may take a few steps (10–11 months).
— if encouraged may walk a few steps between familiar adults (11–12 months).
— kneels alone, "walks" on knees (12–13 months).

Summary (for parents)

These activities involve big muscle groups. As baby grows older performance changes can be noticed. Some parents use this information as the basis for designing games. This is a good idea because unless it is known what is going on within the developmental ground plan it is possible to expect the wrong things. As babies grow we can participate in co-operative activities matched to their capabilities. The relevance of this intervention to crying babies is like many of the others. It helps resolve that awkward question; "Is anything wrong?"

Intervention 9.4 The development of social behaviours: Following the smile

(This intervention is based upon one designed by Margaret McCall, Student, Department of Family Studies, Univeristy of Guelph, Ontario, Canada)

Rationale For parents with a crying baby it is important to give them hope that interactions with their baby can be positive and rewarding. Smiling is one obvious social behaviour that can accomplish this (10). At about six weeks infant smiles seem to be directed toward people and parents begin to feel the baby is a human being rather than just something to care for (14).

Smiles, consisting of a upward turning of mouth corners, can be observed during the first few days of life. However, since these smiles do not involve the entire face, parents do not see these as real smiles and they fail as a social behaviour. Subsequently, over the first two weeks, smiles can be elicited when a baby is neither fully awake nor completely asleep (9). By the third week smiles can be elicited most easily by a female human voice when baby is awake.

These early smiles are believed by some researchers to be not truly social (10). For example a baby will smile at any high contrast stimulus, even a white card on to which two "eye" dots have been painted. As well, babies will smile when they "catch onto" the rules of a game. It is thought by some that through games babies learn to associate pleasure with discovery in the presence of adults and thus learn to smile at them to increase positive emotions. Studies with premature infants and those born after 40 weeks' gestation have shown babies smile fully when they reach the conceptional age of 46 weeks regardless of chronological age (10). Hence it is possible for some infants to display social smiles several weeks post partum and others as soon as three weeks; it all depends on gestational

By and large these findings are not important to parents. What is meaningful to them is to follow the emergence of social smiles. Typically there is a progression from spontaneous unexplained smiles which are made toward unspecific stimuli, to ones that are most likely to occur in the presence of another person and in response to the behaviour of the other. Parents can then feel that interactions with their baby are positive and rewarding and that they are partly responsible for giving pleasure to their baby.

Projected outcomes It is hoped that by understanding what happens as social smiles emerge parents will begin to redirect their attention to positive emotions. To achieve this parents will be encouraged to note and report on different sorts of smiles and when these occurred. In part this means recognising which parent activities seem to be associated with infant smiling. If this happens then patterns of relationships linking adult and infant actions may be recognised. Even if this does not happen parents will at least be looking for positive behaviours from their babies.

Limitations An infant may not smile as soon or as often as expected. A parent who fails to find those smiles which ought to be displayed may become annoyed. Hence it will be necessary to moderate developmental trends with the reality of dealing with a particular parent-baby pair.

Assessment/monitoring The primary assessment tool will be self reports from parents at subsequent meetings. If they feel their interactions with baby are more positive then the intervention will have accomplished what it was intended to do.

Smiling

Background (for parents)

Crying is a baby's main means of indicating its state in the first few weeks after birth. During this time most parents respond to the crying and see baby as needing care and protection. The one behaviour which changes a parent's view, that babies can be social, is smiling.

Smiles of a sort can be seen a few days after birth. They usually occur when baby is asleep or drowsy. Since these expressions involve the mouth only and not the eyes or the rest of the face, they are not usually thought of as being real or social. They are typically caused by "gas" or something other than interacting with people. Some call these "angel smiles".

By about the third or fourth week "real" smiles may be seen. These are short little smiles, quite fleeting, involving the whole face. It seems the voice of a woman is most effective in making a baby smile at this time.

By six weeks of age most full term infants show signs of social smiling. This may be later for premature babies and earlier for those born late. It seems the crucial thing is baby's age since conception; about 46 weeks being about right for social smiles.

Baby now smiles mostly at a human face. This can be very rewarding for those nearby and especially for parents who up till now have received little back from baby in return of caring continuously. At this stage some parents begin playing differently with baby in attempts to draw out more smiles.

Quite soon thereafter the smiles will become even more specific. They will occur most often when the infant can see mother's face or when an adult is playing a favourite game.

A baby's social smiles can make all the trouble and crying seem worthwhile. They are quite magical and wash away the past. If parents begin to look for smiles they will notice which situations prompt these and may work to increase their occurrence. If this happens then everyone is a lot more satisfied with the relationships and parents can enjoy their role much more.

Activity (for consultants)

At the meeting this topic is introduced parents will be asked to reflect back over the previous few days and report on any smiling from their baby. If nothing in this line has been noticed then they can be encouraged to make casual observations over the interval until the following meeting. Specific details are not requested during this time, it is more of an orientation exercise.

If smiling has been reported then more specific directions may be provided. There are two main things to be on the look out for. One is the type of smile observed, the other is the occasion when it happened (what brought it on and stopped it).

To classify a smile into a particular type an observer needs only to be aware of three movements; the tongue, the mouth, the hand. It is quite simple to note these characteristics during smiling since there are only two extremes for each one. The tongue can be in or out; the mouth open or shut; and the hand away from or up to the mouth.

Looking at the situations in which smiling occurs can be more difficult. Here it is necessary to be alert to before and after events as well as how these relate to what type of smile is shown. There are no simple guidelines here. One way to manage this part of the activity is to note the situations which are more play-like; bathing, bouncing, and so on. To recognise when smiles do occur and to make use of these observations is to be aware of what baby can do at any particular time. One of the best indexes of how aware parents are of an infant's developmental status is the ways in which they can capture smiling. Of course this assumes baby is well, parents are willing, and a whole host of other factors which may interfere with enjoying smiling.

Subsequent meetings can be directed to understanding smiles by relating these to events, moods, and other people round about. This can be a gentle way of exploring the well-being of all those involved in family relationships.

Summary (for consultants)

Smiling is like magic, it is the balm which removes negative feelings and encourages positive ones. By watching for different sorts of smiles, asking parents to note what happens and when, it is possible to engage them in mutually satisfying play. Play is the serious business of infancy and favourable attitudes have long-reaching consequences for good health.

Intervention 9.5 The development of social behaviours: stranger anxiety

(This intervention is based upon one designed by Chris Meddick, Student, Department of Family studies, University of Guelph, Ontario, Canada).

Rationale Judy Dunn says in her book *Distress and Comfort* (15) that crying in young babies is often thought of as being mysterious. Yet much of it can be attributed to immediate changes in an infant's physical state. So if a baby becomes hungry, feels pain, or experiences sudden movement she cries. Crying is a signal that something is wrong. It is left to the parent to work out what this is and do something about. However, as babies grow older the causes of crying become much more complicated.

It has been found that at around eight months of age most babies suddenly show signs of "stranger distress". The baby may now protest at being left alone by a familiar mother. A visitor who tries to comfort baby seems to make things much worse (15). When it occurs stranger distress is both startling and puzzling. Now an unfamiliar person who approaches a baby in a friendly manner is likely to be greeted by howls of protest.

Emde et al. (14) suggests there is a specific message to a mother and has two components. First, there are certain situations which upset baby and, second, only a mother's presence will bring comfort. These are highly charged messages and may evoke strong feelings in a mother. Some may be proud their babies preferred them in moments of distress, others can become uneasy about the degree of responsibility which accompanies this special reliance.

It is very important that mothers and others be aware of their feelings and they should be reminded that these are quite normal. Basically, one part of this intervention is designed to answer typical questions which mothers have concerning their infants' reactions to strangers.

The published literature on stranger anxiety reveals two basic methods of confronting infants with unfamiliar adults, each one elicits different responses (16). First, there is the stranger controlled confrontation. Here the manner and tempo is managed by an unfamiliar adult with the common outcomes of increased wariness or outright fear on the part of infants. The second method is infant controlled and entails a passive rather than an active role by a stranger. With this method the infant has unhindered physical access to its mother as well as sufficient space and time to get acquainted with the stranger. The outcomes are typically increased visual exploration, positively curious behaviours, smiling and possibly a spontaneous approach. After a period of infant-regulated acquaintance babies often show little or no distress upon being picked up.

An additional factor which affects the infant-stranger interaction is the availability of the familiar adult, typically the mother. Without mother an infant is much more wary and its threshold is lowered. It seems that as far as many infant are concerned the mother is a secure base from which explorations of the environment can be She is at once a starting place as well as a refuge. This is a normal developmental phenomenon.

Projected outcomes There are a number of outcomes which would be anticipated. These are that parents will:
- be aware of the phenomenon of stranger anxiety.
- be aware that certain situations will make the infant more distressed than others (e.g. stranger approaches when mother is absent).
- know when it typically begins (i.e. 7 to 9 months).
- know what the infants' basic message is.
- know why an infant can be very upset by a stranger approaching.
- be aware that stranger anxiety is quite normal.
- be able to give unfamiliar persons reassurances suggestions to make the situation less stressful for the infant.
- understand that increased frequency of night waking may correspond with stranger anxiety.

Limitations It is not known definitely when the phenomenon of stranger anxiety will disappear or what brings it to an end. Some children will always remain "shy". There are definite problems in trying to understand and identify the dynamics which underlie specific behaviours such as stranger anxiety. It is quite likely a particular infant's behaviour is not shown on the list provided. Nonetheless, the opportunity to follow the behaviour is provided if "comments" are entered by an observer.

Assessment/monitoring As parents attend subsequent meetings they will be able to discuss what happened in the intervening period. This will be of use when different approaches are tried and any consequences observed.

Stranger anxiety from babies

Background (for parents)

Consider the following two situations (adapted from Dr. Dunn's book)

First, a ten-week old baby is lying in her crib and her mother, tidying the blankets, leans over talking and smiling. The baby coos and "talks" back. Then the mother leaves the room to greet a visitor. Quite soon the baby begins to cry. The visitor, who hasn't seen baby before comes over, leans down, smiles, and talks softly. The change is remarkable; baby stops crying and smiles as the visitor picks her up.

Second, an eight-month old baby is playing on his mother's knee. To answer the door bell his mother puts him down on the floor and leaves the room. The baby cries as the visitor enters. But this time when the visitor attempts to comfort by picking up, the baby cries even more frantically. He is soothed only when his mother returns and holds him. From the safety of his mother's lap he first stares and later smiles at the visitor.

There is a crucial difference between these two situations. And it all takes place over a matter of just a few months. On both occasions the babies objected to being left alone. But for the older one it was the mother's departure which was critical. "Strangers" may even be family members but not familiar to baby. Adults are not now interchangeable; for many babies physical separation from their mothers suddenly takes on a new meaning. This is something that matters.

When does stranger anxiety occur? The onset of fearful stranger reactions may occur any time during the third quarter of the first year of life. The onset tends to be more specifically in the seventh or eighth month, but this, of course, varies from one individual baby to the next.

What is my baby telling me? If it could speak the infant is saying something like "I feel secure only with you mother so please don't leave me alone with strange people." In this situation the crying infant generally means "Hey, there are certain situations that upset me and only your presence, mother, will bring me comfort. Do come quickly."

How does this make you feel? Some mothers respond with pleasure to this demonstration of their special magic. They take pride in the fact that their infants prefer them and turn to them in times of distress. Other mothers become uneasy about the added responsibility which accompanies this special reliance. They express this feeling when they say "He is such a baby, always wanting to be cuddled". Other mothers indicate they wished their little girl would soon become more "independent".

Why do infants become upset at the approach of a stranger? Many reasons have been put forward to explain this common infant behaviour. One is that infants are upset because they are uncertain about the strange person and are not sure what to expect. So when a stranger enters a room and keeps some distance away, babies may attend to the stranger with some wariness but don't usually cry until approached quickly or touched. But, alternatively, if the stranger talks with the infant's mother first, smiles and carries on pretty well ignoring baby, then less distress is likely. On these occasions the infant has time to adjust.

It is "normal? Yes, this is a typical, normal infant behavior that occurs between the ages of 7 and 21 months for 70% of babies.

How can I help to make these experiences less stressful for my child? For one thing parents can ask adults who come to the house to talk together for a while before giving attention to the infant. Take time, and let the baby come to the stranger. Alternatively, you could encourage the stranger to play a familiar game with baby or approach holding a peace token, like a special toy.

Activities (for parents)

At the first meeting the topic will be introduced and parental concerns identified and discussed. If a parent recognises a baby is showing signs of stranger anxiety and concern is expressed then this intervention would likely be effective.

It would be helpful to clarify just who a stranger is at this time. A stranger is anybody with whom baby is unfamiliar. Included could be well-intentioned family members such as grandparents, uncles, aunts, etc., as well as other visitors. The important thing to remember is that it is baby's view which is uppermost here.

There are three main situations which a parent can gather information about for any subsequent meetings. These may be identified as follows:

1. Mother present and stranger keeps a "safe" distance from baby. Typically, mother and stranger talk for a while with baby playing nearby. The stranger does not approach the baby who is free to explore and make contact with the unfamiliar person in their own time.
2. Mother present, stranger approaches baby without a preliminary adjustment period.
3. Mother absent, stranger approaches and picks up baby.

The ranges of most likely baby reactions are shown in Box 9.10. For each of the three situations described, an adult simply indicates which ones applied by placing a check mark on the line. These three situations are: mother present, stranger waits (MP + SW); mother present, stranger approaches (MP + SAp); and mother absent, stranger approaches (MAb + SAp).

This can be repeated several times, with a fresh check list provided each time. During the subsequent visit go over the list and discuss what happened in each of the three situations. These findings can be summarised and suggestions offered.

Summary (for consultants)

It is reasonable to enquire about which situations a baby found most distressing, which the least upsetting, why it seemed this happened. Finally, the comments in the background section can be discussed and ambiguities cleared up. This is not an easy topic. Nonetheless, there is a certain sense of relief for many parents when it is made known that there is a strong developmental basis for the onset of stranger anxiety with their babies.

Box 9.10

Stranger anxiety check list

Baby's name:________________________ Date:____________

Where M = mother, S = stranger;
P = present, Ab = absent; W = waits, Ap = approaches

MP + SW	MP + SAp	MAb + SAp	reactions shown
_____	_____	_____	is unaware of strange person
_____	_____	_____	stops what he/she is doing
_____	_____	_____	runs to mother, seeks her attention
_____	_____	_____	begins to fuss
_____	_____	_____	seems anxious
_____	_____	_____	shows signs of distress
_____	_____	_____	is quiet and content
_____	_____	_____	is happy (smiles)
_____	_____	_____	"checks out" stranger
_____	_____	_____	approaches stranger
_____	_____	_____	indifferent to stranger
_____	_____	_____	other: (please explain.)

Comments:

10 FORM

The word "form" is often used to summarise the condition of sports' participants. A gymnast may be said to "show good form", a race horse can be referred to as "true to form". Form refers to general presentation.

For babies "form" is the actual presented behaviour and is what baby does in different settings. There is less by way of interpretation of underlying causes and more by way of direct description. The reason for this emphasis is quite straight forward: Unless we know what baby does it is not possible to offer any suggestions as to why these actions may be occurring.

Seven interventions are offered within this theme. Each one involves adults in a slightly different way. Some are quite passive and these rely on unobtrusive observation. Others are interactive, requiring adults to engage babies in particular ways. Nonetheless, throughout, emphasis is always upon what baby does.

Intervention 10.1 Cry sound descriptions

Rationale One way to capture public attention is to claim a direct link between an event and its interpretation. With regard to cry sounds, it is the "fact" that a particular signal has a definite meaning which is appealing. When correspondence of this sort is established then it seems all the answers are provided.

In some of the early work carried out along these lines various cries from different infants were recorded. For instance "hunger" cries have been obtained from babies due for feeding. "Pain" cries have been recorded from babies whose feet have been "shot" with a rubber band snap, or during immunization "shots", or after ear-lobe pinching. Numerous other cries have been recorded from other techniques as well.

Consider just these two main types at this stage, the so called pain and hunger cries. After recording, different groups of adult listeners have been "tested". Typically, it is reported that those with greater child rearing or handling experience are better at recognising these types than are other listeners. In one type of study in this tradition listeners are provided with the options on a printed page and asked to indicate their selection by circling which one applies (1).

Other researchers have taken this a step further. They recorded cries from babies who are presumed to be from one of three "temperament" groups. (This notion is covered more systematically in Intervention 10.3.) In brief, the purpose was to identify babies who were "easy", "average" or "difficult", and analyse the physical characteristics of their cry sounds (2).

In another study these temperament cries were played back to adult listeners strapped to instruments which measured changes in their physiological responses (3). These results and self-report data, about how the cries could be described and so forth, were analysed according to the three original groups and differences between these types of cries reported.

Other researchers (4) recorded cries from babies with varying birth experiences and whose mothers presented different sorts of backgrounds. These cry sounds have been used in a whole variety of studies (5,6).

Some cries do have distinctive features and may be indicative of handicap or mishap. For the most part however practically all other cries do not have a direct relation with known events. Hence most of the studies already mentioned suffer from a serious flaw. It would be nice to say that all cries mean something. Simply put, this is not the case. Hence results from studies which imply this link ought to be treated with extreme caution.

To understand why these results are for the most part quite meaningless one needs to grasp an essential distinction between different levels of psychological processing. Remember, the implicit claim is that a cry has a definite meaning.

When a person is asked to classify a cry sound at least two mental tasks are demanded. One is to be able to distinguish one sound from another. The second is to allocate one sound with a whole host of others which share the same characteristics. The latter task is much more difficult psychologically speaking, and involves the former.

As a practical illustration, consider a bowl of fruit. If you take any item from the bowl and ask somebody what it is, not only does she need to register the essential physical features (like shape, colour, texture) but also delve into her memories of similar items and then associate it to that class (banana, grape, apple, etc).

A much simpler task is to draw out two items from the fruit bowl and ask the straight-forward question "Are these the same or different?". If enough pairs are taken then it will be possible to put all the "same" ones together. Later one could extend this exercise by asking on what basis the judgements of same/different have been made. So, you could end up with groups created on the basis of colour, then, within each of these, smaller groups formed on the basis of shape and, finally, other ones which have texture as distinguishing features.

Now back to cries. Instead of assuming the cry "meant" something (which is the same as identifying it, believing there is a one-to-one correspondence between the object and its significance) we retreated in the psychological sense and looked at the more primitive process of same/different.

In the first study we took 24 cry sounds and formed every possible pair-wise combination. This included each cry with itself. Each listener heard these pairs and indicated whether the second was the same as or different to the first. Note, we did not say what the cry "meant". In fact at the time of running the study we did not know, as these sounds were kindly supplied by another researcher who did not reveal their identities at the outset. The results were analysed and the "groups" of same sounds formed. Most of them fell into the original groups but there were exceptions (7).

These exceptions deserve attention. According to the listeners' results, formed on the basis of how the sounds were heard, there were some "pain" cries in the mainly "hunger" group and vice versa. If you were a listener and considered a "pain" cry sounded more like a "hunger" one then what, in fact, is the truth of the matter? Well, as far as you, the listener, is concerned it is a hunger cry. Yet, for the researcher this is incorrect as the sound was originally recorded as a pain cry.

As this testing procedure was too long to carry out often we sought alternative methods. When participating in the same/different study it took up to 45 minutes for each listener. As well, preparation of the tapes was very demanding. To make this into a workable technique would be practically impossible; any new sound would have to be paired with all the previous ones.

Attention was then directed to finding a method for distinguishing cry sounds and for grouping those which shared similar properties. One solution lay in using words to describe the sounds with. A listener was presented with a list of opposite word pairs (like "strong....weak"). Then, while listening to a cry, indicated what it sounded like by placing a mark somewhere between these extremes. The results obtained from this approach were almost identical to the earlier same/different study mentioned above. Now it was possible to speed things up and include any cry sound along with appropriate adjectives.

In a whole series of studies I have used different sets of words with the same 12 cries (which were kindly supplied by Mary Lounsbury). Regardless of who has listened the results are practically the same; Canadian students, New Zealand students, parents, and nurses in training all produce similar results. In this study I used the cries which others had employed (2,3). Remember, though that I was simply looking at which cry sounds went together so far as listeners are concerned. They did not know the babies who supplied them belonged to different temperament groups. Indeed, if the cry is the message, then one would expect that the cry groups formed on the basis of listening would be exactly the same as the "easy" "average" and "difficult" temperament ones. What happened was that listener groups contained mixed cries. In fact one group had both the most easy and the most difficult cries.

In short the "problem" here is similar to the pain/hunger one mentioned previously. This is why the results must be treated with caution. So long as cry researchers do not distinguish between what is heard by listeners as belonging together and what researchers believe to be the case (cries represent conditions) then this "error" will be sustained. Unfortunately we have not been able to check out this observation any further since some of the original researchers will not release their raw data for re-analysis.

What this amounts to is that one could design cry-rating scales for specific purposes. The research on this facet has not yet been done. Nonetheless, on the basis of our results to date, it would seem quite reasonable to design rating scales which would distinguish cries according to their sounds rather than their "meanings". This is now an active area of ongoing research, designing scales for wails. In the meantime, some guidelines are available for those listening to unusual cries. These are discussed below (8).

For those who are confronted by a "normal" baby in a home setting three types of responses are needed to establish meaning. I have called this 3-part harmony. It may well be 3-part discord. First there is the sound itself; what are its features? Second there is the emotional reaction of a listener; how does it make you feel? And, finally, there is the situation in which it occurred; what's going on? It is the convergence of answers from these three domains which will help provide meaning. The cries don't mean anything in and of themselves; it is how they are interpreted which provides the major impact.

From our own work it would seem that any particular infant's cry sounds can be stretched out along a single line. At one end are those which are tight, strained and intense. At the other are found those sounds which appear free, loose and positive. The most intense are pain-like, and this is a basic cry pattern which most babies establish if left alone without comforting. Less extreme than these are the so called "hunger" cries. The least intense of all are the whimpering/slight moaning ones.

This range appears to be different between babies. What this means is that the most extreme cries of some infants are only moderately so for others. Hence the amount of overlap between babies' cry extremes should correspond to the capabilities of different mothers to recognise similar patterns. Although the research on this possibility has not been carried out, it may account for the cry misclassifications we found in the laboratory studies.

Projected outcomes Through using the descriptive scales provided parents will begin to understand the distinctive features of different cries and the effects these have on a listener. Then, by combining these effects with the situations in which the crying occurs (like middle of night; after bathing; after feeding; before feeding... see 10.3 for other examples) recognition of a particular infants's cry repertoire may occur.

Essentially, what is aimed at is the provision of a scheme which will show personally meaningful discriminations to be made by a parent.

Limitations Unknown. Some people will have difficulty using the scales and may wish to modify the procedure.

Assessment/monitoring Primarily by follow up at the next meeting. If in doubt; and the cry does seem a typical advice ought to be sought from other professionals.

Describing cry sounds

Background (for parents)

There is little doubt that infant crying can be a very stressful sound for parents. It is a complex noise which cannot be described easily. We do not have a way of describing cry sounds easily.

The purpose of this exercise is to provide a means to help people describe cry sounds with. There are at least three things involved when trying to make sense out of a baby's crying.

First, there is the nature of the sound itself. Simply taken as a sound, how can it be described? Second, there is the effect a particular sound is having on a listener, what is the reaction of a person hearing a cry? Finally, there is the situation when the cry occurred. By putting these three together it may be possible to begin to notice similarities and differences which will influence the way baby is handled.

For example, it has been noted that pre-term babies seem not to have much variation in their crying. All their crying is said to be intense, high pitched and monotonous. By having available a means of distinguishing different cry sounds a parent may recognise important variations between them.

It is said that some parents can tell what is the matter by the sound of the cry. To do this they have learned to select the main characteristics. The words provided below are designed to provide a means to help parents tell the difference between various cry sounds of "normal" babies.

There are some babies for whom the cries offer an indication of something being amiss. Although these do not mean there is something definitely "wrong", it is a good idea to seek further advice if these are present in your baby.

Box 10.1

Cry characteristics which may relate to malfunctioning CNS

1. Either of two extremes in the pitch of the cry. They may be either thin, high, squeaky or thick, low and harsh.
2. Either of two extremes in their variation. They can be either flat and monitone-like or they can rapidly shift between the extremes described in 1. above so there is no steadyness.
3. The cries are dull; they have no richness nor colour.
4. There is no rhythm to the cry, there is no sense of timing.
5. The cry breaks the sound barrier and seems distorted and turbulent, bouncing above a "normal" range.
6. There are massive differences in the length of each cry burst. Some may be short and snappy others long and drawn out as if baby cannot regulate crying with breathing.
7. Either extreme of sensitivity where a slight movement or bump leads to crying, or practically no crying to quite severe pains.

Adapted from Lester (8)

Activity (for parents)

For each cry sound to which the descriptions are to be provided it will be necessary to indicate listener/date/time/what soothed baby. Some parents may wish to add more details about the occasion (see Box 10.2). As one set of words is to be used for a simple cry it may be necessary to make copies and use these.

The words are arranged into two groups. For the first group the heading is: "this cry can be described as....". It deals with the physical nature of the cry.

The second group is headed as: "for me this cry is...". It aims at finding out a listener's feelings about the cry.

If a listener believes a word *does* apply to a particular cry then place a mark to the *right side* and on a line under the heading "very much".

On the other hand, if a word *does not* apply then a check should be placed on the left side *on* the line under the heading "not at all".

The spaces between these two extremes should be used as considered necessary. There will be one mark placed against each word, somewhere on a line.

Start at the top of the page. Make sure each word has a check mark on the line.

Box 10.2

Rating scales for cries

(Permission to is granted to make copies for personal use providing source is acknowledged)

	not at all						very much
	this cry can be described as...						
strong	____ :	____ :	____ :	____ :	____ :	____ :	____
shrill/piercing	____ :	____ :	____ :	____ :	____ :	____ :	____
strained/intense	____ :	____ :	____ :	____ :	____ :	____ :	____
urgent	____ :	____ :	____ :	____ :	____ :	____ :	____
screaming	____ :	____ :	____ :	____ :	____ :	____ :	____
choking	____ :	____ :	____ :	____ :	____ :	____ :	____
	for me this cry is...						
tiring	____ :	____ :	____ :	____ :	____ :	____ :	____
upsetting	____ :	____ :	____ :	____ :	____ :	____ :	____
demanding	____ :	____ :	____ :	____ :	____ :	____ :	____
unpleasant	____ :	____ :	____ :	____ :	____ :	____ :	____
irritating	____ :	____ :	____ :	____ :	____ :	____ :	____

person listening/rating:
date: time:
what successfully soothed baby:

From: Kirkland, J. (1984) *Crying and Babies.* London:Croom Helm.

Outcomes (for parents)

This is a complicated activity to follow and apply. However, if the instructions can be followed and several cries are rated on the scales it is likely differences between these will emerge.

It should be possible to:

— understand the two groups of terms and how these focus on different aspects; describing sounds and feelings
— if carried out over a period of time to notice changes in the sounds and feelings toward these
— to begin to understand differences between cries
— to begin to understand babys' range of cries and what these mean in different situations.

Intervention 10.2 Daily baby plotting record

Rationale George Kelly's (9) psychology of personal constructs has many implications for those who work with crying babies. Kelly's notion is that it is the way people understand their various worlds which largely determines their courses of individual participation. Since there are many different views of the same situation then to be effective one needs to understand the framework which any individual utilises in order to make sense of it. Once a particular viewpoint is recognised as an elaboration of an individual's construct system then interventions may become more effective.

Parents trying to cope with irritable babies are often unwilling victims of the crying baby syndrome. Although their reports are quite accurate these are couched within the syndrome. Hence a consultant not only has to understand the general dynamics of processes occurring within the syndrome but also of an individual's interpretation of these. Although an impartial observer may comment about "bias", "contamination" or "unbalanced" nature of these parental reports this is not very helpful. The situation *is* as a parent describes it. And this is what has to be understood by a consultant.

The greater the correspondence between the views of different people, the greater their mutual communication. Hence, although there are unique aspects of any situation there are also channels of communication established through agreed upon similarities. Patterns of communication emerge when individuals share construct systems. Briefly, what one person makes of a situation is shared when others apply the same frameworks which generate similar meaning.

In order to release a parent from the destructive effects of the crying baby syndrome a scheme which lies outside of it needs to be provided. If a frame of reference which is not bound to personal views can be provided then it may serve as a life line of hope. This can become a way out of the syndrome, an escape route to family health.

One effective technique is to reintroduce the notion of time by the keeping of a simple diary. Other researchers have designed daily diary forms for parents to record what goes on in the home (10).

On the face of it this intervention may appear simplistic. Nonetheless it has been very effective. For one couple it was the primary means a mother could show her partner what happened each day upon his return from work. For others it offers a chance to recognise patterns emerging from the days of many crying bouts. Indeed it is precisely because the diary is so straightforward to use that parents often begin to search for patterns themselves. They can see the data and begin to interpret them without outside assistance.

Projected outcomes The diary provides a convenient focus for subsequent consultations. For any one week the diary offers a means for making enquiries about what happened. For some parents it may well be a realisation along the lines "I don't seem to have a crying baby after all." This in itself is not a sufficient reason to terminate meetings. A baby who seldom cries for long periods but does so during "social" times can be hard to handle and places the family under enormous stress. So it is not only the amount of crying, but when it occurs which can be devastating.

When diaries from several weeks have been completed these can be laid one beneath the other in the order of completion. If the pages are folded just below the bottom line of "Saturday" then week-by-week changes become even more obvious. Patterns or the lack of them are quite striking.

Through inspecting the completed diaries opportunities are provided for:

— talking about crying episodes
— identifying repetitive patterns
— noting times of extreme family stress
— looking at possible alternatives for coping with the crying
— providing parents with an activity which they can go on with during the week
— offering a means of noting other disruptive infant behaviours
— promoting a positive approach to escape from the crying baby syndrome.

Limitations Some parents may get so tired they cannot keep track of clock time needed for accurate diary entries. If parents miss a day they will volunteer explanations. There is no need to chastise them for non-cooperation.

If the symbols used are too difficult to remember errors tend to increase. Initially it is better to stick with a maximum of four different symbols and provide a careful explanation of what each one stands for. As parents become more proficient at diary keeping they may wish to add extra ones in order to capture a greater range of infant behaviours.

Box 10.3

A blank diary form

(Permission is granted to make copies for personal use providing source is acknowledged. If necessary, use a photocopier to enlarge).

Diary form Parent name: ____________ baby's name: ____________

Start date: __________

For the present form: X = crying; / = feeding related crying;

________ = sleeping ; f = feeding

	mid-night					morning							mid-day	afternoon					evening						
	12	1	2	3	4	5	6	7	8	9	10	11	12	1	2	3	4	5	6	7	8	9	10	11	12
Sun																									
Mon																									
Tues																									
Wed																									
Thurs																									
Fri																									
Sat																									

Comments:

From: Kirkland, J. (1984) *Crying and Babies.* London:Croom Helm.

Sunday:

Monday:

Tuesday:

Wednesday:

Thursday:

Friday:

Saturday:

Assessment/monitoring Verbal reports by parents at subsequent meetings offer an opportunity to find out how things are going. Any difficulties regarding the mechanics if keeping the diary can be clarified on these occasions.

Daily diary record

Background (for parents)

One difficulty many parents have when dealing with a crying baby is keeping track of what is going on from day to day. Some have commented that with increased tiredness a dull greyness settles over everything and nothing makes sense anymore.

With twins this problem simply becomes greater. In fact some parents of twins get so tired they cannot remember what happened to which twin when.

The cry diary form was designed to help parents keep a note of what is happening. Although it is designed for crying episodes the form can be used to record other behaviours as well, like sleeping, feeding, bathing and so on. At the outset it is helpful to make a note of up to four different activities only. These are; "crying", "feeding related crying;", "feeding" and "sleeping/down to rest".

Activity (for parents)

The diary form shows 15 minute blocks for the seven days of the week. Across the page is a daily clock. It begins at midnight, goes through the morning to noon in the centre and then shows afternoon and evening. Down the side of the page are shown the days of the week. Now, since today is ......, let me strike out the previous days for this week. This is done to remind you to begin another page at the beginning of next week rather than the start of this one.

When making your entries it is not necessary to keep a close eye on the clock. If a particular behaviour occurs within the quarter hour block then indicate this by printing in the box. So, it is not for how long something happened but whether it did or not within any of the time periods. A cry of 5 minutes gets the same entry of one lasting 10 minutes if it falls into one of the 15 minute slots provided on the diary form.

There are three or four things which I'd like you to enter. One refers to sleeping. Just use a straight line to show this. Draw it right through the box from one side to the other. This means a continuous bout of sleeping has a long line drawn through several boxes in a row.

The next thing to show is "crying". You could make a distinction here between "crying that upsets me" by printing a cross in a box, and "other crying" (like feeding-related crying) by entering in a slash (half a cross).

The final thing to show is feeding. To do this simply print a small letter "f".

Later on we can talk about adding more things on the diary form. You may like to consider some extras during the week. In the meantime it's best to stick with the ones indicated above.

So, start this form tonight. Then starting on Monday begin another sheet. Bring all diary forms to the next meeting. Finally, at the bottom of each form is a space to write comments for each day. You may like to include visits, doctor's prescriptions tried, other drugs used, or other events which may provide us with some clues about the crying. Even a change in your (or baby's) diet should not be overlooked.

Summary:
The basic idea here is quite straightforward. A diary form is provided for you to indicate when each of three or four different infant activities occurs. By keeping the diary for a week or more similarities will become clearer. Weekly diaries can be laid one under the other. If the pages are folded across at "Comments", the weeks can be seen as a continuous calendar.

Intervention 10.3 Infant profiles

Rationale The concept of infant temperament was introduced in the mid-1950's (11) to counter a dominating environmental view of human development. According to the latter position individuals had more or less equal opportunities to develop. Hence it was as a consequence of environmental differences that any variations between people occurred. The notion of *temperament* changed this bias. It introduced the idea that basic personal differences could exist from very early on in life. In other words, people are not born equal.

According to temperament theorists, research has provided evidence for three main categories of infants. Although a broad range of different techniques have been designed to assess infant temperament they are largely in agreement about these major groupings. First, there are the so called *easy* babies. These are positive in mood, approach events/people, are rhythmical in their actions (have regular schedules for eating, sleeping, etc.) and adjust quickly to new surroundings. These typically account for around 40% of infant groups. These babies, while a joy to be with, are a nuisance; parents both adore and attempt to make their baby into this ideal.

Another temperamental group is characterised by the label *difficult*. This includes around 10% of babies. Their behaviour is opposite to the "easy" babies; They are negative in mood, avoid/withdraw, are non-rhythmical, and settle in slowly. These are the babies most consultants will deal with; they are the good criers, poor sleepers, bad feeders.

Between these two extremes are several other groups of infants. One is known as the *slow-to-warm-up*. As the label implies these infants are initially wary but gradually ease into co-operation. Some researchers have lumped these in with the "difficult" babies (12). Other temperament groups have been described and are of little importance here.

There are several competing explanations for the concept of "difficult" temperament. One is that the source of this trend is firmly based within the baby, and is part of the overall genetic design (13). Another is that it is a parent's view of the baby which is the main contribution to its "difficult" temperamental status (14). It is important that these different explanations are known since the belief a consultant has about one or other of these views will influence the sorts of interventions which will be implemented. For those who embrace a constitutional explanation emphasis is on encouraging a parent to weather out the situation.

The danger of suggesting the inside "baby" position is that nothing can be done since temperament is inbuilt and relatively fixed. Contrariwise, those who locate an infant's difficult temperament within a parent's view will select and apply interventions which attempt to alter these views. The danger in adopting the second view, of parental views making temperament, lies in blaming parents and of perpetuating their feelings of inadequacy and guilt.

One resolution of this dilemma is to aim at a maximum gain/minimal loss approach. This means making the most out of what is presented. It is to accept the merits of each position and design interventions which include both sets of participants, babies and their parents.

The present intervention aims at a dual approach by using a parent's descriptions of what baby is doing in different settings. There are 24 settings about which information is requested. Some situations will not apply to a particular baby and are simply discarded.

Behind the decision to ask parents to provide information about their babies are two reasons. First, parents tend to be accurate reporters of what is going on in the home, especially if there is a definite task clearly described. Second, there is Kelly's personal construct theory (9). Kelly's constructs are based on the idea that people can relate significant values and/or events to one another in order to grasp what is going on in their worlds. In the present setting it applies to relating infant behaviours exhibited in different situations to ways of describing what these are.

From different sources it is apparent that the notion of difficult temperament includes dimensions of behaviour. Incidently, these dimensions refer to the way in which behaviours are described rather than the particular behaviours themselves. Thus a distinction is made between "ways of seeing events" and the "events" themselves. Hence, from a "difficult" temperament perspective the "ways" or descriptions of displays are said to include those already mentioned, namely; high intensity, high activity and withdrawal. Several studies have provided evidence to support the organismic specificity hypothesis; that temperament describes something going on within the baby. Two possible explanations have been advanced by researchers (12). One was that as a group difficult babies are less sensitive to social interactions and more sensitive to overstimulation of the physical environment. A second explanation was that difficult babies are so directed to their internal discomforts they tune out of social interactions. Quite clearly the main point is that for whatever reason, difficult babies are not receptive to social activities.

Projected outcomes For any particular parent who is trying to cope with a crying baby it is important to find out just where the strain is occurring. The present intervention is designed for this purpose.

After having results analysed parents will be able to comment on various prospects of their situation. This means affirming areas of difficulty as well as those which are more positive and even enjoyable. Since infant crying can destroy a person's feelings of pleasure it is important to find out which situations are pleasurable. In some cases these have been completely obliterated by the crying, and a parent can no longer recognise or participate in them even though in fact they are still present.

In brief the technique:

— provides a means of reorganising views about distressed babies by
— enabling a parent to see related aspects of infant behaviours in various settings, and
— showing where adjustments to ways of handling babies may be effective
— serves as a vehicle for monitoring different infant behaviours as baby grows older
— provides a basis for ongoing discussions

Limitations It can take time to show parents how to make a record of their observations, to complete the forms and supply relevant information. Second, at the outset any possible benefits to parents are not immediately obvious. Finally, as parents get accustomed to the task they may change the criteria for making their ratings, but is of little consequence in this context.

Assessment/monitoring The responses obtained from parents about their infants' behaviours in different settings will be unique. Monitoring of the technique can occur only within each situation.

If the infant profiles are completed at regular intervals then the results will provide a more or less continuous monitoring of changes which occur as baby grows older. Hence the assessment of the technique itself is ongoing and corresponds with parental involvement.

To begin with the procedure for making sense of the data will take time and effort. Quite soon, after about half a dozen analyses, consultants will find their speed increases dramatically. To help in this matter short cuts will become apparent and consultants will learn to "read" the data as well as use it beneficially.

What is actually done with the information is up to each consultant. From experience I tend to begin with the most negative incidents and work toward the more positive ones. A good part of the time at subsequent meetings is spent talking about what is half known to a parent already. Take your time, parents will readily volunteer information about what seems to be going on. In part, the technique is designed to guide parents to make their own choices. By finishing with the positive situations, parents can be reassured that everything is not as bleak as they imagined. Mind, it could be worse.

With gentle encouragement, ask parents to complete another profile in preparation for the following week. Remember, you may ask for it to be posted. I sometimes supply a self-addressed envelope for this purpose.

There are many ways for parents to lessen the impact of a stressful situation. For example baby may have changed since the form was completed. This is helpful to know and makes a convenient and acceptable excuse to talk about something other than what the results show. However, to get some practice ask a friend to complete it initially and go over the results with her. In the end you'll have to rely on your own judgement of the situation.

Assume you have a completed data sheet. In each of the little boxes will be either a letter "1" (for yes) or "0" (for No). First off you probably won't "see" anything at all except when the whole sheet, or a good part of it, is made up entirely of 1 or 0.

Now, once the entire form has been completed your task is to put together situations which are similar.

In order to sort out what might be going on, each situation has to be separated from the other. First, cut the page in half lengthwise. This action separates the numbered boxes half of the page from the printed descriptions of the various situations. Note, even though the page has been cut in half, a duplicate set of identification tags (the numbers 1–24) serves to link parental replies (1's and 0's) with the original printed descriptions. Next trim off the page heading. Look down through, the replies and note consecutive rows which have identical answers. If there are some the same this saves cutting in the following step. For every different pair of strips separate by cutting across the rows. The result is lots of strips, each with a parent's replies and an identification tag.

Your task now is to arrange these reply strips using the answers provided. Place the strips onto a sheet of blank paper in an orderly manner.

I make a basic left/right distinction on the page when placing the strips. If the focus is on "grizzly, grumpy, crying" (the sixth column) then all the strips with zero in column six go to the left and those with 1 are placed on the right. (For other specific topics make this left-right distinction sorting on another column; such as column 1 if it is a high activity which is particularly annoying.)

A second distinction is made using the top-bottom dimension on the page. As there are six response boxes on each strip there are actually seven amounts of the answer 1 available (from none at all through to six). For sorting purposes focus only on the entries of 1, ignoring for the meantime the zeros. Within groups strips are arranged using their identification tag sequence.

The strips with seven 1's will be placed at the top right of the page and those with no 1's at all at the bottom left. Other groups, formed on the basis of 1's will be arranged in between. Where the same number is 1's are provided but in different sequences for a group, simply arrange strips across the page while retaining groups. A bit of pushing and shoving will settle these difficulties, which are not crucial anyway since the general overall pattern is what matters.

Once these strips have been sorted out stick them in place using clear tape before a draught scatters them. Now, by repeating the whole process for the other half of the response sheet, the names of each situation can be taped onto another sheet of paper in the same order by matching identification tags. This pattern becomes the focus of discussion at the next meeting. An illustrated example of the whole process is shown in Box 10.4.

Occasionally some aspects of the situations emerge very clearly. It may be feeding sessions which are troublesome. In another case it may well be that this particular baby reacts to being dried/changed. Or there may be something about missing close, warm, physical contact. Other babies may be observed to be non-sociable, or non-cuddly.

There are dozens of leads which are thrown up by this technique. Some of these will require more systematic assessment. Others can be followed through the weeks with subsequent profiles, and changes noticed. Indeed, it is common for parents to start interpreting the results themselves. They tend to latch onto the ways different situations produce predictable behaviours and get a handle on what seems to be going on. Once shown what to do with scissors and tape, some parents can make up and interpret the profiles themselves. This is a useful strategy if baby is having on-days and off-days. Here a daily summary of each day is helpful to get a handle on what seems to be going on.

Box 10.4

An illustrated example of sorting parent replies using infant profile form

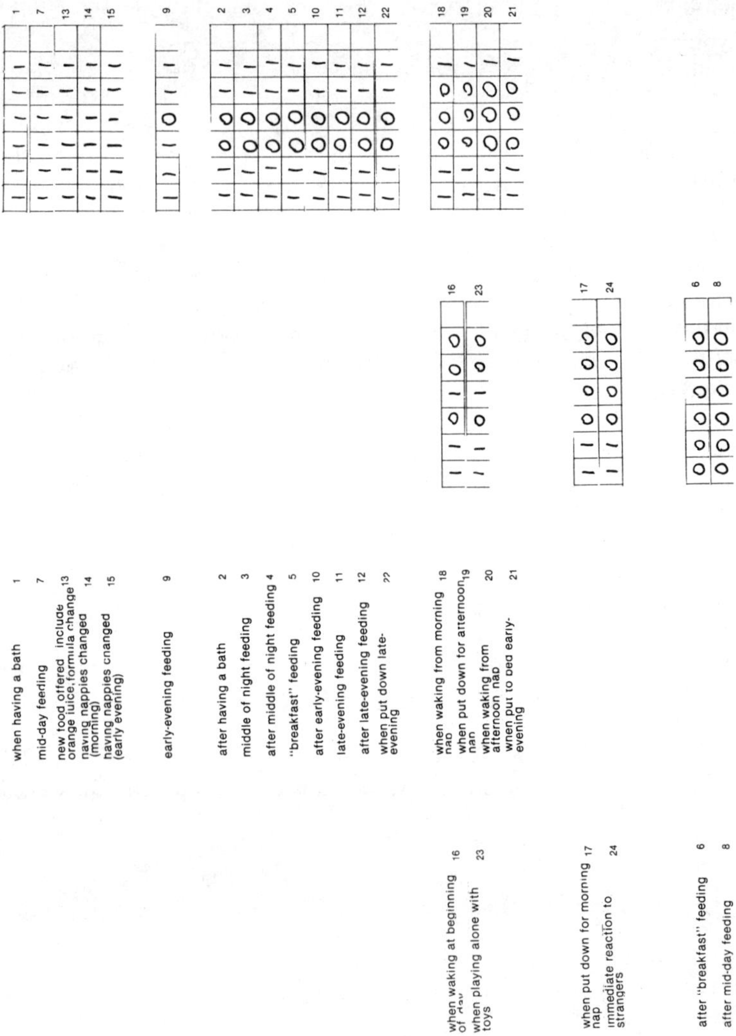

Describing baby's behaviours

Background (for parents)

When living with a baby who is crying a good deal it is hard to make much sense out of the day to day things that go on. When parents get tired all that seems to meet them is the constant crying. Sometimes babies can be doing other things but these are just not seen because the crying takes over completely and seems to block out anything else.

The task tries to get over this problem. It does so by asking you to note what you see as going on in the day to day business of handling your baby. If you can do this in the next few days and then post me the slips of paper I'm about to show you then I could have something else we can talk about at the next meeting. The reason for my wanting these posted is that I can do some homework to save time when we next get together.

Activity (for parents)

There are two ways to look at the different things which babies can do. First there are the different situations in which babies find themselves. On this sheet of paper 24 different situations are listed. Now, let's look over each one and see if it will apply to your baby. I'll read each one out and you tell me if it applies or not. I'm doing this because some may not be useful, and if they are not I can simply cross these out.

(Read down the list slowly, one situation at a time. Pause after each one and explain further if necessary. It is a parent's view which is important here. Each can decide when "early morning" or "breakfast" or "late evening" is during the day. You may like to make a note on the form to help fit these situations to particular babies. If a situation does not apply just draw a line across the page. Extra situations can be added; although unlikely the first time, parents may wish to include more subsequently.)

As well as these situations there is what is done in each one. This is the second way of looking at what babies may do. There are six different ways to describe a baby's actions. These are as follows.

1. They can "move much" by being very active, or move hardly at all.
2. They can be "loud and noisy" or quiet.
3. They can "turn away from and avoid" something as if to get away from it, or they can approach it positively.
4. They can "adjust slowly, taking time to settle in" or take things in their stride.
5. They can be "rigid and tense" or relaxed and comfortable.
6. They can be "grizzly, grumpy or crying" or happy and pleasant.

These six ways of describing behaviour are shown across the top of the page. Now, what I'd like you to do is to print 1 or 0 in each box. Put "1" for Yes and "0" for No. One way to remember this is with the expression "Oh, no".

Let us take as an example the situation "Having a bath". Now think

Box 10.5

Infant profile form

Please fill in every box with either 0 or 1

		moves much	loud	turns from, avoids	adjusts slowly	takes time to settle in	rigid, tense	grizzly, grumpy, crying	
when having a bath	1								1
after having a bath	2								2
middle of night feeding	3								3
after middle of night feeding	4								4
"breakfast" feeding	5								5
after "breakfast" feeding	6								6
mid-day feeding	7								7
after mid-day feeding	8								8
early-evening feeding	9								9
after early-evening feeding	10								10
late-evening feeding	11								11
after late-evening feeding	12								12
new food offered include orange juice, formula change	13								13
having nappies changed (morning)	14								14
having nappies changed (early evening)	15								15
when waking at beginning of day	16								16
when put down for morning nap	17								17
when waking from morning nap	18								18
when put down for afternoon nap	19								19
when waking from afternoon nap	20								20
when put to bed early-evening	21								21
when put down late-evening	22								22
when playing alone with toys	23								23
immediate reaction to strangers	24								24
	25								25
	26								26

Baby's Name: ______

Today's date: ______

Parent Name: ______

Remember 0 = NO 1 = Yes

(Permission is granted to make copies for personal use providing source is acknowledged. If necessary, use a photocopier to enlarge).

From: Kirkland, J. (1984) *Crying and Babies.* London:Croom Helm.

back on the last couple of days or so and tell me about the bath. Did baby: move much, be loud and noisy, turn away from and try to avoid it, adjust slowly and take time to settle in, be rigid and tense, be grizzly, grumpy, crying. (While going through these print a big "1" or "0" in the corresponding boxes.)

Now, does that seem to make sense? It will take about quarter of an hour to fill it in. So, I'd like you to take it away and fill in each and every box on the page. When you've done that post it to me using this envelope. Once I get it back I'll do some homework and we'll talk about it at the next meeting.

Summary (for parents)

For the situations you indicated which apply to your baby show whether or not the six behaviours happened by putting a "1" or an "0" in the box. You can add extra situations or delete those which don't seem to apply. When completing the form think back on what tended to happen during the last few days. After you have filled in every box post the form to me and I'll sort something out to talk about the next time we meet. The upshot of this will be a sort of map about what seems to be going on.

Intervention 10.4 Introduction to infant states

Rationale From the early 1960's the idea of infant state offered clinicians and researchers a scheme which enabled them to make greater sense of what was happening. By classifying an infant's ongoing behaviours into one of six or so states greater precision was obtained in neurological assessment (15) and related psychological processes (16).

Most people now engaged in the study of babies include descriptions of state. Although different schemes have been designed it is generally accepted that for most purposes half a dozen capture most of the variation.

Projected outcomes Although designed as a prelude to subsequent interventions, the present outline of infant states is likely to be quite effective in and of itself. By providing a general descriptive framework, observers who use it can appreciate the significance if attending to baby's contributions during interaction.

Limitations Unknown. One possibility is that a particular infant's behavioural repertoire cannot be contained within the categories provided. Verbal reports from adult observers will provide an ongoing evaluative guide.

On seeing baby's behaviours I: an introduction to state.

Background (for parents)

This introduction will deal with the idea of infant state. Many other activities planned for involving parents with their babies depend upon an awareness of what infant state is about.

There are six well known infant states which will be described below. Each state is a description of what a baby may be doing at any given time. By knowing about infant states a parent can begin to see similarities between activities on different occasions. For instance the state known as "deep sleep" can be seen during most sleeping sessions. So the idea of infant states makes it possible to notice regularities in what otherwise may seem haphazard events. This can lead a parent to seeing something predictable in what appears to be nothing more than random activities.

In part, awareness of an infant's various states depends upon the extent to which a parent can recognise them. For once these are recognised, then it is possible to deal with baby in a sensitive way. For example, it is no use trying to interest baby in following a brightly coloured toy with its eyes if it is almost asleep. To get the most from baby it is a good idea to make your requests when it is most receptive. But, as will become clearer, not all states prime an infant for positive action. Good lusty crying is a state too.

As well as the way baby is handled, a baby's states are set by and controlled from things going inside it — for example, food related activities (such as time since last feed; amount and type of food; water balance); its general health (infections, illness); maturity (teething); how it is feeling; drugs given; and what happened in its immediate past (previous state). All these and many more have a bearing on present state exhibition.

But it is a parent's alertness to and capability for noticing differences in baby's total behaviour range, and of bringing similarities together into recognisable states which is the first step. After that, being able to follow a baby's changes in state is important. For it is then that events can begin to be seen to be related to one another. How baby got to where it now is, what can be expected now it has got here and where will it go to from this present state (as well as of being able to make good guesses about the likelihood of one state changing into another), can open the door for positive interaction between parent and baby. For if states cannot be seen, if a parent does not see how these are linked one to the other and how they are related to the things which are done to and come from baby, then it is as if little at all makes any sense.

Activity (for parents)

The six infant states are typically divided into two which are related to sleeping and four to wakefulness:

Sleeping related states

A. *Deep sleep.*

This looks relaxing and peaceful. Baby's breathing is regular, its eyes are closed and there is little movement except for an occasional startle or jerk. Bumps and noises can lead to startles, but not immediately.

B. *Light sleep.*
Baby seems to give the appearance of suddenly going to wake up, and frequently does. The eyes seem to flutter about under closed eyelids. Breathing is hesitant and irregular, there are bursts of sucking. Startles can lead to waking. Other movements are regular and slow.

Awake related states

C. *Dopey, drowsy or sleepy.*
As the description indicates, baby is in between sleeping and waking. May or may not be fussing, or moving. Altering position will often change to a another state; otherwise can drift off to sleep.

D. *Quiet alert.*
A rather special state which can at first be quite fleeting tends to arise when baby has been fed and is comfortable. During this time its eyes will tend to track moving objects, it will imitate face movements, and generally direct attention to the source of influence. There is little body movement.

E. *Restless.*
Lots of big body movements and occasional startles, both of which tend to increase as extra stimulation is provided. Fussing may be present or absent.

F. *Crying.*
There is no need to provide any description here.

Summary (for parents)

Its all very well listing these states. But remember that any infant may not show the same pattern of state change from day to day. In addition, there are some infants who seem to be happier overall than do others. The usefulness of the state idea lies in allowing a parent to observe baby, to see how these states slide one into another, and to see how they can be influenced.

Being able to recognise different infant states is a start. The next step is to match parent behaviour to an infant's and to see how much each person is changing the other. This is much more difficult to grasp. Remember, to a large extent baby depends on you for its state alterations. Don't expect baby to enter the quiet alert state by simply asking it to do so. There are no rules which can be given or followed for encouraging a quiet alert state. You'll need to be sensitive enough to find out for yourself when to expect this and how much baby can take before changing into a restless or crying state.

After reading and understanding these notes you should be able to:

— describe six different infant states
— recognise which state a baby is in
— realise how one state can change to another
— begin to understand what leads to infant state changes
— notice how your actions and baby's are tied together as each of you influences the other.

Intervention 10.5 Observing infant states

Rationale This intervention builds upon the previous one (10.4) which dealt with infant state descriptions. The Neonatal Behavioral Assessment scale (16) is well known in the research and clinical literature. In two recent reports an innovative approach to applying this scale was adopted. In one (17) mothers were provided with a printed copy of a modified version of the scale without any training whatsoever. They rated their babies twice, shortly after birth and at 4 weeks. The full Brazelton scale was applied to these same infants independently by qualified examiners. Surprisingly, there were few differences between trained and untrained assessors. Then, in another study (18) first-time mothers and fathers of newborns were trained to apply the Brazelton scale as an intervention procedure. These infants were all full term, healthy, and were involved in the programme while still in hospital following delivery. It was reported that treatment parents had increased knowledge about and were more confident and involved with their babies than their non-participating partners.

The items for the present intervention are drawn from Field (17) and are directed toward an infant's state control and activity processes.

Projected outcomes An increased involvement by infant caregivers.

Refer to *Summary* section of attached document for general outcome predictions. In addition this will provide an initial screening for psycho-developmental handicap, an outcome which can be followed up systematically.

Limitations Unknown.

It is assumed adult participants can follow the instructions provided.

Assessment/monitoring Through discussion of results obtained and by a brief check it will be possible to assess reliability of observations. This would be an ongoing activity.

Observing infant states

Background (for parents)

The present notes offer guidelines for making observations about your baby. There is no need to complete all these observations at one sitting. Instead, watch baby and play at different times during the week with half a mind on the items listed below. Then complete the observations when you are both comfortable with one another. Do remember that these are just guidelines for making observations, there are no right or wrong answers.

To be able to make full use of these guidelines you should be familiar already with the notion of infant state. If not, read the information contained in intervention 10.4 (Introduction to infant state).

Some of the observations mentioned below can only be carried out when baby is in a particular state. Others ask you to indicate the states baby is in when the actions can be seen. Beside each item number the desired infant state is shown by a letter (in brackets).

I'd suggest you make your observations and note the replies to each section on a separate piece of paper. Simply put the item numbers down the left side, in the margin perhaps, and then put your observation and any extra comments on the same line. Put the date and baby's age at the top of the page. Then next week make another set of observations, but use a fresh page for replies. This way you can compare baby's changes week-by-week.

Activity (for parents)

1 (State F)

When crying vigorously which of the following will quieten baby:

1. nothing
2. pacifier/dummy
3. holding upright
4. holding upright and rocking
5. holding upright, rocking, talking/singing
6. gentle but firm hand pressure on tummy while talking to it
7. (other)

2 (State D)

How long can baby engage in a quiet alert state after your best feeding session.

1. 0 minutes
2. 1–3 minutes
3. 3–5 minutes
4. 5–10 minutes
5. more than 10 minutes

3 (All States)

How extreme are baby's daily states?

1. not at all (sleeps soundly, feeds well, hardly cries)
2. minor (tends to drift between sleeping and waking without vigorous crying)
3. moderate (hard to settle to sleep, even when drowsy)
4. high (many state changes during a day)

4 (All States)

During the following times which state is baby mostly in?

1. ——— night
2. ——— early morning
3. ——— morning
4. ——— afternoon
5. ——— late afternoon/early evening
6. ——— evening

5 (All States)

During which states does baby bring hand(s) to mouth. (Show more than one if necessary. Circle answer.)

never; A; B; C; D; E; F;

6 (All States)

During which states does baby smile (show more than one if necessary. Circle answer.)

never; A; B; C; D; E; F;

Summary (for parents)

If there are any other observations about state changes you wish to make then do so. For as you become tuned to the idea of noticing states all sorts of other adventures will follow.

You may have the impression that baby can only show the quiet alert state when held in your arms or playing actively with you. Of course while this happens it is not always the case. There are times when baby will be in a quiet alert state without anybody else being around at all. For example, when alone in bed baby may be quite content to look about, finger toys, suck hands, or gaze at and play with a mobile hung overhead.

One way to spoil a baby is to interrupt its own contentment, to infringe upon its peace. Waking a sleeping baby to feed on schedule is one way to do this. Another way is to barge in and pick up a happy infant, especially when parents wish to show it off to visitors. So be sensitive to any disruptions you make when interrupting baby's contentment. On the other hand, as a parent you must expect your own peaceful times to be disrupted by baby. It does seem unfair that this is one-sided. But that's the way it is. Sorry.

After reading this section you should be able to:

— make observations of baby's states
— begin to realize there are some patterns to baby's daily activities
— notice that some things you do to baby are directly related to state changes
— be able to compare week-by-week changes
— by asking another person (like partner or friend) to make separate observations on the same items, to discuss any differences and similarities

Intervention 10.6 Looking, listening, and copying

Rationale The present intervention builds upon and extends the previous one (10.5). As in the (17) report where mothers were provided written instructions to guide them in administering the Brazelton (16) neonatal assessment scale, the main divisions within that scale are maintained here. In 10.5 the motor and organisational processes were discussed. For the present intervention attention is directed toward interactive processes, and primarily those concerned with orientation.

Separate interventions are designed (10.5, 10.6) which make use of divisions within the Brazelton scale. There are two reasons for dividing this up and dealing with the components independently. First, all interventions must be mangageable by participants. To help meet this objective an extended explanation which introduces planned activities is offered as background information. In addition, since the Brazelton scale terminates with 4 week old babies and we are dealing typically with a 3–30 week age range some items have been modified and extra ones included. Second, there is a ''natural'' break between the two planned interventions (10.5, 10.6) as there is an increasing emphasis on ascertaining infant preferences (for instance to animate and inanimate sound production) rather than descriptions. Overall a general trend toward understanding the emergence of baby's thinking is emerging, a course which is more evident with another intervention (9.1).

Projected outcomes Broadly stated objectives are outlined in the *Summary* section below. Consistent with an emphasis on involving people with their infants, the planned activities help to direct attention toward practical involvement.

Limitations There may be some reluctance for people to follow the elaborate instructions. Nonetheless, these can be modified to suit participants. Practical demonstrations can be offered when requested, or when these appear necessary.

Assessment/monitoring Parents will not be left completely alone to engage this topic. Hence it will be possible to find out from their verbal reports where strengths and weaknesses in the procedures lie. Consultants will need to be sensitive as to how much is a practical work load for any given period. It is likely some work will need to be put into designing record sheets. At present this will be left to participants to arrange for themselves.

Looking, listening and copying

Background (for parents)

It was once suggested that human babies are born about six weeks too early. This is because they are typically so helpless for that period of time following birth. Although we know babies can do some ''smart'' things, like copying tongue poking when in the quiet alert state, they are very dependent on adults for survival. Perhaps we should think of ''birth'' occurring when the social smile appears, at about six weeks. At least by doing so we need not feel guilty about attending to baby's demands, however unreasonable these seem to be.

As a baby grows older it becomes more responsive. Its actions change from being simple reflexes (like turning its head to gentle cheek pressure).

They become intentional and are done on purpose. So instead of just reacting to outside stimulation older babies can decide some things for themselves.

There is a great danger here. People may come to expect things from their babies which cannot be delivered. For example if a baby shows so much cleverness at being able to follow a human face with its eyes then why will it not stop crying when told to do so? The danger is that adults will tend think of babies as being responsible for all the things they do, including feeding, crying, sleeping as well as smiling. Just because a baby demonstrates co-operation at one time is no reason for us to expect this all the time.

One challenge to any parent is to be sensitive to a baby's unreasonableness and to be gentle and comforting regardless of baby's mood. This is an impossibility. Nonetheless it still exists as a challenge, to capitalize on the co-operation of babies and to respect them even when they won't go to sleep, won't feed, or cry all the time. This all boils down to a simple point: you will get the best from baby when it is in the quiet alert state. Of course there are other times to treasure too, like the sheer enjoyment many babies get from splashing in the bath or the sense of togetherness you feel when a baby drifts off to sleep in your arms.

The title of the present section is "Looking, listening and copying". This topic is commonly referred to as "orientation". As you will remember, what baby does depends upon its present state. (For an overview of the idea of state check Intervention 10.4). For practically all of the activities outlined below baby should be in state D, the quiet alert one. This is not absolutely necessary. There will be occasions during other states when baby will orient to objects and to people.

Two cautions should be mentioned and kept in mind while you are encouraging a baby to take part in orientation activities. The first is not to overdo things and tire baby to the point of crossness, fussiness or crying. This requires a certain sensitivity on the part of the adult being alert to those subtle alterations which signal state changes. It is a good idea to have comfort available if baby does get upset. Perhaps a snack feed, or another routine (like picking up, rocking, bathing) which can be applied quickly in the event of unfavourable reactions.

A second caution applies to baby's capability. Adults often like to make comparisons between different babies on the basis of what they are able to do. For the purpose of the present activities the only useful comparison to make is with what could be done by the same baby at an earlier time, for example yesterday, last week, or the week before. So don't push baby too hard and do not demand a performance. Your task is to adjust to baby's capabilities by finding out what are its possibilities. Parents who set up various tasks often intrude too far and make mistakes without realizing it. Remember to show your pleasure to baby by rewarding it for work well done.

In summary, be aware of two likely dangers when taking part in these activities. First of not overdoing it by demanding too much from baby who may be in a non-playful mood. And, second, of not comparing your baby with others. Instead compare it to itself at different times, in different moods, and/or with different adults.

Finally, remember you are trying to find out what is baby's best performance. It may be necessary to repeat any one task on several different occasions. So don't be put off by baby's inactivity or lack of co-operation. Bide your time and take each opportunity as it comes to hand. You can participate with baby in these activities in any order, there is no need to follow the list exactly.

Activity (for parents)

1. Capture baby's attention by holding (or shaking gently) a colourful toy about 25 cm from its face. A small plastic/paper plate or a ball works well as babies seem to be attracted by circles. Then when baby's eyes are fixed on the object move it slowly back and forth (from ear to ear with the nose as centre to this imaginary circle). Now what did baby tend to do?
   a. ignored the whole process, didn't look at all
   b. became quiet (or stayed quiet) and looked at object to begin with
   c. followed with eyes but jerkily through part of the circle
   d. followed with eyes smoothly through part of circle
   e. followed the object smoothly with eyes and head at least once from side to side
   f. (other)
2. Same procedures as for 1 above. But this time move the object up and down after capturing baby's attention. Again, keep the object about 25 cm from baby's nose. Indicate baby's best performance.
   a. didn't look at all, ignored every attempt
   b. became quiet (or stayed quiet) and looked to object at the start
   c. followed with eyes, but jerkily up and down
   d. follows with eyes smoothly up and down
   e. follows the object smoothly with eyes and head at least one complete pass
   f. (other)
3. Use a small tinkling bell (not a big noisy one as its sound cannot be pin-pointed easily) and shake it first on one side of baby's head, then on the other. Repeat this several times. What do you notice when this is done?
   a. nothing at all, perhaps a blink
   b. became quiet, or stayed quiet at start
   c. turned eyes and head to the sound once or twice
   d. turned eyes and head to sound source more than two times
   e. (other)

4. As for 1 above but using your own face instead of a hand held object. This time hold baby about 25 cm away from your own face and shake your head slowly from side to side keeping eyes on baby. At the mid-point of these movements your noses will be directly opposite one another. What does baby do when watching?
   a. ignored everything, refused to looked at all
   b. becomes quiet (or stays quiet) and watched to begin with
   c. followed your movements briefly
   d. followed movements practically all of the time
   e. (other)
5. As for 4 above but talk to baby at the same time as shaking your head from side to side. Keep an eye on baby throughout and see what happens.
   a. ignored all actions
   b. became quiet (or stayed quiet) and looked at the start
   c. followed head movements with eyes briefly
   d. followed your movements practically all of the time
   e. (other)

There are other variations you can design on this theme. For example hold baby in front of you but keep your head in the same place (talking, not talking, singing, etc.) and rotate baby's body. Does baby not look at all, break eye contact after brief glance, or get locked onto your face and stare continuously? It doesn't take much imagination to make up your own act. Just don't be embarrassed. This can be a lot of fun.

Now for copying activities. For a long time it was believed babies could not copy facial expressions or sounds until several months of age. This view has now changed. There are some delightful pictures of babies doing things which had been thought impossible by researchers just a few years ago. The best state in which to see these things is D, the quiet alert one. If baby will not co-operate, don't force it.

6. Hold baby about 25 cm in front of your face. Keep your head still and decide to do one of the following movements several times. Repeat each phase slowly several times in succession. Count to yourself to set up a regular pattern. Hold each phase for about 5 seconds.

   Movement 1 Tongue poking
   phase 1. Face at rest, lips parted slightly.
   phase 2. Poke out tongue as far as it will go.

   Movement 2 Surprise
   phase 1. Face at rest, lips closed (you may need to swallow)
   phase 2. Open mouth to full round dentist's delight, keeping tongue down. At the same time open both eyes wide.

   Movement 3 Lip pouting (kissing)
   phase 1. Face at rest
   phase 2. Push your lips out for a big smoochy kiss (without making contact).

I'll leave you to wonder what baby might be imagining with all these movements. In any case, what was baby's reaction for each one?

a. didn't look, no reaction at all
b. became quiet (or stayed quiet) and watched to begin with
c. remained quiet and kept looking
d. mouth moved slightly, almost to point of doing something
e. copied briefly
f. made at least two full copying actions one after the other
g. (other)

Summary (for parents)

After reading, understanding and carrying out these activities you should:

— be aware of baby's orienting reactions in different states
— notice any differences and preferences baby has with regard to orienting to things and/or to people
— be able to compare changes each week as baby grows older
— manage and extend the quiet alert state
— other cautions: 1. If baby is completely non-responsive to any of these activities then mention this to your doctor. 2. Some babies sleep with their eyes open; is the non-response due to sleeping?

Intervention 10.7 Night Waking

(This is an extended version of an intervention designed by Janet Hambly, Student, Department of Family Studies, University of Guelph, Ontario, Canada).

Rationale The triad of "difficult" infant behaviours most consultants encounter consists of crying, poor feeding, and night waking. These are the things which distress parents. Hence consultants need to know either how to deal with these directly or to whom referral may be made. Attention in this section is directed toward night waking.

In her Ph.D. study Fay Deane (19) reports that the one dominant aspect of mothering anticipated by pregnant women was that baby would sleep during the nights. More than any other this belief was the hardest to come to terms with when babies did not "conform". Babies do not sleep for as often or for as long as most expectant parents believed. The beliefs we have about events goes a long way toward explaining our reactions towards them. Indeed, parents who accept as part of their role getting up to a distressed baby in the night are less affected by sleep disruption than those who do not hold this view. Yet, even duty can fail. This is especially so if fatigue becomes unbearable and others, like partner, are unwilling or unable to help out. The plight of these parents is made even more acute by the knowledge that friends' babies slept through the night from quite an early age. In the end it comes down to an individual mother and her handling of the situation.

It is difficult to find reliable information about night waking in babies because evidence is often interpreted in favour of the authors' views. In one report on behavioural management of night waking (20) where parents were encouraged to leave children to "cry it out", literature was carefully selected and interpreted to support this position. There may be occassions when leaving a child seems to be the only course of action left. For older children this procedure can have the desired effects. So far any evidence about long term consequences of adopting this strategy with younger babies (of, say, less than a year old) is just not available. And, in spite of the claims about successful outcomes with older children who have been left to cry it out there is little about later effects on them either. The point is, one can engage in a particular course of action which appears to alleviate a situation, which in this case is stopping night waking by parental non-compliance, but still miss any underlying dynamic which is actually going on.

This developmental puzzle gets even more complicated. What may have started out as a particular reaction in the first place may be kept going by something quite different. In other words the original behaviour seems to have picked up other "benefits" and is now sparked off by quite different events. So, locating the cause of night waking can be very difficult. Indeed this may not even be particularly useful if the original "cause" is now only marginally related to that which does directly influence what is going on in the present context. A case example will provide a good illustration.

Parents of a nine month old baby came to seek assistance with regard to handling night waking and crying. For the remainder of the day baby was a delight, easy to handle and positive of mood. At nights it was a different story; she awoke crying every hour and could only be soothed by a breast snack. After reviewing the case my suggestion was to continue getting up in the night and offer the breast for comfort. Eventually the night routine changed and baby once again slept through. A consultant's role in a case like this is to offer as much support as possible and to relate some observations about babies' development in general.

First, there are about 10% of babies who seem never to sleep regularly through the night for the whole of the first year. It is not known why this is so and appears to be related to constitutional factors. Some authors report no association between amount of day sleep and broken nights (21).

Second, there is a gradual developmental drift toward longer periods of sleeping during the night as babies grow older. However, for some inexplicable reason, there is a relapse at around 13 weeks of age. This happened for almost a half of one group of infants participating in a longitudinal study (21). It is suggested that new causes of night waking are involved in the 6–9 month period. When one links this observation to the onset of stranger anxiety (Intervention 9.5) then quite obvious parallels emerge; there is a major reorganisation going on within the baby.

This reorganisation seems to have been at the root of what was going on in the case mentioned above. Looking back on one particular evening the parents remembered going out for dinner. As before they took baby too. Although they had done this many times previously, baby had always been awake. This time baby was asleep. At their host's place the sleeping baby was put into a separate room. After an hour or so it awakened, screaming. No amount of social comforting would placate the crying. Finally, the mother decided to offer a breast feed, which was accepted. Baby dropped off to sleep. Thereafter at home it awoke several times each night. One way to manage what appears to be a massive change and reorganisation is to provide close support by way of night feeding. Indeed this was at the back of my suggestion to continue snack feeding on demand. But this can be a risky venture. Some parents believe the best way out of a situation like this is to leave the baby to "learn" that no amount of crying will bring any comfort so it may as well give up.

Even changing a room about, altering the bedding, moving into another sleeping location seems to spark off night waking during this 6–8 month period. This is a major step in baby's own development; becoming aware of the surroundings. Nonetheless, the disruptive effects from this increased "awareness" as well as adverse reactions to the apparent loss of familiar others in strange settings can be very time-consuming for all concerned. One way to think of this strong sudden reaction is as if it was a phobia. The main point about calling it a phobia is to indicate that this is neither intentional nor rational on the infant's part. In other words baby has not carefully thought this all out beforehand and is now using it as a means of getting adult company in the middle of the night. No, not at all. This is just the way babies are made. At this time in their lives they appear to have a "biological" need for comfort from those they recognise and know as theirs. They are extremely sensitive to disruptions which throw them off balance.

Third, there does seem to be a relation between adult attending and night crying. It has been reported that parents who either left, or attended to all episodes of night waking had less disruptions subsequently than those who were undecided, coming in on some occasions but not on others (21). Most parents will try anything. Some are strongly urged by friends as well as health and allied professionals simply to leave their babies to cry it out, mainly because it is believed these infants are only trying to get the upper hand and must not on any account be spoilt. This fear of spoiling is endemic to our society. It is premised on the belief that what baby is doing now it will always do. This is wrong on at least two counts. First, there is no evidence to indicate night waking in the latter part of the first year of life can be predicted from what happened in the first three months.

Second, there are rhythms in development, like the spontaneous "relapses" which occur even after a period of baby sleeping through. With close support, feeding and comforting, even following many nights of distress, baby will "suddenly" stop and be at peace.

Another pair of paradoxes emerges regarding this topic. One is that it seems to be not only the fact of getting up and feeding a night waking baby which is important, but also the associated socialising (21). Those babies who were fed either the least or the most had far greater tendencies to wake than those who were fed and had between 10 and 20 minutes extra time spent with them. So it seems there is something else going on besides just waking in the night. These results indicate that quite contrary to what many parents are led to believe by the threat of spoiling, spending more time in gentle and reciprocal social interaction is beneficial in the long run.

The second paradox is that infants who are either first or second born tend to be more disruptive than those who are later born. There seems to be a pattern of handling babies which comes only through experience. Perhaps there is less tension in the whole system, a greater amount of flexibility in adapting one to the other without unnecessary strain. Possibly it is the knowledge that what is happening now is part of an evolving plan of mutual development, that now is not for ever. And this allows parents to participate rather than try and force or control maturational thrusts.

A quotation from the discussion by a couple of researchers is appropriate here. Moore and Ucko (21) note:

> Finally, we have to remember that sleep is by no means an invariable sign of good health nor of good adjustment. Indeed, many children suffering from faulty adjustments of various kinds seem to sleep particularly soundly, as though recovering energy expended in crying or otherwise combating their difficulties. On the other hand, in a well and happy infant, even nightly waking need not be regarded as too serious a problem, provided the parents can accept it without resentment, self-reproach or other ill-feeling, deal with it efficiently and get enough sleep. Prolonged spells of waking more than once in the night are, of course, likely to indicate some faulty adjustment in the child or family calling for a thorough review of the whole situation with professional advice." (p. 342)

Projected outcomes To help parents recognise that night waking is a part of infant growth and development there are several approaches available. Apart from bodily discomforts, such as being too hot/cold and/or medical ailments, some infants' continued night waking appears to be constitutional. It is just part of the way they are built. For others it is a parent's inexperience which is the main contributor to mutual disruption.

Of the many ways to ease these situations the most consistent and reliable is feeding coupled with socialising.

Limitations Due to the complex nature of night waking no single remedy can be applied by all parents to their babies. A consultant will need to explore each situation carefully and then offer recommendations which make sense to those participating. The need for caution is warranted; remember most cot-deaths occur in the midnight to dawn period. Although there may well be times when a parent ought to leave a crying baby alone, like when their feelings of violence are upper most or it is an older child,this is not generally a beneficial procedure.

Concerning as it does a period of time when parents are likely to be "low", they may have neither the interest nor the energy to sustain positive involvement. One approach is to find other parents who have already achieved a healthy, positive resolution to this topic and then have them provide essential personal social support.

Another limitation is that there will be numerous sources of conflicting advice. This emerges both from the literature and from friends, acquaintances, in-laws, parents and medical professionals. All have an answer, yet none works for all.

Assessment/monitoring Basically the "success" of any intervention aimed at minimising the detrimental effects from night waking will become obvious to parents. An open approach at subsequent meetings can resolve minor difficulties. Parents have a right not to comply. So accept any reluctance gracefully without making them any more guilty.

Night waking

Background (for parents)

Parents often seek professional advice to help them cope with night-waking babies. The first person contacted is usually a doctor. But once baby has been checked out and nothing medically wrong is found then the night-waking no longer remains in the medical court. At this point many doctors give up. Unfortunately there are few other professionals available who can offer guidance on this matter. Apart from using some form of medication to sedate these babies most people who are not directly involved encourage parents to "be cruel to be kind". In short, to let the baby cry it out.

The strength of this societal force to let crying babies lie alone is very strong. There are some people who believe parents have a duty to see that their babies are not spoilt. This is shown in the belief that if you get up to baby now you'll always be getting up. Forever. And since parents are often so weary at this time, sick and tired of getting up night after night, the word "forever" is the the closest thing to hell on earth imaginable. Others come from a religious background and interpret selected biblical quotations to press their advantage. The most frequently heard misquote is "Spare the rod and spoil the child". The "rod" in this case is a parent's firmness in not giving in nor getting up to a night-waking baby.

Then there are others who say parents have got their priorities wrong. These people make it quite clear that if you don't get your act together now then you never will. Strangely enough some people even believe that a rigid approach is going back to "good old basic times when people knew what was what". They are wrong. The "old times" means babies in arms and not imprisoning them in separate rooms.

Then there are the people who use a soft-sell approach to the topic. Some of these are likely to be bringing their own guilt forward, disguising it as a "natural" thing to do. "Look at the children of Mrs so and so. She left them all to cry. They cried for a while but finally learned what was what. Now you never saw such a nice family". Of course leaving a baby alone to cry it out "works"; so does torture. Another approach is to claim an attending parent is being soft; the baby has to be toughened up.

There may be times when it is advisable not to pick up a night-waking baby. For example if a parent is so tired and they may do the infant harm because they are pushed beyond the limits of reason.

What seems to be going on? According to the research which has been reported on this subject you can take any position you like and find some support for it. In a sense one has to go beyond the research and look at broader issues.

For example there does seem to be an inclination for about 20% babies to begin night-waking in the 7–13 month period. This includes those "angels" who slept through the night from their earliest days. One suggestion is not to move things about baby's room during this period. If you go out visiting at night see that baby is awake and aware you are present. Otherwise the sudden shock of waking in a strange room could be too much. It seems babies are very sensitive during this phase of their lives, they are finding out about trust and building up hope. So the short answer is to provide support and comfort, then rest assured it is nothing but an essential phase which will pass away.

For younger night-waking babies it is often hunger which prompts their urgent cries. There is only one remedy for this; food. As babies grow there is a natural tendency for them to drop the feed after midnight. Incidently, sleeping through the night means an unbroken period between midnight and about 5 am. Yes. *That* is sleeping through, all five hours of it. So, don't expect too much.

One comment many mothers make about their babies is that they expected them to sleep more. This is the one thing which upsets parents more than anything else, except their crying. Yet crying, night-waking and poor feeding seem to go together.

Some babies are easily startled. They jump to the slightest of sounds or movements. It seems that these infants are "keyed up", their bodies are tuned up for reaction to the slightest changes. So far we don't know why this is. For some it may be linked to the birth itself; those on some drugs during delivery or who suffered long drawn-out births seem much more sensitive. It is as if their bodies are still not quite settled down. As for parents, the challenge is to help these babies to help themselves settle down. Swaddling (Intervention 8.6) can work wonders. In the early weeks the mouth seems to be the door to the world. This may be why sucking and dummies/pacifiers are so successful (see Intervention 8.4). As babies grow so these doors change. The mouth seems to lose its charm. Now it seems to be upright movement which is the most soothing (see Intervention 8.2). And so it goes on; what once worked no longer has the essential magic of bringing about.

There are some older babies for whom night-waking becomes a routine with little merit. As soon as a parent enters the room the crying stops. Baby is ready to play; smiling and gleeful at the chance of having a companion. This seems to be nothing but pleasure on the child's part. But it is most wearing on parents already too tired to take part in "the game". Although it's hard to believe; this is part of an unfolding developmental plan as well.

That's all very well, of course, but what do you do about this so as to get an unbroken night? One suggestion has been to go in before the child awakes and to gently arouse it and play on your terms (22). The idea here is that by doing this you are actually encouraging further sleeping. The argument goes as follows. If playing is such fun then why not do it after some sleep because then in this way, the child learns that more sleep leads to more play. The scheme is based on the same sort of psychology as leaving a baby to cry it out, but it is far more humane. All the same it is hard to know when night-waking is an essential part of parent-infant growth and when it has become a habit for all these involved. Up until about 12 months it is best to think of night-waking as an essential part of infant development. After that age, and depending on the circumstances, assistance may be needed to change this routine for family health. Perhaps even of adopting a ruthless "leave'em to cry" approach.

Medication can offer temporary relief for parents and older babies caught in the bind of night-waking. This may provide essential temporary relief. But this ought to be done cautiously. Otherwise parents and their children may come to rely on drugs as the only "solution". If drug dependency occurs then more and more is given at stronger and stronger levels. This is a trap which should be avoided.

Sickness, moving rooms about, visiting places unfamiliar to baby, visitors and visiting may each interrupt continuous night sleeping. The upshot can be a triggering of spontaneous night waking. Of course this does not mean parents should stop exploring new situations and broadening baby's horizons. What it means is that if night-waking does begin then be very prompt in attending to it at the outset. Although the research data are not available it seems that any delay in comforting a baby during this period (typically between 7–12 months) will make it worse rather than better. It is as if baby is demanding reassurance.

Finally, a baby who sleeps through the night need not be a healthy one. By the same token one who wakes is not necessarily ill or spoiled. What matters above all else is how parents react to the night-waking. Some are better than others. Those who cannot cope should not be blamed.

It seems that babies sleep in cycles much as adults do. After drifting off to sleep they stir and surface to a near-waking state about an hour later. Any sudden change at this time can snap them awake. It may be a tightening of the gut, a startle, or a noise. The hourly waking business appears to be a pattern which exists during the sleep cycle itself.

Activities (for parents)

There is nothing "wrong" with you if after repeated days of night waking you feel tense, irritable, tired, and/or depressed.

The first thing to do is to find out what seems to be going on. The easiest way to do this is to keep a daily record (as outlined in Intervention 10.2) which has night-waking as a definite symbol.

Since night-waking seems to be influenced by so many things it is helpful to get a handle on what happens. The following questions are designed to find out more about what is going on. Thereafter other interventions may be relevant. Select those which match the situation.

1. What do you do when baby wakes crying that night? The idea here is to note the actual procedure. For example do you; get up right away, pick baby up, feed, change, turn over, put firm hand pressure on the tummy, pace the floor? It is helpful to go over each of these steps, finding out what is and is not done as well as outlining alternatives.
2. Is there any particular order in which you attempt things to try and soothe baby and/or yourself)? The order may change from night to night, or from waking to waking. This depends on many things. Again the search here is for some sort of pattern which makes sense of what is going on. Of course there are no right or wrong patterns. The enquiry is directed to describing the events.
3. How long does each activity last? The question is aimed at finding out what leads from one thing to another.
4. How often do you try any one activity? This question can refer to either a single episode or to many different ones. For instance; if different people are available to help out what do they do, are some things tried earlier in the night but others later.
5. How successful are these activites? Of course it all depends on what one means by the word "success". For parents it may mean a good snatch

of missed sleep; for babies it may mean soothing without leaving them crying. Maybe success is the gentle adjustment from one infant state to another (Intervention 10.4). Once aware of what "success" is, then a start can be made to look for what brings it about.

6. On some occasions and for some babies it is as if a "change" in routines helps settle baby. One mother let her baby cry, but went in every 15 minutes to stroke his back. The change here was not picking up and not feeding. Although the crying went on for some time the mother checked in regularly to stroke and talk. After two hours of this Merbentyl was given. These changes "worked". The next night no medication was given and baby cried less. Mother still came by to confirm her presence by making physical contact. On the third night there was hardly a whimper. This whole topic is quite confusing and more research is needed. In the meantime people will do what they can.

Summary (for parents)

Night-making can become a crisis in parent-infant development. Handling it "successfully" and without guilt is an important accomplishment for those involved.

As babies grow older different things bring about night waking. Each situation is unique. There are no easy solutions.

Perhaps the parent dealing with night waking babies is like a magician who may be called upon at a moment's notice to perform not knowing how the audience will react. The more "tricks up the sleeve" the more likely it is that the performance will produce the desired effect. Remember, if you don't quite get it right the first time your audience will demand a repeat performance. So there will always be the prospect of a second chance, and a third, and a fourth ....

CREATING A BASIC LIBRARY

Suggestions for books and resource materials

Bower, T.G.R. (1977) *A Primer on Infant Development*. San Francisco: Freeman. A good, sound overview of infant development.

Bower, T.G.R. (1982) *Development in Infancy*. San Francisco: Freeman. For those who would like more on infant development, this book extends the primer mentioned above.

Bowlby, J. (1979) *The Making and Breaking of Affectional Bonds*. London: Tavistock (and Penguin). A collection of Dr. Bowlby's lectures. These serve as a handy introduction to attachment theory for readers wishing to consider theoretical matters. The book is lucid, logical and readable.

Curtis Jenkins, G., and Newton, R.C.F. (1981) *The First Year of Life*. Edinburgh: Churchill Livingstone. For those wishing to have a well-written book with a medical orientation. Although prepared to up-date doctors, this book is not too difficult.

Furuno, S., O'Reilly, K.A., Hosaka, C.M., Inatsuka, T.T., Allman, T.L., and Zeisloft, B. (1979) *Hawaii Early Learning Profile (HELP)*. Write to VORT Corporation, P.O. Box 60880, Palo Alto, California 94306, U.S.A. Written in plain English with large format. Many practical suggestions are provided for the items described.

Graves Medical Audiovisual Library. Holly House, 220 New London Road, Chelmsford, Essex CM2 9BJ, England. An excellent brochure outlining many tape-slide programmes for use with small group or personal tuition.

International Childbirth Education Association (ICEA) has a bookcentre and publishes *Bookmarks* three times each year. Bookmarks contains news and reviews of new books in the areas of childbirth preparation, family-centered maternity care, breastfeeding, and related subjects. Write to ICEA, P.O. Box 20048, Minneapolis, Minnesota 55420, U.S.A. For ordering purposes, major credit cards are accepted.

Leach, P. (1979) *Baby and Child: from Birth to Age Five*. Penguin. This, and other books by Dr. Leach, are popular with many parents. Watch for the latest editions.

March of Dimes, Birth Defects Foundation, 1275 Mamaroneck Avenue, white plains. New York 10605, U.S.A. Well worth writing to for their excellent catalogues. The information books/reprints and so forth are mostly free.

Minchin, M. (1983) *Food for Thought*. Sydney: Allen and Unwin. And at special discount rates for self-help or parents groups: Alma Publications: 5 Meredith Court, Alfredton, Victoria 3350, Australia. This is an excellent readable book with helpful suggestions for those involved with allergies.

National Institute of Mental Health publish many documents. Some of these materials are free. Write for a copy of *Development of Mental Health in Infancy*. (Science monographs 3, ADM, 80–962, stock number 1017–024–00996–2) and their list of publications with ordering procedures to:

National Institute of Mental Health
Division of Communication and Education
Science Communication Branch
Public Inquiries Section
5600 Fishers Lane, Rm. 15c–17
Rockville
Maryland 20857
U.S.A.

REFERENCES

Chapter 1

1. *New Zealand Listener* (1983) 105 (2287), p.21.
2. Chess, S., Thomas, A., and Birch, H.G. (1956) *Your Child is Different; a Psychological Approach to Parenthood without Guilt.* Penguin Books.
3. Lewis, P.J.E., Ironside, W., McKinnon, P., and Simmons, C.W.R. (1974) The Karitane project: psychological ill-health, infant distress and the postpartum period. *New Zealand Medical Journal 79* (517), 1005–1009.
4. Kirkland, J. Child abuse: the crying baby at risk. In A. Neale and R. Renwick (Eds.) *Early Childhood in New Zealand: Their Needs — Our Concern.* Proceedings of Second Early Childhook Convention. Christchurch, New Zealand, August 1979, pp. 114–132.
5. Leach, P. (1979) *Baby and Child: from Birth to Age Five.* Penguin Books.
6. Teuting, P., Koslow, S.H., and Hirschfeld, R.M.A. (1981). *Special Report on Depression Research.* Rockville, Maryland: National Institute of Mental Health.
7. Phillips, J. (1983) *Mothers Matter Too.* Wellington: Reed.
8. Dalton, K. (1980) *Depression After Childbirth.* Oxford: University Press.
9. Lewis, M., and Rosenblum, L. (Eds.) (1974) *The Effect of the Infant on its Caregiver.* New York: Wiley.
10. Frodi, A.M., and Lamb, M.E. (1980) Infants at risk for child abuse. *Infant Mental Health Journal, 1* (4), 240–247.
11. Newberger, E.H. and Bourne, R. (1978) The medicalization and legalization of child abuse. *American Journal of Orthopsychiatry, 48*, 593–607.

Chapter 2

1. Ashton-Warner, S. (1963) *Teacher.* New York: Simon and Schuster.
2. *Oxford American Dictionary* (1980)
3. Thomas, L. (1980) *The Medusa and the Snail.* New York: Bantam.
4. American Psychological Association (1981) Specialty guidelines for the delivery of services by clinical psychologists. *American Psychologist, 36* (6), 640–651.

Chapter 3

1. Asnes, R.S. and Mones, R.L. (1983) Infantile colic: a review. *Developmental and Behavioral Pediatrics, 4* (1), 57–62.
2. Glaser, J. (1956) Colic in infants. *Pediatrics, 18*, 828–829.
3. Weissbluth, M., Christoffel, K.K., and Davis, A.T. (1984) Treatment of infantile colic with dicyclomine hydrochloride. *Pediatrics, 104*, 951–955.
4. Jones, S. (1983) *Crying Baby, Sleepless Nights.* New York: Warner.
5. Weissbluth, M. (1984) *Crybabies: Coping with Colic.* New York: Arbor House.
6. Brazelton, T.B. (1962) Crying in infancy. *Pediatrics, 29*, 579–588.

7. Thoman, E.B., Acebo, C., and Becker, P.T. (1983) Infant crying and stability in the mother-infant relationship: a systems analysis. *Child Development*, *54*, 653–659.
8. Buss, A.R. (1978) Causes and reasons in attribution theory: a conceptual critique. *Journal of Personality and Social psychology*, *36* (11), 1311–1321.

Chapter 4

1. *Webster's New Twentieth Century Dictionary* (Unabridged, second edition) (1966) The World Publishing Company.
2. Deane, F. PhD. dissertation in progress, Massey University, Palmerston North, N.Z.
3. Bassett, G. Personal communication, January 1984.
4. Bowlby, J. (1969) *Attachment and Loss Volume 1 Attachment* (Pelican, 1971)
5. Essen-Moller, E. and Wohlfahrt, S. (1947) Suggestions for the amendment of the official Swedish classification of mental disorders. *Acta Psychiatrica Scandinavica* (supplement) 47, 551–555.
6. Kirkland, J. and Morgan, G. (1984) A multi-axial scheme for assessment and intervention. *Early Child Development and Care*, *14*, 1–12.
7. Von Bertalanffy, L. (1956) General system theory. *General Systems*, *1*, 1–10.
8. Sameroff, A. (1975) Transactional models in early social relations. *Human Development*, *18*, 65–79.

Chapter 5

1. Kirkland, J. (1982) Co-ordinating CrySOS perspectives. *Cry Research Newsletter*. *5* (1), 16–18.
2. Asnes, R.S. and Mones, R.L. (1983) Infantile colic: a review. *Developmental and Behavioral Pediatrics*, *4* (1), 57–62.
3. Sluckin, W., Herbert, M., and Sluckin, A. (1983) *Maternal Bonding*. Oxford: Blackwell.

Chapter 6

1. Anastasi, A. (1958) Heredity, environment and the question how? *Psychological Review*, *65*, 197–208.
2. Scarr, S., and McCartney, K. (1983) How people make their own environments: A theory of genotype —> environment effects. *Child Development*, *54*, 424–435.
3. March of Dimes. *Genetic Counseling* (Available from March of Dimes Birth Defects Foundation, 1275 Mamaroneck Avenue, White Plains, N.Y. 10605, U.S.A.)
4. Gottlieb, B. (1970) Conceptions of prenatal behavior. In L.R.Aronson, E. Tobach, D.S.Lehrman, and J.S.Rosenblatt (eds.) *Development and Evolution of Behavior: Essays in Memory of T.C. Schneirla*. San Fransicso: Freeman.

Chapter 7

1. Minchin, M. (1983) *Food for Thought*. Sydney: Allen and Unwin (and at special discount rates for self-help or parents groups write to: Alma Publications, 5 Meredith Court, Alfredton, Victoria 3350, Australia).
2. Curtis Jenkins, G., and Newton, R.C.F. (1981) *The First Year of Life*. Edinburgh: Churchill Livingstone).
3. Dickin, K.L., McKim, M.K., and Kirkland, J. (1983) Designing intervention programs for infants at risk: considerations, implementation and evaluation. *Early Child Development and Care*, *11*, 145–163.
4. American Psychiatric Association. (1980) *Diagnostic and Statistical Manual of Mental Disorders* (3rd edition). Washington, D.C. :APA.
5. Kirkland, J., and Deane, F. (1984) A rejecting baby in a twin set. *Infant Mental Health Journal*, *4* (4), (in press).

Chapter 8

1. Zeskind, P.S., and Lester, B.M. (1978) Acoustic features and auditory perceptions of the cries of newborns with prenatal and perinatal complications. *Child Development*, *49*, 580–589.
2. Beintema, D.J. and Prechtl, H.F.R. (1968) *A Neurological Study of Newborn Infants.* (Clinics in Developmental Medicine, No. 28). London:Heinemann.
3. Brazelton, T.B. (1973) *Neonatal Behavioral Assessment Scale.* (Clinics in Developmental Medicine, No. 50). London: Heinemann.
4. Field, T.M., Dempsey, J.R., Hallock, N.H., and Shuman, H.H. (1978) The mother's assessment of the behavior of her infant. *Infant Behavior and Development*, *1*, 156–167.
5. Prechtl, H. and Beintema, D. (1964) *Neurological Examination of the Full Term Newborn Infant.* (Clinics in Developmental Medicine, No. 12). London: Heinemann.
6. Wilson, J. (1978) A developmental reflex test. In Shirley G. Vulpe. *Vulpe Assessment Battery.* Toronto: National Institute on Mental Retardation, pp. 342–364.
7. Ambrose, A. (Ed.) (1969) *Stimulation in Early Infancy.* New York: Academic Press.
8. Bryne, J.M. and Horowitz, F.D. (1981) Rocking as a soothing intervention: the influences of direction and type of movement. *Infant Behavior and Development. 4*, 207–218.
9. Ter Vrugt, D., and Pederson, D.R. (1973) The effects of vertical rocking frequencies on the arousal level in two-month-old infants. *Child Development*, *44*, 205–209.
10. Detterman, D.K. (1978) The effect of heartbeat on neonatal crying. *Infant Behavior and Development*, *1*, 36–48.
11. Brackbill, Y., Adams, G., Crowell, D.H., and Gray, M.L. (1966) Arousal level in neonates and preschool children under continuous auditory stimulation. *Journal of Experimental Child Psychology*, *4*, 178–188.
12. Brackbill, Y. (1971) Cumulative effects of continuous stimulation on arousal level in infants. *Child Development*, *42*, 17–26.
13. Brackbill, Y. (1973) Continuous stimulation reduces arousal level: stability of the effect over time. *Child Development*, *44*, 43–46.
14. Jones, S. (1983) *Crying Baby, Sleepless Nights.* New York: Warner.
15. Leach, P. (1977) *Baby and Child.* Harmondsworth: Penguin.
16. Fraiberg, S. (1959) *The Magic Years.* London: Methuen.
17. Anderson, G.C., Burroughs, A.K., and Measel, C.P. (1983) Nonnutritive sucking opportunities: a safe and effective treatment for preterm infants. In Tiffany Field and Anita Sostek (eds.) *Infants Born at Risk: Physiological, Perceptual and Cognitive Processes.* Grune and Stratton.
18. Anderson, G. (1983) Infantile colic: a possible solution. *American Journal of Maternal Child Nursing. 8* (3) 185.
19. Heinl, T. (1982) *The Baby Massage Book.* London: Angus and Robertson.
20. Auckett, A. (1982) *Baby Massage: The Magic of the Loving Touch.* Wellingborough, Northamptonshire: Thorsons.
21. Lipton, E.L., Steinschneider, A, and Richmond, J.B. (1965) Swaddling, a child care practice: historical, cultural and experimental observations. *Pediatrics*, *35*, 519–567.

Chapter 9

1. Alperon, G.D. and Boll, T.J. (1972) *Developmental Profile Manual.* Indianapolis, Indiana: Psychological Development Publications.
2. Bayley, N. (1969) *The Bayley Scales of Infant Development.* New York: The Psychological Corporation.
3. Frankenburg, W.K., and Dodds, J.B. (1970) *Denver Developmental Screening Test.*
4. Amdur, J., and Mainland, M. (1980) *Developmental Inventory Scales for Children* (DISC) Kitchener, Canada: Unpublished document.

5. Uzgiris, I.C., and Hunt, J. McV. (1975) *Assessment in Infancy*. Chicago: University of Illinois Press.
7. Vulpe, S.G., Rollins, E.I., and Wilson, J. (1978) *Vulpe Assessment Battery* Toronto: National Institute of Mental Retardation.
8. Elkind, D, and Sameroff, A. (1970) Developmental psychology. *Annual Review of Psychlogy*, *21*, 191–238.
9. Bower, T.G.R. (1980) *Development in Infancy*. San Francisco: Freeman. (2nd edition).
10. Bower, T.G.R. (1977) *A Primer on Infant Development*. San Francisco: Freeman.
11. Furuno, S., O'Reilly, K.A., Hosaka, C.M., Inatsuka, T.T., Allman, T.L., and Zeisloft, B. (1979) *Hawaii Early Learning Profile (HELP)*. Palo Alto, California: VORT.
12. De Lissovoy, V. (1973) Child care by adolescent parents. *Children Today*, *2*, 22–25.
13. Graves Medical Audiovisual Library, Holly House, 220 New London Road, Chelmsford, Essex CM2 9BJ, England (phone 0245-83351). Write for brochure and price list. Their tape-slide programmes are available for use in small group or personal tuition.
14. Emde, R.N., Gaensbauer, T.J., and Harmon, R.J. (1976) *Emotional Expression in Infancy: A Biobehavioral Study*. New York: International Universities Press *(Psychological Issues*, Monograph 39).
15. Dunn, J. (1976) *Distress and Comfort*. Cambridge, Mass.: Harvard University Press. (and Penguin).
16. Horner, T. (1980) Two methods of studying stranger reactivity in infants: a review. *Child Psychology*, *21*, 203–219.

Chapter 10

1. Wasz-Hockert, O., Partanen, T., Vuorenkoski, V., Valanne, E., and Michelsson, K. (1964) Effect of training on ability to identify preverbal vocalizations. *Developmental Medicine and Child Neurology*, *6*, 393–396.
2. Lounsbury, M.L. and Bates, J.E. (1982) The cries of infants of differing levels of perceived temperamental difficultness: acoustic properties and effects on listeners. *Child Development*, *53*, 677–686.
3. Boukydis, C.F.Z. and Burgess, R.L. (1982) Adult physiological response to infant cries: effects of temperament of infant, parental status, and gender. *Child Development*, *53*, 1291–1298.
4. Zeskind, P.S., and Lester, B.M. (1978) Acoustic features and auditory perceptions of the cries of newborns with prenatal and perinatal complications. *Child Development*, *49*, 580–589.
5. Zeskind, P.S. (1980) Adult responses to cries of low and high risk infants. *Infant Behavior and Development*, *3*, 167–177.
6. Zeskind, P.S. (1983) Cross-cultural differences in maternal perceptions of cries of low — and high-risk infants. *Child Development*, *54*, 1119–1128.
7. Brennan, M., and Kirkland, J. (1979) Discrimination of infants' cry-signals. *Perceptual and Motor Skills*, *48*, 683–686.
8. Lester, B. (1983) There's more to crying than meets the ear. *Child Care Newsletter*, *2* (2), 1–5.
9. Kelly, G. (1955) *The Psychology of Personal Constructs*. New York: Norton.
10. Brazelton, T.B. (1962) Crying in infancy. *Pediatrics*, *29*, 579–588.
11. Thomas, A., Chess, S., Birch, H.G., Hertzig, M.E. and Korn, S. (1963) *Behavioral Individuality in Early Childhood*. New York: New York University Press.
12. Wachs, T.d., and Gandour, M.J. (1983) Temperament, environment, and six-month cognitive-intellectual development: a test of the organismic hypothesis. *International Journal of Behavioral Development*, *6*, 135–152.
13. Thomas, A., Chess, S., and Korn, S.J. (1983) The reality of the difficult temperament. *Merrill-Palmer Quarterly*, *28*, 1–20.

14. Bates, J.E. (1980) The concept of difficult temperament. *Merrill-Palmer Quarterly*, *26*, 299–319.
15. Prechtl, H., and Beintema, D. (1964) *The Neurological Examination of the Full Term Newborn Infant.* (Clinics in Developmental Medicine, Number 12) London: Heinemann.
16. Brazelton, T.B. (1973) *Neonatal Behaviour Assessment Scale.* (Clinics in Developmental Medicine Number 50) London: Heinemann.
17. Field, T.M., Dempsey, J.R., Hallock, N.H. and Shuman, H.H. (1978) The mother's assessment of the behavior of her infant. *Infant Behavior and Development*, *1*, 156–167.
18. Myers, B.J. (1982) Early intervention using Brazelton training with middle-class mothers and fathers of newborns. *Child Development*, *53*, 462–471.
19. Deane, F. (1984) Ph.D. study in progress. Massey University, Palmerston North, New Zealand. 20. Seymour, F.W., Bayfield, G., Brock, P., and During, M. (1983) Management of night-waking in young children. *Australian Journal of Family Therapy*, *4* (4), 217–233.
21. Moore, T., and Ucko, L.E. (1957) Night waking in early infancy. *Archives of Disease in Childhood*, *32*, 333–342.
22. McGarr, R.J. and Hovell, M.F. (1980) In search of the sandman: shaping an infant to sleep. *Education and Treatment of Children*, *3*, 173–182.

INDEX FOR TOPICS

INDEX FOR NAMES

CRY EDUCATION AND RESEARCH TRUST

CRY EDUCATION AND RESEARCH TRUST

Dear Supporter,

As most parents know, the stress generated by a crying baby has an impact on every member of the family.

All too often mothers become exhausted and depressed because they don't know how to cope with their baby's crying. Fathers often have to begin the working day feeling worn out and their work performance and job competence can be impaired. Family relations can be damaged and even violence triggered by the strain of a baby's incessant crying.

These are some of the important reasons why it is necessary to support and promote significant educational and research programmes as soon as possible.

We are sure that you will support us by taking an interest in our work and talking to others who may be just as concerned. But, as you will realise, we need financial support as well as good will, and we hope you will feel able to contribute. Please take the time now to complete the enclosed trust supporter reply form and post it to us. Your support will help us to boost our level of activity and the commitments we can undertake. Further details about the Trust are enclosed.

Thankyou for caring enough to give us your support.

Yours sincerely,

John Kirkland

Ian Ferry

Stuart Malcolm

Ephra Garrett

CERT, P.O. Box 718, Palmerston North, New Zealand. J/48

The Cry Education and Research Trust (CERT) serves parents and others who are involved with crying babies in both family and community settings. It does so by designing educationally relevant applications as well as by initiating research with the object of giving a greater understanding of what is happening within the Crying Baby Syndrome.

EDUCATIONAL

From an educational perspective the Trust provides support for students and others involved in designing practical techniques which can be applied by those dealing with crying babies.

- designing practical techniques for families
- merging techniques with other community services
- reporting about techniques (locally, nationally, internationally)
- training others to use the techniques
- offering direct assistance to those with crying babies

RESEARCH

Additional research is required to investigate which components of infant cry sounds are disruptive, how these may be modified by parent education, and what the sounds are informing us about infant status.

- cry signal analyses (perceptions, descriptions, technology)
- building up the cry signal library (recording, editing, filing, etc.)
- evaluating the techniques
- examining the use of cry signals as a diagnostic aid
- collaborative work with others

Already an international reputation has been established in this field. A cross-section of papers which have already been published is listed below. A gift to the Cry Education and Research Trust is money invested for delivering practical preventative aid.

Complete details below.

CREDIT CARD DONORS

Please invoice my .... Credit Card.

Expiry Date ....

Card Number:
(include all digits)

| | | | | | | | | | | | | | | | | | |

Signature ....

Amount of Donation $..